Jessie Homer French

Jessie Homer

FRENCH

Fish, Fire, and Death

SKIRA

Cover
Blowout (detail), 2020
Oil on canvas, 36 × 36 in. (91.4 × 91.4 cm)

Editorial Coordinator
Flavio Del Monte, MASSIMODECARLO
with Kelley Camberos, Various Small Fires

Texts Editor
Agatha French

Art Director
Luigi Fiore

Copy Editing
Andrew Ellis

Layout
Elisabetta Presotto

First published in Italy in 2023 by
Skira editore S.p.A.
Palazzo Casati Stampa
via Torino 61
20123 Milano
Italy
www.skira.net

© 2023 Jessie Homer French
© 2023 MASSIMODECARLO
© 2023 The authors for their texts
© 2023 Skira editore, Milano

Printed and bound in Italy. First edition

ISBN: 978-88-572-5024-3

Distributed in USA, Canada, Central & South America by ARTBOOK | D.A.P. 75 Broad Street, Suite 630, New York, NY 10004, USA.
Distributed elsewhere in the world by Thames and Hudson Ltd., 181A High Holborn, London WC1V 7QX, United Kingdom

This book has been published thanks to the generous contribution of MASSIMODECARLO and Various Small Fires. The galleries would like to thank first and foremost the artist Jessie Homer French and her family, Robin French, Spencer French, Agatha French and Ryan Schude, Amy French, and Wendy and Billy Al Bengston for their support. This book wouldn't have been possible without the commitment of Nich McElroy.

Contents

7   Jessie Homer French
Louise Farr

13   Above, Under and In-Between
The Paintings of Jessie Homer French
Francesco Bonami

15   Our World, On Fire:
Jessie Homer French in the Arc of
Self-Taught Artists in the United States
Jen Sudul Edwards

19   **Works**

127   Biography

Jessie Homer French

Louise Farr

Anyone who has known Jessie Homer French for more than a few years—and I've known her for more than sixty—will have amassed folders that bulge with her correspondence: birthday cards painted with images of layer cakes and glowing candles; cartoons based on the latest global or local disaster; sinister Valentine cards in which hearts drip with blood; photos of her latest work, with hand-written musings on the back.

"It's quite large—36 by 60 inches—with infinite layers of compulsively painted leaves—took months," she wrote, circa 2008, about a brooding painting of an island in Oregon's Willamette River, the sky lowering, the water rippling with beauty and faint menace. "I really was wishing I was an abstract expressionist. Painting like that would be fun & freeing," she continued. "Maybe."

That "maybe" is crucial. If Jessie had really wanted to become an abstract expressionist, she would have become one.

Instead, as a self-described "narrative regional painter," she offers us people, rivers, fish, creatures of all kinds, cemeteries, swaths of greenery, and mountain vistas, painted in oil in her characteristic flat yet vivid style.

When I first met Jessie, in Los Angeles, we were in our late teens, working as fashion models—not out of vanity or a craving for fame, but out of the simple need to make a living. She was Jessie Sanders then, a sophisticated-looking ex-New Yorker who was stashing her work savings while plotting for a time when she could do nothing but paint. This she did on weekends, disguising herself as a boy so that men wouldn't hit on her when she visited the hardware store for supplies.

A prodigious reader of history, biography, and Agatha Christie mysteries (her childhood bedtime stories were Grimms' fairy tales and *The Decameron*), she also consumed volumes of science fiction and concluded that things were not going to turn out well for the universe. That theme haunted her then and haunts her still.

"Very sensible, if you ask me," she says today, of that attitude.

Before she met Robin French, the prickly, funny, and remarkably generous British-born Hollywood agent whom she married in 1969, she lived in a cabin in the bucolic Echo Park hills, as close to the country life she had grown up in as was possible in a metropolis such as Los Angeles.

Later, she and Robin bought an old estate bunkhouse that sat on two and a half acres, within Beverly Hills but far from the popular image of that city's ostentation. There were chickens, geese, peacocks, wildflowers, children, dogs, and a herd of wooden cows that Jessie painted and placed on the hillside, simply because she thought the hillside needed them.

But for the six tragically short years in the life of Valentina French, a radiant little girl born with cerebral palsy, Jessie was so focused on caring for her and her younger brother, Spencer, that she could rarely paint. Later Amelia and Agatha were born, and with the children at school, Jessie worked in an old decagon cabin that Robin had trundled up the hill from a shopping center on Sunset Boulevard. Increasingly, her work focused on death and resurrection.

Jessie always favored the motto, "Idle hands find the devil's work to do." She was constantly busy, whether that meant baking an apple pie or creating some object out of rocks or garbage cans. Decades later, the "Idle Hands" quote found its way onto one of the rugs she makes that are less objects to step on than works of confrontational art. After a day in her studio, once Jessie's scrubbed off the paint, finished dinner (made from scratch, of course), and done the dishes, she's incapable of settling down to merely watch the evening news. Instead, she quilts, hooks a rug, or stitches one of her fabric, paint, thread, and ink "mapestries" that chart California's river systems or earthquake fault-lines; safer than paintings, she thinks, to hang over a bed in the event of an inevitable temblor. Just one more worry taken care of in a fearsome world.

To this day, Jessie insists that she is a coward, which is absolute nonsense. On the other hand, self-deprecation is one of her specialties. So she discounts the solo camping trips she used to take deep into the High Sierra and the wilds of Oregon, with only the smell of bear forcing her off her path in search of the beloved trout that populate so much of her work. She mustered the courage to make those trips, she says, because she could feel the safety of Robin, waiting for her at home. True. But it is still an act of bravery to venture into the wilderness alone. And it has taken a different kind of bravery to persevere, over decades, as unshakable now as ever, in her vision as an artist, even within the void left by Robin's death.

In a note accompanying an image of one of her Chernobyl paintings, with its nuclear power plant, wolves, elk, and wild boar, she wrote to me that the Exclusion Zone "now rivals the world's most abundant nature preserves: A 'Garden of Eden' for the 21ˢᵗ Century." About that Garden of Eden comment, she noted, "Half hopeful—half ironic." Not unlike Jessie and her paintings.

Louise Farr: I know you're not a fan of artists' statements, but can you talk about being a regional narrative painter? You moved from New York to California, to Canada, to Oregon, to the California desert, and then to the mountains. So I guess you were regional by necessity.

Jessie Homer French: My painting was always narrative, and always regional. If the narrative is not self-explanatory, you screwed up. So, no, I don't like artists' statements. If artists were good at explaining, we might be writers.

LF: You've said that you don't believe in perspective, either. Why not?

JHF: Because I like the way shapes get spread out on a flat surface. I think perspective is annoying. As far as flat surfaces with no perspective, the influence would be medieval art.

LF: I've always wondered if there's a clear narrative in your mind when you conceive of a painting?

JHF: Yes. Some paintings just appear to me. You'll be walking along or driving along, or sitting there, and they just appear.

LF: There's a great deal of religious imagery in your paintings. A painting in your Chernobyl series, with a crucified Jesus, moved me to tears the instant I saw it in your studio, and I'm not remotely religious. You've painted nuns and priests, church bell-ringers, references to the Garden of Eden. Several of your paintings are actually in a church in Oregon.

JHF: Christ on the cross, which I draw and paint a lot, I think of as representing all humanity. A lot of my paintings are symbolic, but I have no idea what they're symbolic of. But you can feel the symbolism when you look at them.

LF: Did you always want to be an artist?

JHF: No, I wanted to be a cowboy first, obviously. Who wouldn't? I wanted to be a biologist, which would've been a terrible mistake since I'm allergic to animals. But becoming an artist never occurred to me. Well, maybe it did, because I wanted to paint the dioramas that you see at the Museum of Natural History. I just didn't know then that that made you artist. My father would take me when I was very little, four or five, before we lived in the country all the time. We'd walk across the park to the Metropolitan Museum of Art, and the next week we'd go to the Museum of Natural History. Later, I never thought of getting married or having children. My plan was to just make art. I don't know if I wanted to be an artist, because that seemed to involve a whole other thing, with lifestyle, and people, and shit you have to do that I don't like.

LF: You've spoken about hearing colors. You heard paintings when your parents took you to museums. Do you still hear colors?

JHF: I mostly hear tinnitus now. I don't think I hear colors anymore, but I cannot listen to music and paint at the same time. But, yeah, everybody in the family has synesthesia.

LF: You always say you moved so often because of Robin, but you had a touch of wanderlust. You ran away from New York's Little Red Schoolhouse when you were little.

JHF: I was out with a group of children in Central Park. I wandered away to explore. And I was found by a policeman on the other side of Fifth

Avenue. Obviously, they can't have little children escaping, so the school had my parents take me to a psychiatrist. She had white hair, and a sandbox in her office, which had really bad lighting. I always cared about lighting, no matter what age I was, and I would escape, mentally, through the windows out over the roofs.

LF: But indirectly, her advice ended up influencing the kind of artist that you became.
JHF: She said, "Just let her go. Let her be a feral child." Because we had a house up in the country, that was perfect. I was a feral child from then on. I played in an abandoned cemetery next to our property. I'd take my clothes off, I'd wander in the forest, and nobody paid any attention to me. I was very lucky that I got to live in the wilderness, grow up in the wilderness alone. Feral children develop a little compass in their heads. They always know where they are. So I can't get lost in the mountains. And I think that's why I paint that kind of stuff.

LF: Much has been made of Robin's work as an agent, his time as Paramount production chief, and his famous clients, who included Marlon Brando, Gene Hackman, Elizabeth Taylor, and Richard Burton. But I don't feel as if Robin's world influenced your art.
JHF: How would it?

LF: You could have made wooden cutouts of movie stars instead of interesting-looking people who captured your imagination. You could have painted the estates of famous actors. Picfair, say, or L.A.

landmarks like the Chinese Theatre, instead of your series of peaks in the Hollywood Hills.
JHF: I was not a Hollywood person. I was *not*. I thought having to go to those Hollywood things, like the Academy Awards, was work. The people I did like were writers, artists, and I guess some producers. I am definitely not a party girl. But, remember, that was in the Seventies. It was like we were all hippies. Life was fun. People weren't on their iPhones all the time. People had time to hang out. There were important deals made on the porch while people were eating, petting the dogs. But I was never involved in any of that, because I was always cooking or taking care of the children. People always ask if it's possible to be an artist and a mother, and I say I don't think so, unless you have help. I had help.

LF: The writers Christopher Isherwood and Michael Crichton were friends. I remember meeting them at your taco parties. But you've also been linked to the group of West Coast artists now referred to as the Cool School: Ed Ruscha, Billy Al Bengston, Joe Goode, Laddie John Dill, Chuck Arnoldi. Some critics have even suggested Ruscha influenced your use of fire and letters.
JHF: It's totally unconscious. I did not use letters thinking of Ed Ruscha at all. A lot of people use letters. I started painting fire while seeing a prescription burn while hiking. And I didn't know about them being the Cool School. They were all friends through Billy, who was our best friend for fifty-three years. Later so was his wife, Wendy Al. We ate tacos and drank. Some of them smoked pot. Billy gave me my how-to

art books: *The Artist's Handbook; Materials of the Artist*. You could look up how you want the paint to last, and how not to fuck it up. If I had a question, I'd ask Billy. I could ask him how to do anything, and he was very kind. He always had the answers.

LF: He described you to Wendy as "a monster."
JHF: Wendy said it was a good thing, so I was flattered. I don't know what he meant. I think he was talking about how hard I worked, all the time.

LF: You've always had a rich dream life. Do paintings ever come to you as you sleep?
JHF: Only paintings about the hidden magic of water and magical hidden fish. Because when you're walking along a creek, aren't you imagining what's underneath? Fish under water are supposed to be symbolic of the subconscious.

LF: Fish may be symbolic, but they're also a real part of your life, and so often they make their way into your work: Atlantic cod below a burning oil rig; fat brown trout in Rush Creek in the Sierra; sharks; and giant mutated wels catfish in the Chernobyl cooling pond.
JHF: My first fish, I think it might have been a small-mouth bass, I caught with my hands. I must have been about three. I always fished with a stick and an eagle claw hook, and worms. I fished for chub and ate them. I always fished, but I didn't discover fishing again until the early Seventies, after I came to California. Fly fishing is a totally other thing, but any kind of fishing is a thrill.

LF: You've said that it takes time to internalize a landscape. I imagine that must apply to rivers, too, when you're painting them, and fish as part of the waterscape.

JHF: You do get to know a river. You know every inch of it, every undercut bank, every tailout, every riffle. The Cowichan River, in Canada, is an amazing river. It has steelhead. It has giant, voracious browns. It has a few rainbows. I love that river. I walked it. I floated it.

LF: I don't think I've ever seen you as happy as when you're sitting on a riverbank trying to choose the right fly to cast. It must make a big difference to a painting when you know and understand the entirety of a river, even if you're painting only one section.

JHF: You paint the caddis hatch, you know where the steelhead hang out, and the tailouts, I painted all of that. Of course, you know the colors if you've walked it year-round. You know how all the colors change, and when the skunk cabbage comes up in the spring. The bears wake up, and they eat the skunk cabbage. I painted that. It was exciting learning the Cowichan. It was my home waters for ten years and there's nothing like home waters that you love, like Rush Creek.

LF: Can you talk a little about being self-taught?

JHF: I've said before that I do think all artists end up being self-taught. But I was always trying to make stuff. We won't go into the time I smashed all my toys. I was maybe seven or eight. I was locked in my room, and I was angry, and I ended up making my own toys to replace the ones I de-

stroyed. I started making all kind of things. I made dolls out of wood and grass. I used to burn wood. Glue things together. I was always trying to do carpentry and I was really bad at it. Like everybody, I made a raft out of inner tubes and wood.

LF: Not everybody makes a raft out of inner tubes and wood! Did you learn to draw and create things at school?

JHF: When I was about twelve, I was given one of those paint-by-numbers things. I was sitting at the desk in the country house trying to paint this snow scene, paint by numbers, and I looked out the window and saw the snow. I thought, *wait a minute*. And so I tried to paint the real snow, and I wasn't very successful, but I painted things like the special kind of light over the beaver dam in November. I still can't paint snow. I actually made my first money as an artist at that age by drawing penises, at a nickel at a piece, for the girls at school. In grammar school we were told to outline everything in a black line and that probably could have been fun and interesting, but that's not what I wanted to do, so I did something else. The teacher gave me a zero and told me I did it all wrong. I thought, *I'm never going to listen to any of you*. I would never teach a child to paint or draw.

LF: So you don't approve of art school?

JHF: I do. My grandchildren are going to art school. I wish I had gone to art school. I told my mother I wanted to, but she wanted me to become a secretary, so I left home. When students come out of art school and start doing things in

their own original way, that's good. But some of them don't. They just keep making what they've been taught. You look at their work and it's skillful, and good, and clever, but you think *why*? Why are they doing it if they don't really mean it? I think people can be brilliant, but derivative.

LF: You're a news junkie, also unusually well-read when it comes to politics and history. You've said that whatever happens in the world will find its way into your paintings. So often that is darkness and destruction: fire, burning oil rigs, ghost guns, assault rifles, the devastation of climate change, the Chernobyl landscape, even threats to the U.S. Post Office.

JHF: When the Ukrainian war started I was really upset, like most of the world, so I made a painting with a lot of death in it. All the things that humans do to kill ourselves and destroy ourselves: stealth bombers, religion, nuclear towers. But I painted them in a sort of timeless green world to remind us of the world we used to live in. I don't know if it'll still be there when this war's over.

LF: How do you feel when you start a painting and how do you feel when you finish it?

JHF: The thing I like about painting, or fishing, or reading, is that you cease to exist. Anyone who paints will recognize that. I've said before, when I start a painting I feel really hopeful: it's going to be great. I get a little way in, and I think, *Uh-oh*. Then I get farther in and, *Oh, it's just not working at all*. And then at the end, sometimes I think, *Well, it's ok-aay*. Or not too bad, or the colors are good.

Sometimes you look back at them years later and they're a little better than you thought they were when you finished them. That's why Robin didn't like me to burn them or throw them away. He'd say, "You'll change your mind."

LF: You and Robin had a remarkable partnership. I remember he'd drop into the studio a few times a day to chat and see how your work was going.

JHF: When Robin and I lived here in the mountains together, it was our very happiest, joint productive time. As always, he was in charge of everything. I'd ask him questions like, "What about the rays on that painting? That's not working." Or we'd talk about titles. He was such a help. We worked on everything together. He did his stuff—he was database guy—and I did my stuff. It was a job that was much more successful with two people working on it.

LF: So what next?

JHF: I don't think I'm going to live long enough to paint everything I want to paint. There's work I've been meaning to do my whole life and haven't got around to.

LF: Do you want to say what that work might be?

JHF: No, I don't. I'm not sure I could even do it. I might try, though, before I die.
I've always had an urge to do one giant painting, but I don't think it's going to happen.

LF: Why not?

JHF: Well, I'd have to get it in and out the studio door.

Above, Under and In-Between
The Paintings of Jessie Homer French

Francesco Bonami

Some might say that it's taking a shortcut to rely on geometrical abstraction in order to escape the conflicts that surround us—conflicts for which we are at times even responsible. I think of Agnes Martin in the middle of the New Mexico desert seeking solace in the simple gesture of drawing a line. Reality is not simple, whereas our gestures can be. Jessie Homer French toes the line between isolation and remoteness, and yet does not shrink from reality. Her paintings cannot be boxed within the confines of either outdoor art, or naïve. She paints not as soliloquy, but to establish a conversation with her surroundings, suspending judgment. Her art is a matter of exquisite balance between happiness, sorrow, and boredom—three elements we all must deal with at some point in our lives.

Jessie Homer French's work involves first negotiating a balance among these three elements, and then negotiating a balance between catastrophe and hope. Her small canvases embrace the possible evil of human intervention and tame it into an improbable harmony between the animal world, the environment, and structures of disruption devised by the hand of man: destruction mirrored by rejuvenation. In a memorable video work from 2008

Migration (part of his *Empire* series), Los Angeles artist Doug Aitken tells a story of an animal kingdom taking over human infrastructures in a world where all humans have disappeared. Humans have not, yet, disappeared completely from Jessie Homer French's narrative, but the majority are lying underground in graves that look like smartphone screens. We die, at least in this life. We mourn the dead, while they listen to us mourning.

Painting is not a matter of survival, but a way to gather time. Animals do not know what a painting is. Animals cannot heal their wounded identity. Animals do not understand the difference between life and death any more than they can distinguish the flames of an oil refinery from the fire rising from a parched tree, an act of immolation, sacrifice and protest against the deafness of humankind. Animals view the artist as a presence, as prey, as an alien element amidst a Nature they believe should belong only to them. Reality can be painted in its essence or in its presence. Jessie Homer French adopts the latter. Remaining within the presence of the real allows the artist to create in total acceptance of the looming possibility of an unavoidable Armageddon, whilst also allowing that the unavoidable could

be delayed indefinitely. Her visions are never grim or dark, in fact they emanate the luminosity of a relentless optimism. On top of the graves, flowers keep growing. Life, mysteriously, goes on.

A painting cannot put out a fire. A painting cannot prevent a pipeline from crossing a prairie. A painting cannot halt death. A painting can only help us to cope with all of this without judgment or resistance. Jessie Homer French slices up the world like a birthday cake, revealing the layers and the flavors. The layers of life are the "above," the "under," and the "in-between." The "under" where our destiny sinks and rests. The "above" where our dreams rise like kites to dissolve or disappear into either nothingness or eternity. The "in-between" where we stand in the present. Animals have no awareness of the above or the under. They roam the present in-between, oblivious and entirely belonging to it. Because our own consciousness is unbearable, we indulge in projecting onto the animal world. We want these animals to share the burden of fear, the burden of loneliness, while we keep the bliss of solitude for ourselves.

With her work, Jessie Homer French celebrates the bliss of solitude, the beauty of a remoteness that defeats both loneliness and isolation. Each painting is a journey pioneering the frontier of the mind. Life inside life, inside life, inside life. Nature inside nature, inside nature, inside nature. Paintings like Russians dolls concealing and containing the same simple, unavoidable meaning: we come into, and leave, the world alone. Life is a journey in which the "I" ceaselessly strives to become a "we," and by the time we believe we are a "we," we are on the threshold of death, forced to cross over alone, leaving behind the "we" and all who were part of it. This is what the small fairytales depicted by Jessie Homer French represent: souvenirs and postcards from a collective reality to which we never really belong. The animals, the burning woods, the man-made aggressions, the weather, the climate, the environment—these are nothing but disconcerting set-designs for this comedy or tragedy (or both) in which we play characters for a short time. All of Jessie Homer French's art generates this wonderful quilt made of wondrous backdrops before which people, animals, nature and human hardware perform their part before the curtain falls, and the souls crowding the hall of the universe's theater explode in a standing ovation, celebrating the successful failure of that exceptional play called life.

Our World, On Fire:
Jessie Homer French in the Arc of
Self-Taught Artists in the United States

Jen Sudul Edwards, Ph.D.

"You know, the world keeps burning, so I keep painting fires."[1]

I am consistently astounded by humans' disregard of Nature. Is there a bolder act of hubris? The fires, the floods, the dry lakes, the atmospheric rivers, the earthquakes shaking land after we frack and drill. To bring William Butler Yeats-via-Joan Didion's cautionary line into the present: the center will not hold.[2] Homer French documents it all—the burning trees (*Wind Whipped*, 2015; *Endangered*, 2020; *Red Moon Rising*, 2020; *Forest Blaze*, 2022), the oil fires out of control (*Oil Pipeline Fire*, 2014; *Oil Platform Fire*, 2019; *Blowout*, 2020). She also depicts the natural world implacably surviving despite deforestation (*Clear Cut*, 2017) and humans destroying their habitat (*Chernobyl Spring*, 2018). Her animals—human and other—stand resolutely, calmly. This is why I find the works so consoling, even with destruction, death, and desolation as subjects. To remain can be a form of resistance, its own strength. But the wild animals give me hope—a legion of furry and scaly Zen masters. As Los Angeles critic Michael Slenske has written, "they're the perfect antidote to a world on the brink of collapse."[3]

"If I start a painting, I always start it with great hope. You know, I think it's going to be wonderful, but then I don't really know what I'm doing, so every time I start a painting I feel that I'm starting from scratch. You're hoping it's going well when you start and you shape it out and then you get to the middle and you're kind of disappointed and then sometimes at the end it's ok or it's not. What are you gonna do?"

– Jessie Homer French[4]

The artist describes herself as "a regional narrative painter," aligning herself with two traditions.[5] The first is the untrained artist, sometimes labeled outsider, naïve, vernacular, or folk. Because these artists do not formally study perspective and figure modeling, their paintings are often distinguished by appearing flat, with depth implied by figure placement or objects simply reduced in size, not scaled via perspective with gradually receding depth. Figures appear flat, too, forward-facing or in profile with a hard-edged silhouette and stiff poses without gradations or shadows. These artists generally paint what they know, though this could mean what they see as they walk the world, or in their imaginations. "Regional narrative painter" also recalls the American Regionalist movement of the first half of the twentieth century. These artists popularized rural and landscape scenes—farms, hills, hoedowns—often with aerial perspectives and flat treatment of space, light, and figures. Most studied in art schools and on trips to Europe, but also incorporated the subjects and aesthetics of untrained folk artists—which, from the 1920s, were becoming the vogue in antique shops and museums. Commercial and institutional attention collided, but it's unclear which came first—the market, the approval, or the artists leading the way.

"If I'm a regional narrative painter I'm going to be painting the region I live in. In the beginning, it was West Mountain in Upstate New York and then when I moved to California it was California and then when I got to Oregon it was, you know [Oregon], and Canada it was Canada. You paint what's around you, whatever landscape you're in, you internalize but sometimes it takes a few years to internalize a landscape."

— Jessie Homer French[6]

Folk art exists wherever and whenever there are people, but the tradition had an unusual evolution in the early centuries of the United States. There was not a single tradition or artistic style to represent the colonized Americas; instead, there was a collision of Indigenous, European colonist, and enslaved African cultures. The art historian and dealer Jane Kallir posited that folk art evolved in the United States specifically because it allowed each faction to preserve the cultural heritage from their homeland, while inflected by the other influences.[7]

Although many of the European immigrants were from predominantly conservative Protestant sects, American folk art took on more secular subjects—portraits, historical subjects, landscapes and town scenes—instead of the religious topics popular among European folk artists. Morality appeared through allegory, or Old Testament stories, as typified by the sign-painter-turned-museum-staple Edward Hicks. There were exceptions, especially with visionary artists in the South where there was a stronger Catholic presence through Spanish and Portuguese colonizers. Many of the styles imported by the dominant immigrant population in a particular region evolved with Western expansion.

Centuries later, a similar family tree of arts lineage can be traced through Homer French's body of work. Like Edward Hicks, she sometimes balances the gentle integration of biblical references into paintings that also imply secular leanings—*First Creatures – Vancouver Island* (2005) presents the region's indigenous creatures in Noah's ark; *Genesis* (2017) is both Bible quotation and textbook illustration of the lakes-rivers-ocean flow; *Death & Resurrection, Chernobyl* (2018) partners a crucifix and stag in the snowy, deserted intersection of forest and building. Homer French folds into this the American lineage of Regionalist painters and folk traditions, and also the California-specific painter Ed Ruscha, whose carefully articulated typography and LACMA-on-fire come to mind when seeing Homer French's paintings. The quilted "mapestries" like *The Salton Sea* (2016) and *Mapestry of California with Fish* (2016) acknowledge the "women's work" tradition championed by the CalArts feminists Judy Chicago, Miriam Shapiro, and Faith Wilding, to name a few.

Homer French also benefits from the United States' special relationship to landscape painting. In the nineteenth century, landscapes and scene-paintings became a favorite subject for folk artists and buyers. The landscape proved the perfect antidote to the photograph with distinctive colors and textures that Daguerreotypes could not capture. A landscape could offer an idealized, nostalgic presentation of the charm of the New World before the settlers altered it irrevocably. Unlike most parts of the world, the United States did not have any art academies until the Pennsylvania Academy of Fine Arts was established in 1805; therefore, folk art was seen not only as viable, but a homegrown creative product. This made it easier for the American Modernists to reintroduce the aesthetic into high-art circles shortly after World War I. Decades before Abstract Expressionism became the proposed visual language of the United States, this folk art tradition could be held up as stylistically unique to the country.

This is not to say that acceptance was instant or common. Since most self-taught artists worked other jobs, the time to make art was scarce, and recognition could come at mid-life or even later. Grandma Moses had her first one-woman show in New York City at seventy-eight years old, after a lifetime of being a farm wife; her life-story even defined her first exhibition in 1938 at Galerie St. Etienne, entitled *What a Farm Wife Painted*. John Kane was sixty-seven when he was accepted into that first Carnegie; Bill Traylor began making work in his eighties; Henry Darger's masterpieces were discovered after his death; Jimmy Lee Sudduth was relatively young at fifty-eight when he had his first exhibition; William Edmondson started sculpting in 1934 at sixty and had a MoMA retrospective three years later. Clementine Hunter started painting in her fifties and first received museum attention a decade later with a 1956 show at what is now the New Orleans Museum of Art. Indeed, Homer French had a successful first career as a model, and painted while raising four children, yet did not exhibit at the Biennale until she was in her eighties. While many self-taught artists find acclaim late in life, many start late too: and when seen in parallel with those who receive formal training, the ten- to twenty-year career arc is the same.

"The confusion caused by the various descriptive terms for self-taught artist leads one to ponder the problem of a name that will convey without ambiguity his place in the world of art. … A variety of names has been used, none of them adequate."

– Sidney Janis, 1942[8]

I am fundamentally uncomfortable tagging Jessie Homer French an outsider, folk, naïve, or whatever label we prefer. So is she. Those labels suggest that the artist created based on compulsion—the need to expel something out of their system. While this is certainly true for Homer French, I have yet to meet an artist—trained or not—who doesn't fit that description.
These labels also imply creating in a vacuum, without the influence of art history or other makers. This is often not true—and clearly not in the case of Homer French, who is thoroughly familiar with works by her California contemporaries Billy Al Bengston, Peter Alexander, Ed Ruscha, Joe Goode, Laddie John Dill, and Don Bachardy, many of which she has hanging in her home. Her relationship to Ruscha's lettering and treatment of fire has been noted by many.

The labels also connote a simplistic approach to material and composition. Yet that, too, is misleading. Like many artists in that category, Homer French has been practicing her craft for decades; she has painted over 1,200 works in the past fifty years. She is not only highly trained but limber enough to make choices as to how she will depict and deliver her message, even if each new painting feels like "starting from scratch."
How does that on-the-job training compare with someone only five years into a Master's degree? And in how many other artistic fields do we make a division between self-taught and formally schooled? Pop singers and musicians, woodworkers, actors, writers, filmmakers—we may cite their training, but it's not required and not surprising to find they were practicing privately until discovered by the public. However, those in the more formal modes—classical musicians, Shakespearean actors, opera singers—usually come with an expectation of formal, rigorous training. These genres have also been designated as elite art forms, requiring money and mentors. In the visual arts, the division between trained and untrained is a modern construct; as Kallir has noted, "In the Middle Ages there was no nonacademic art because there was no academic art. Artists were simply craftsmen."[9] Homer French speaks of the struggle she has with each painting, even after a long career: "I don't know how the style developed at all because I just keep trying to do each one right and then never feeling I get it right and then I don't know. It does seem to end up to be recognizable."[10] But here I am, with others, marveling at the power of her im-

ages, investigating their coded messages and analyzing their emotional punch and balm. Is the difference between schooled and untrained not skill or talent, but confidence?

"There can be no very black melancholy
to him who lives in the midst of Nature and
has his senses still."

– Henry David Thoreau.[11]

Nevertheless, Homer French draws on consistent elements found in self-taught artists: straightforward simplicity that delivers moral messages with highly personal subject matter. She also incorporates craft techniques, as in her early shaped animal paintings and the quilted "mapestries," which are both her impressions of the lands close to her home and artworks that she treats as "safe art for above one's bed in case of tremblors," in her earthquake-prone region of Southern California.[12] Fault lines prominently cut through the land in her quilts.
There are also the biblical references often found in early folk art, in paintings like *Mojave Burning* (2021) depicting the 2020 Dome Fire that destroyed much of the Mojave National Preserve. While Homer French claims the painting is more documentary than morality tale, it is hard to not find religious references—the Joshua Trees' biblical name, the allusion to the Burning Bush.[13] Will we wait to heed the message emanating from these flames?
Her treatment of space, in which figures confront us calmly, can result in deceptively quaint scenes. But the post-office series (*Piñon Crest Mailboxes,*

2021) is, in fact, political critique "delivered sideways," as Homer French describes her approach to topical subjects: here, a comment against Trump-era cuts to the postal system on which she depends.[14]

Like the twentieth-century American Regionalists, Homer French incorporates the static essence of the flattened perspective and frontal figures to evoke stasis, merging nostalgia with timelessness. If it weren't for the traces of industry, these paintings could be by a United States painter in the 1920s, 1820s, or 1720s. Those paintings, too, often wrestled with mortality and morality—typical themes included human insignificance in the larger arc of time, the continuum of nature, and the idealization of the American Dream versus its harsh reality. These motifs can be found in Homer French, too, but she introduces subjects unique to her lifetime: the climate crisis and the challenge of our moral responsibility toward Earth, a subject rarely seen in painting.

When the image is of a forest denuded or on fire, that nostalgia and timelessness become the ominous and urgent now and forever; our natural world being destroyed before our eyes. Or at least changing before our eyes. Homer French's straightforward depiction is both convincing and embarrassingly simple—how could we deny this obvious truth?

So, what are we going to do?

[1] Jessie Homer French, https://www.ryanschude.com/motion--jessie-homer-french#1.

[2] When I look at Jessie Homer French's paintings, Joan Didion's opening sentence from *Slouching Towards Babylon* always runs through my mind, but French points out that Didion, in fact, was quoting Yeats's poem "The Second Coming." Joan Didion, *Slouching Towards Babylon* (New York: Farrar, Straus, and Giroux, 1961), 84; William Butler Yeats, "The Second Coming," https://www.poetryfoundation.org/poems/43290/the-second-coming.

[3] Michael Slenske, "French Lessons," *Los Angeles Magazine*, April 22th, 2022.

[4] Jessie Homer French, https://www.ryanschude.com/motion--jessie-homer-french#1.

[5] Ibid.

[6] Jessie Homer French, https://www.ryanschude.com/motion--jessie-homer-french#1.

[7] Jane Kallir, *The Folk Art Tradition: Naïve Painting in Europe and the United States* (New York: Galerie St. Etienne and Viking Press, 1981), 21.

[8] Sidney Janis, *They Taught Themselves: American Primitive Painters of the 20th–21st Century* (New York: The Dial Press, 1942), 11–12.

[9] Kallir, 12.

[10] Ibid., Jessie Homer French, https://www.ryanschude.com/motion--jessie-homer-french#1.

[11] Henry David Thoreau, *Walden Pond* (New York: Open Road, 2010), 133.

[12] Jessie Homer French quoted in Jessica Gelt, "Stitching the Fault Lines," *Los Angeles Times*, January 24, 2016, F2.

[13] Jessie Homer French in conversation with editor Agatha French. For more on this painting specifically, Hannah Rotwein provides an excellent deep-dive analysis into the historical and social significance and the Dome Fire in her August 7, 2022 article for the online journal, *Glasstire*. https://glasstire.com/2022/08/07/beauty-and-unease-jessie-homer-french-at-various-small-fires-dallas/.

[14] Slenske.

Works

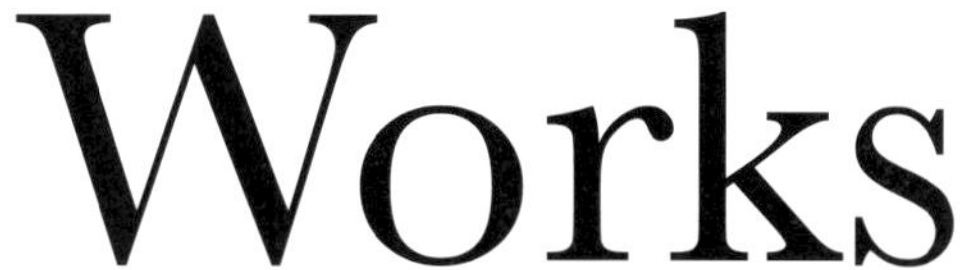

All works courtesy the artist, MASSIMODECARLO, and Various Small Fires.
The selection of works and their sequence were decided by the artist.

Looking at these hundreds of paintings I feel "my life flash before my eyes." My assistant, Nich, and I seem to agree on the ones we like the best, which is reassuring. We've winnowed it down to a couple of hundred or so, as I don't have good photos of everything.

People always ask me if I miss my paintings once they are gone. No. When I feel I've done the best I can and a painting is okay, I forget about it. (If I hate it I want to burn it. Sometimes I'm wrong about that.)

But, seeing these old paintings of my "home waters"—the Cowichan River, the McKenzie River, the High Sierras—I'd like to have them all around me for some "armchair fishing." (I have lots of fishing books for when I can't go fishing, and that's called "armchair fishing.") When I look at photos of these paintings I feel I am there. I can smell the river, the season, time warp to when the brookies are spawning in the high country of the Eastern Sierras, a brookie shooting up from the depths of a lake at 10,000ft to hit a 'hopper on the surface. There's one painting of browns in Rush Creek—my favorite summer fishing spot—an evening caddis hatch and alpenglow…

I won't go on. People's eyes glaze over when you talk about fishing, unless they are another fly-fisherman, of course.

Jessie Homer French

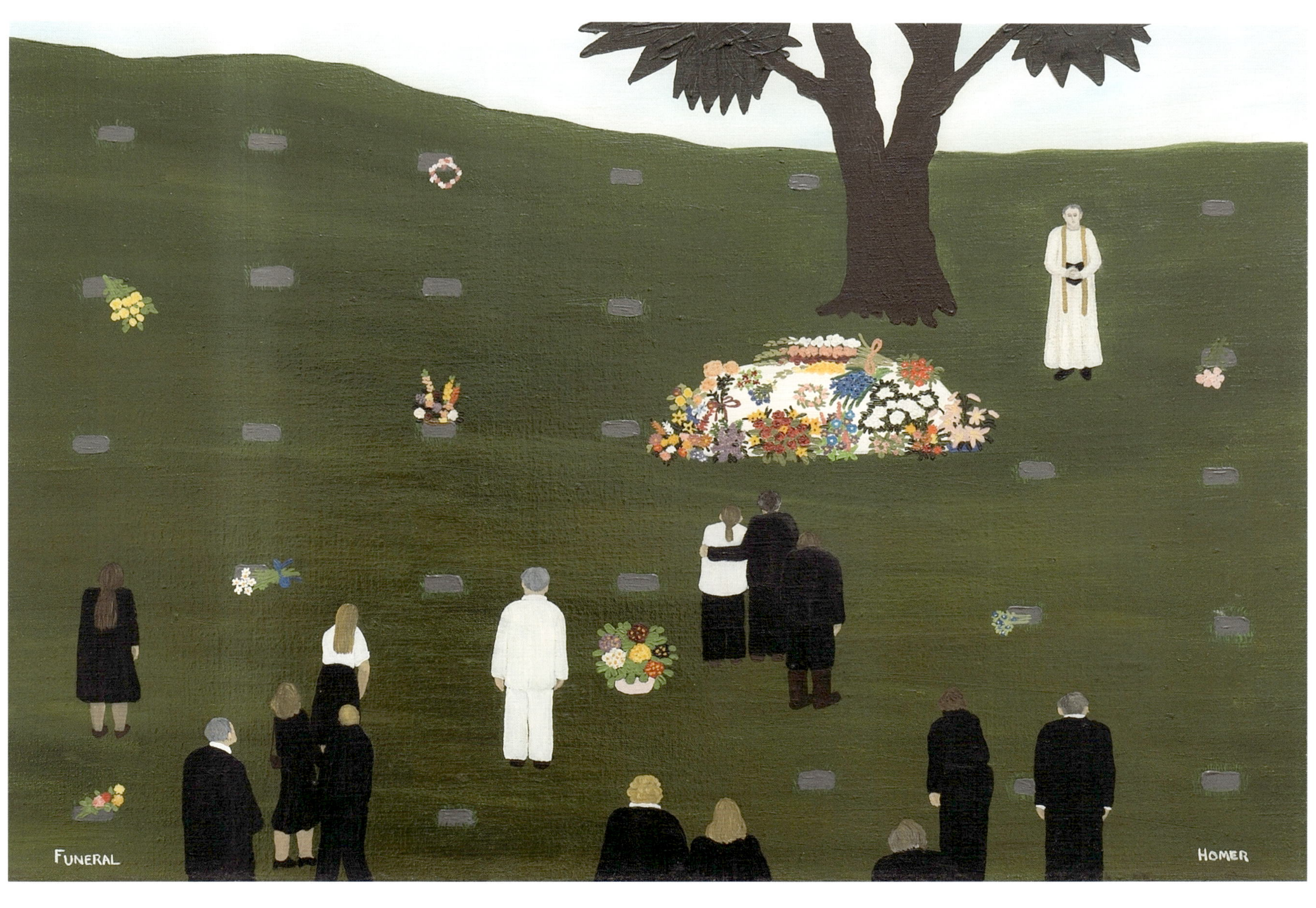

1. *Funeral*, 1978
Oil on canvas, 24 × 30 in. (61 × 76.2 cm)

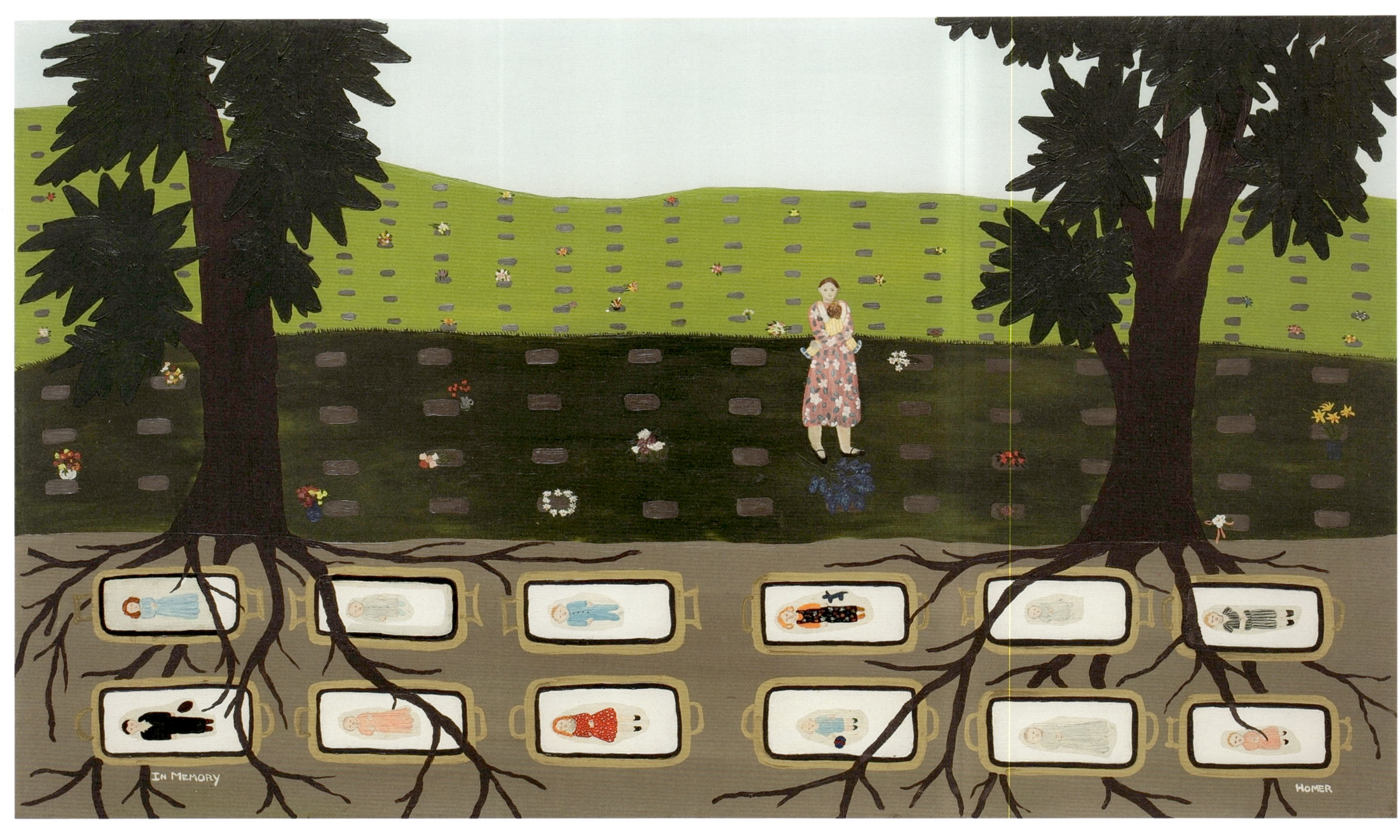

2. *In Memory*, 1985
Oil on plywood, 18 × 30 in. (45.7 × 76.2 cm)

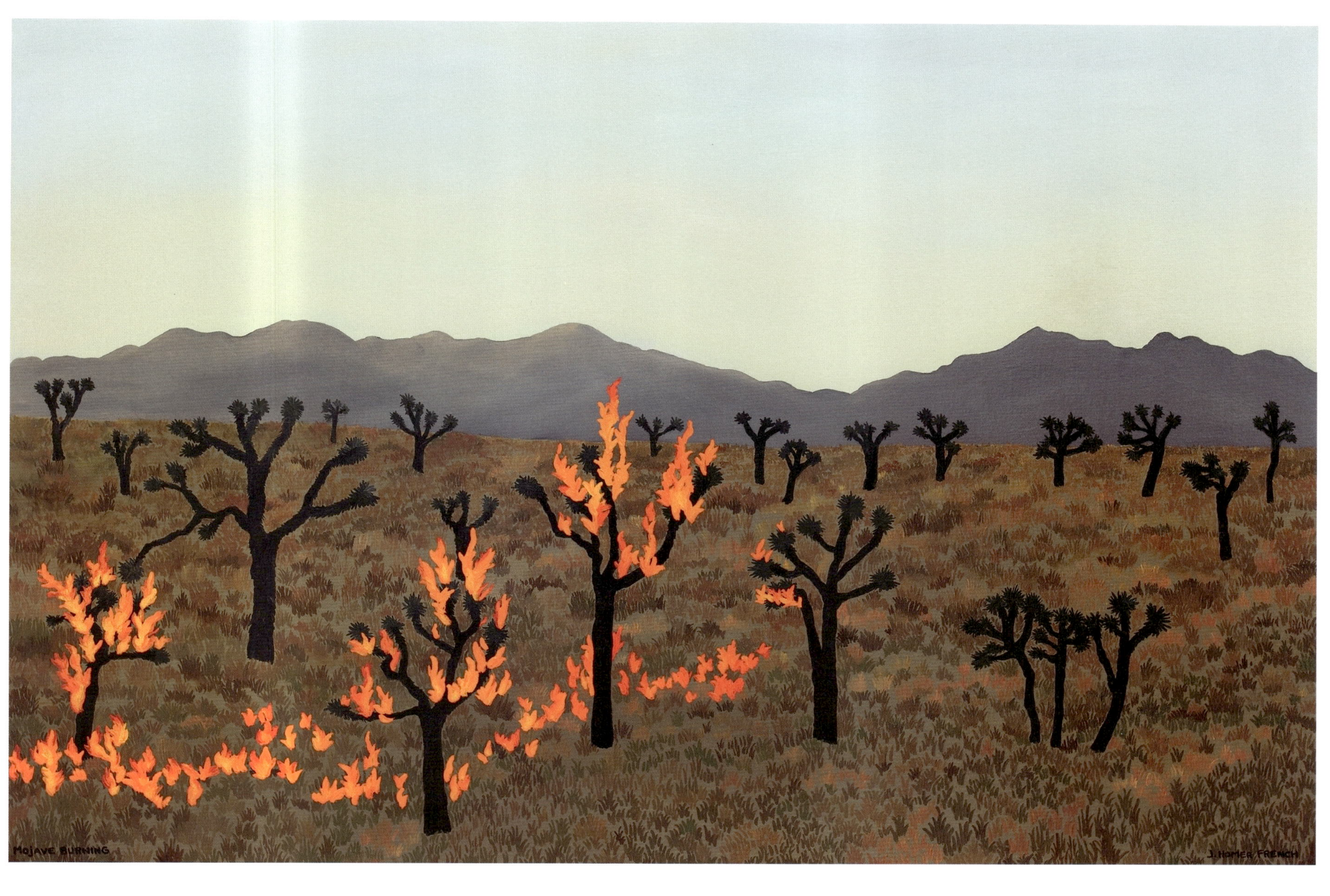

3. *Mojave Burning*, 2021
Oil on canvas, 24 × 36 in. (61 × 91.4 cm)

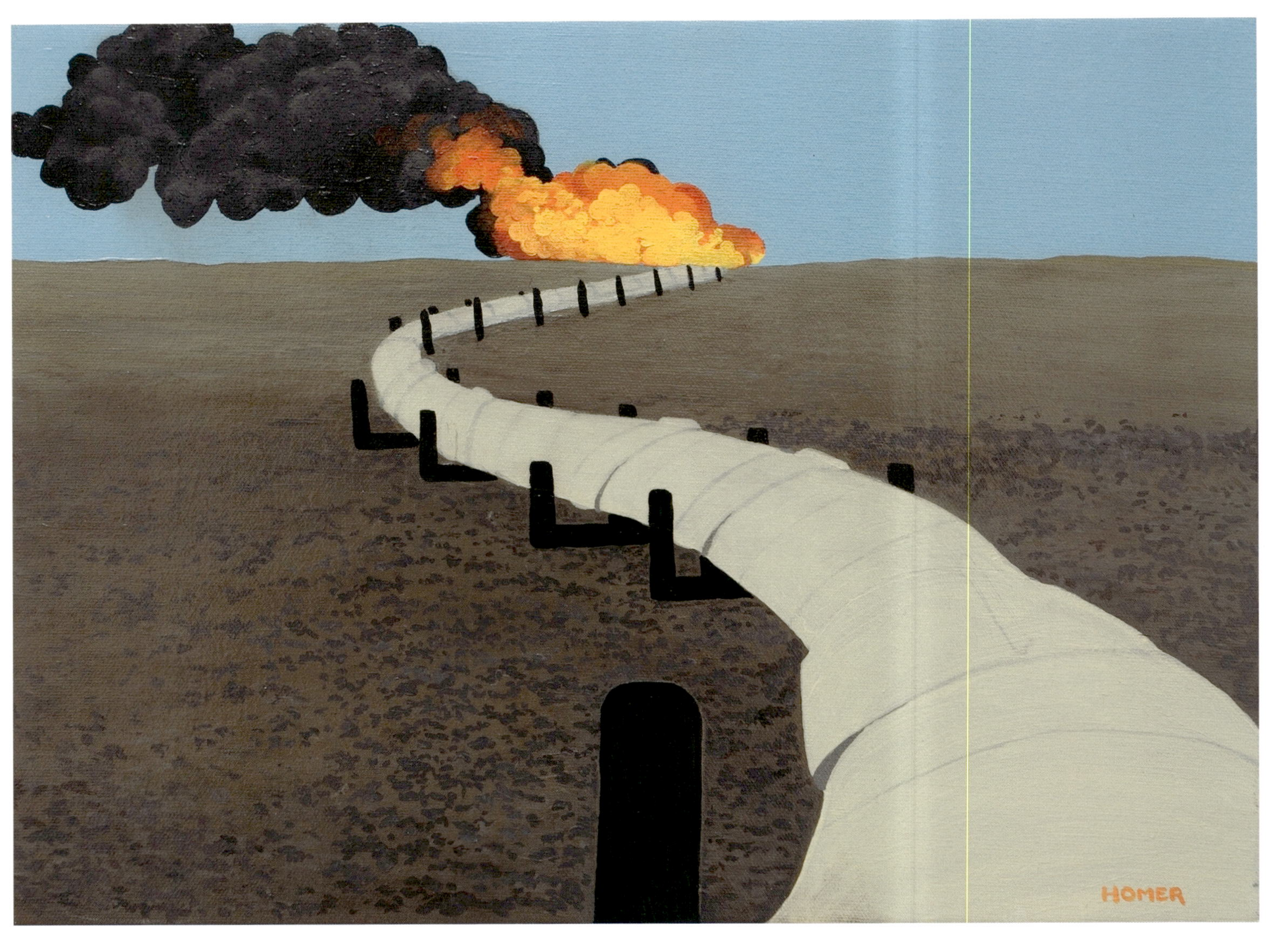

4. *Oil Pipeline Fire*, 2014
Oil on canvas, 12 × 16 × 1 in. (30.5 × 40.6 × 2.5 cm)

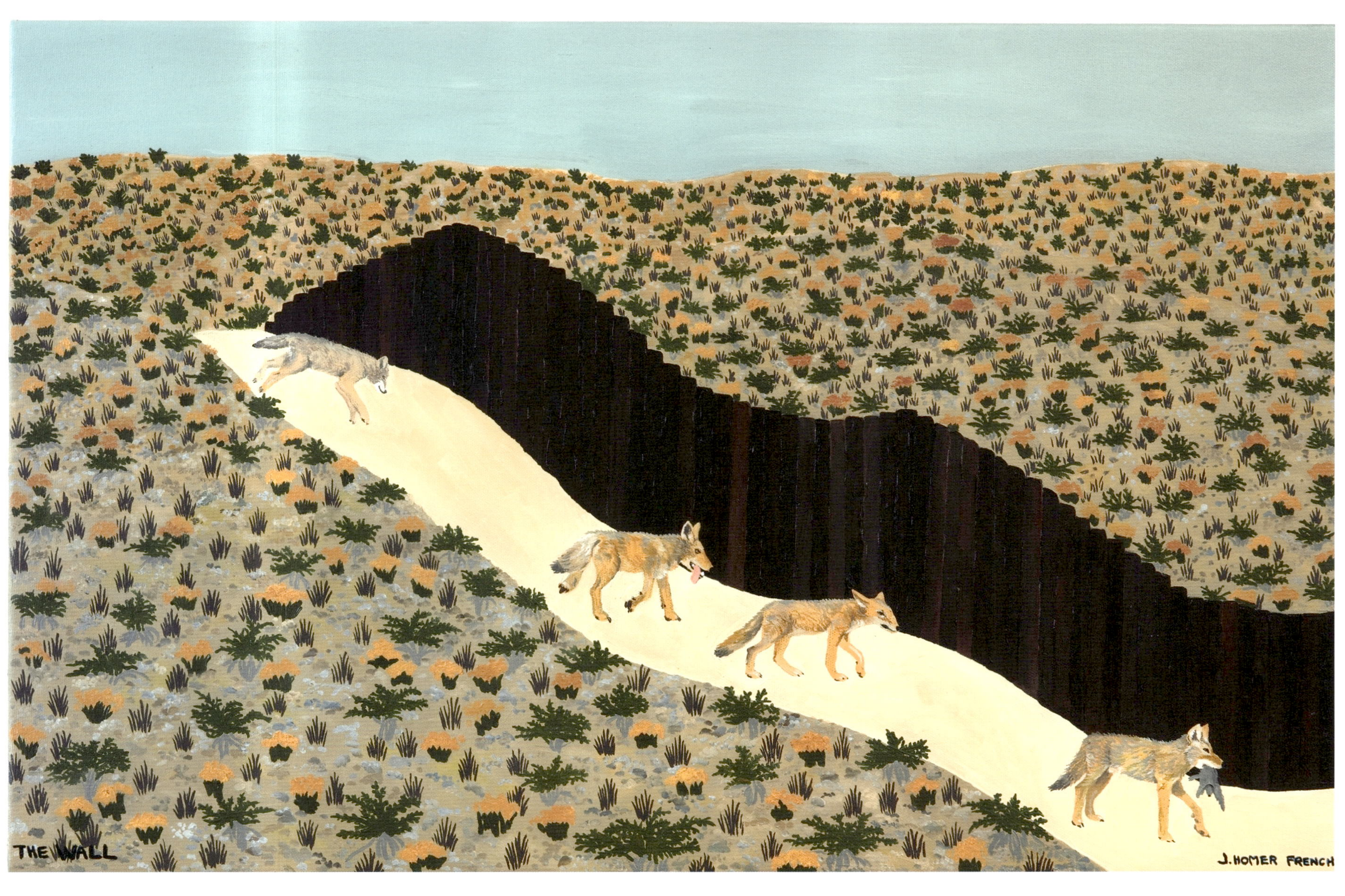

5. *The Wall*, 2021
Oil on canvas, 16 × 24 in. (40.6 × 61 cm)

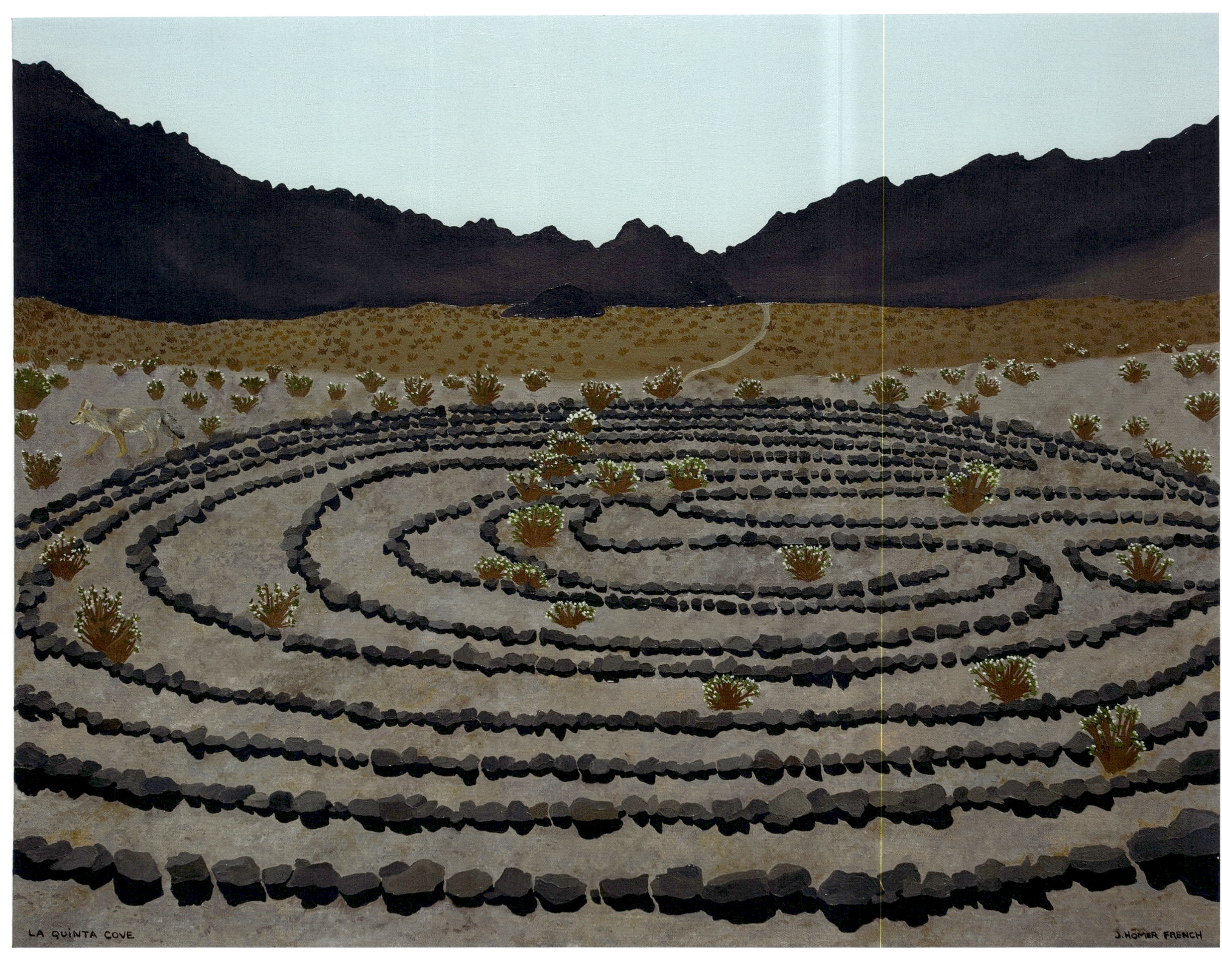

6. *La Quinta Cove*, 2021
Oil on canvas, 24 × 30 in. (61 × 76.2 cm)

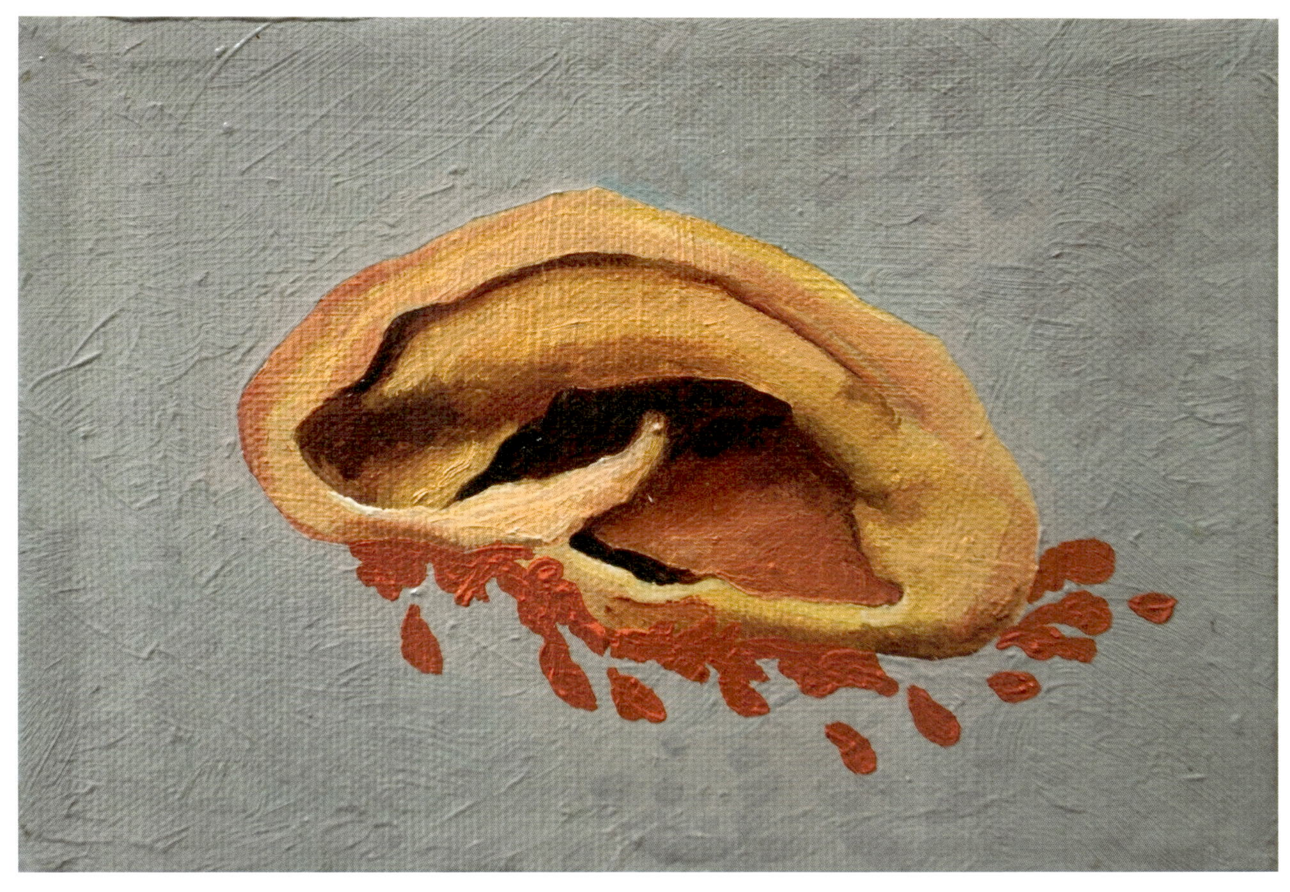

7. *Vincent's Ear 5*, 2012
Oil on canvas, 5 × 7 in. (12.7 × 17.8 cm)

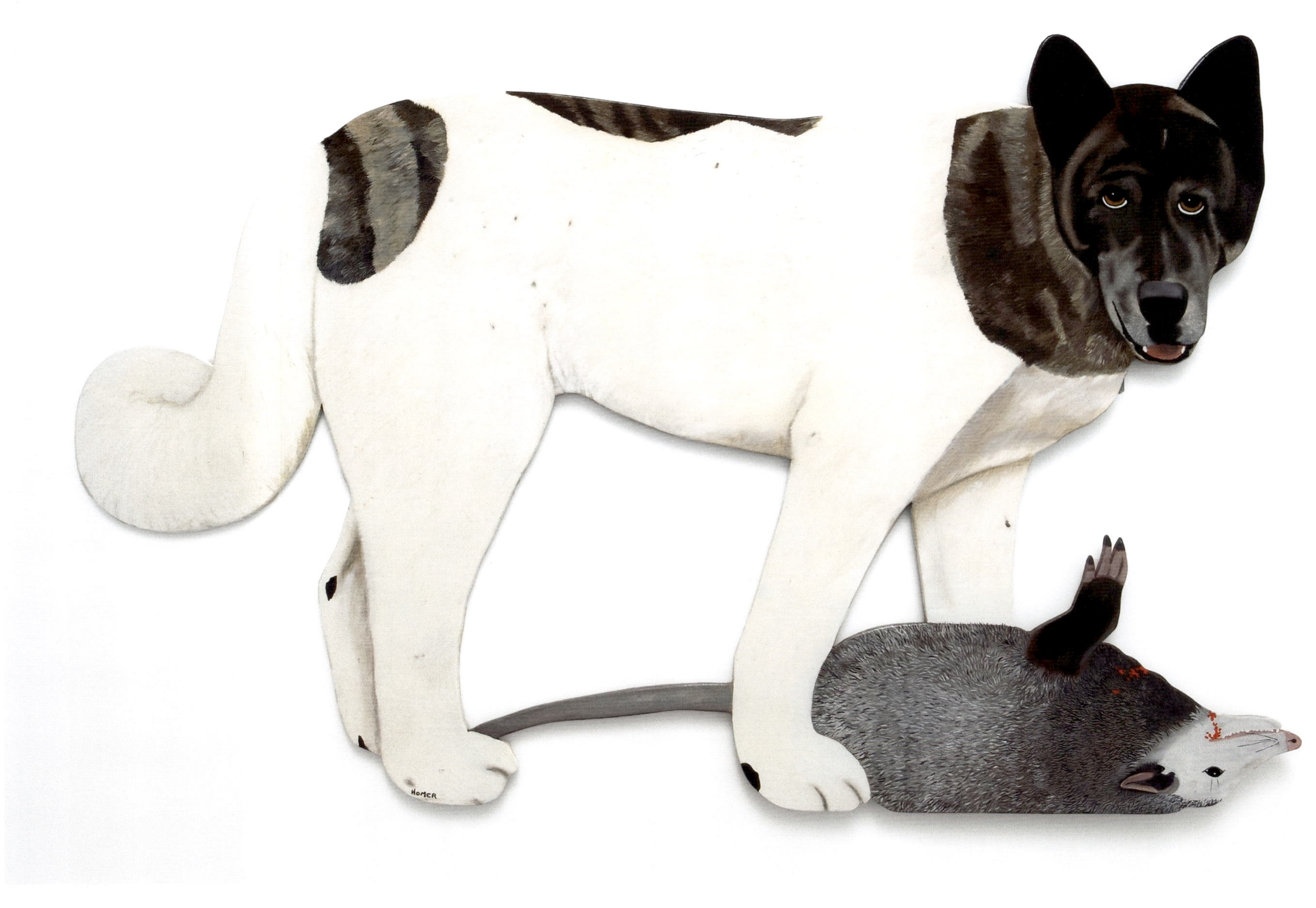

8. *Possum Killer*, 1993
Acrylic and oil on plywood, 42 × 68 in. (106.7 × 172.7 cm)

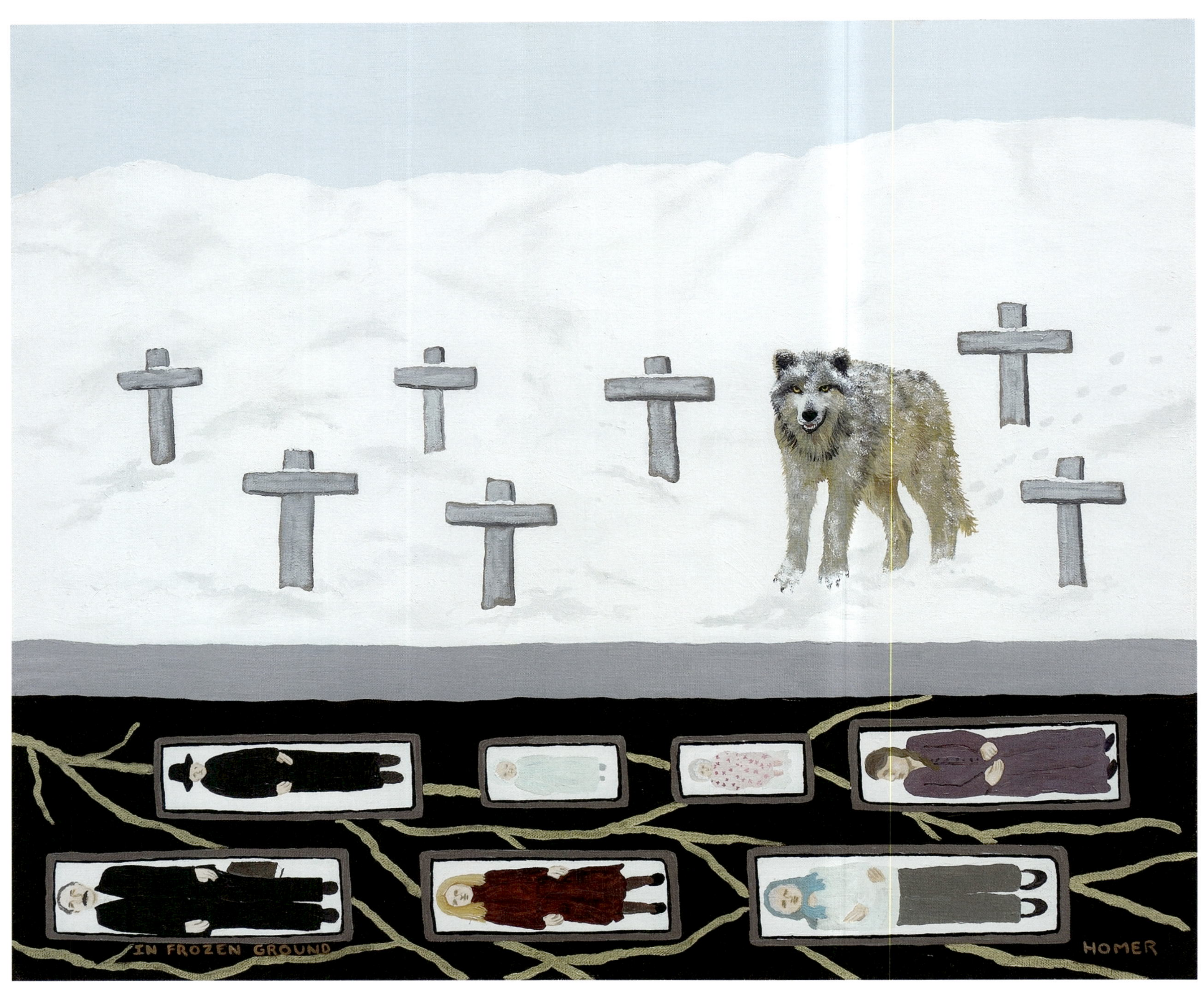

9. *In Frozen Ground*, 2003
Oil on canvas, 20 × 24 in. (50.8 × 61 cm)

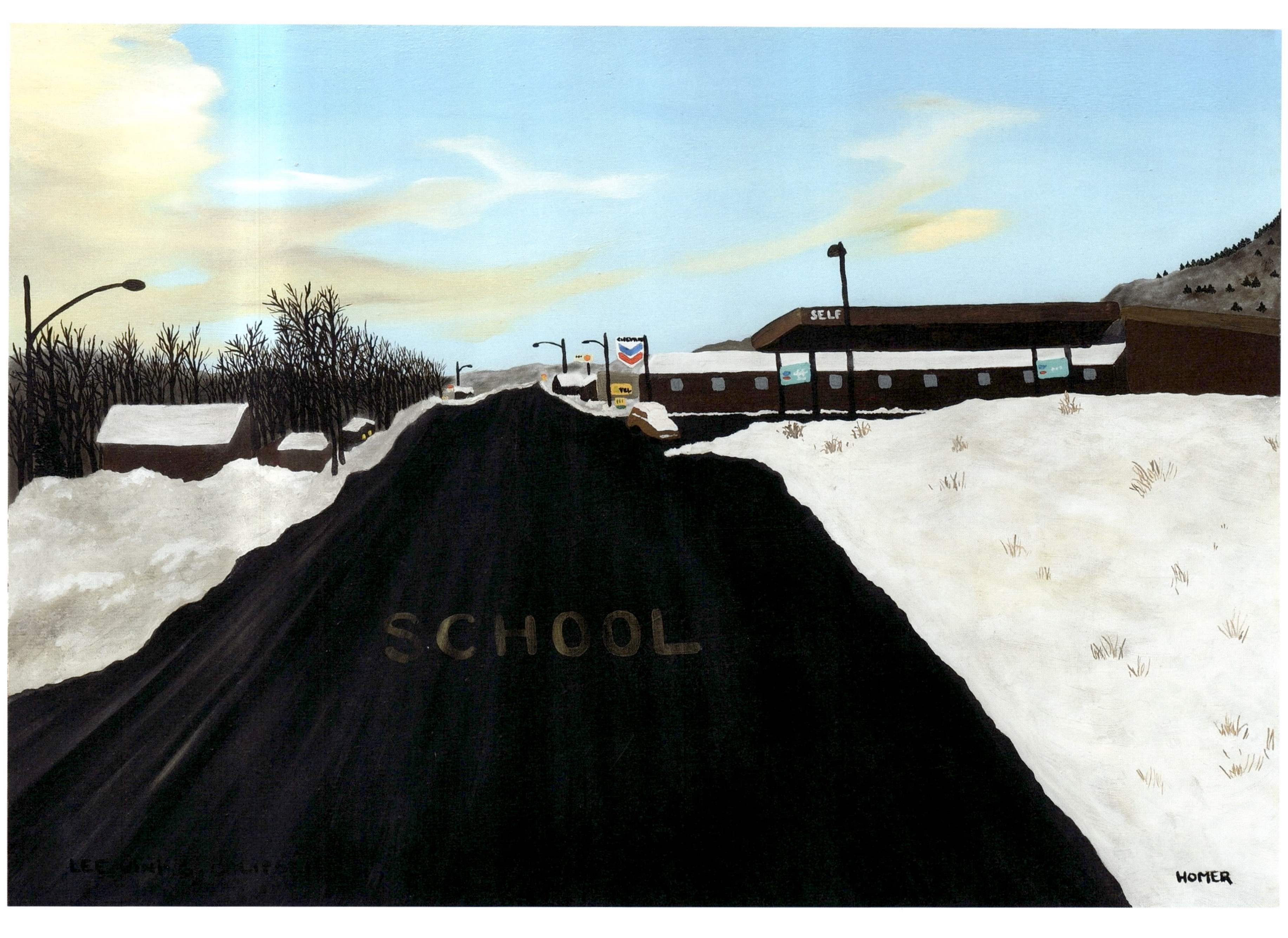

10. *Lee Vining, California*, 2000
Oil on plywood, 17 × 24 in. (50.8 × 61 cm)

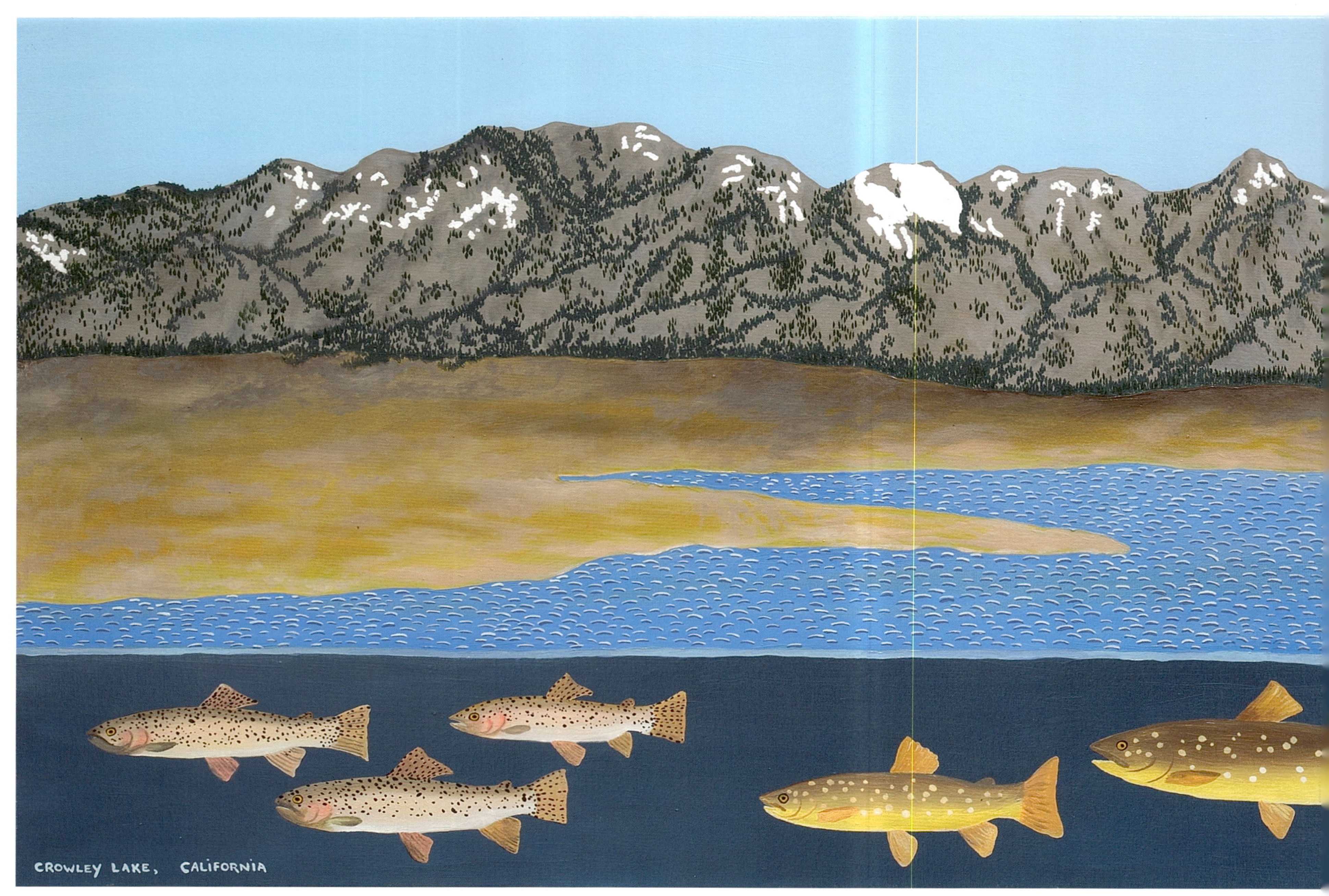
CROWLEY LAKE, CALIFORNIA

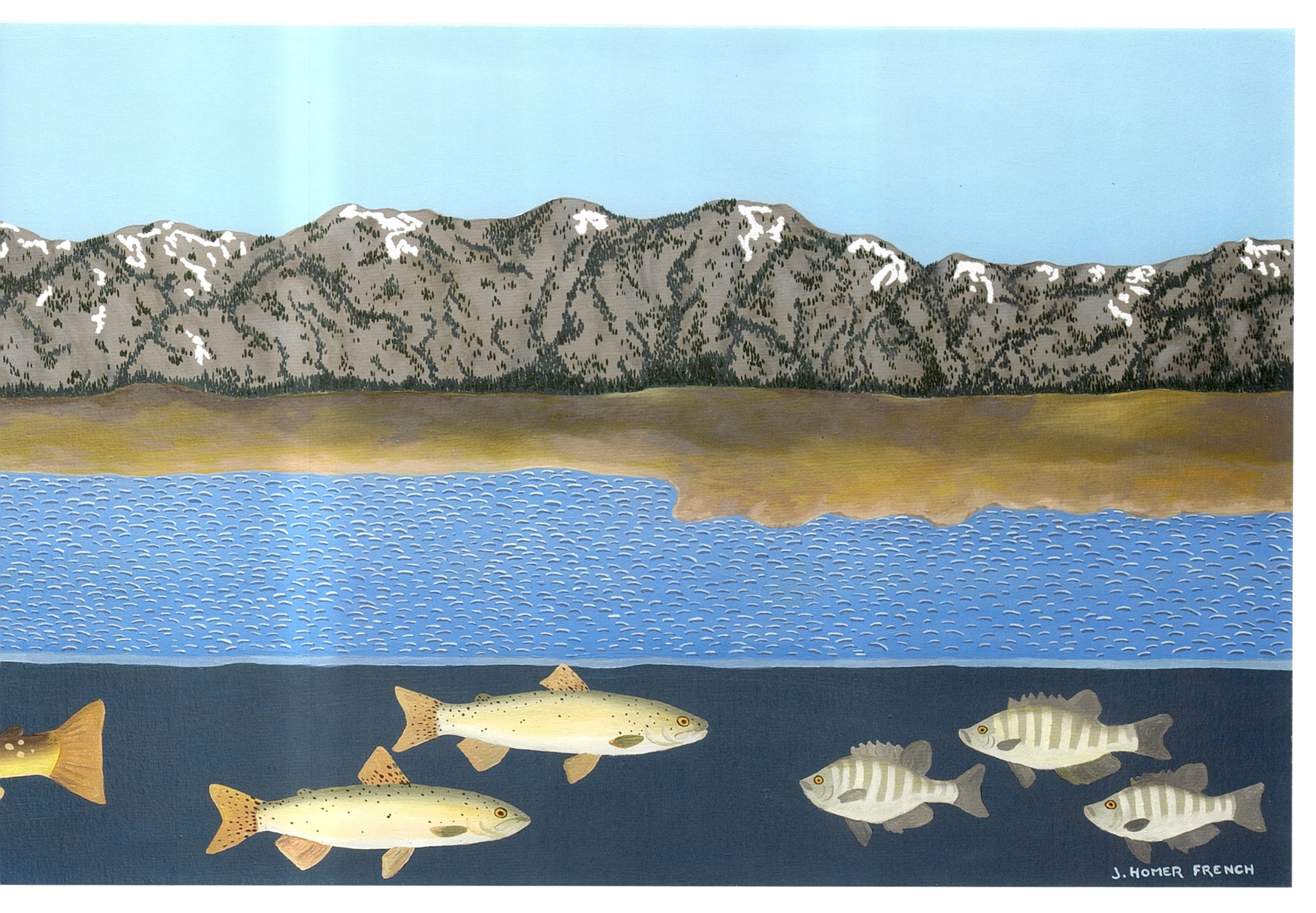

11. *Crowley Lake, California*, 2022
Oil on canvas, 20 × 60 in. (50.8 × 152.4 cm)

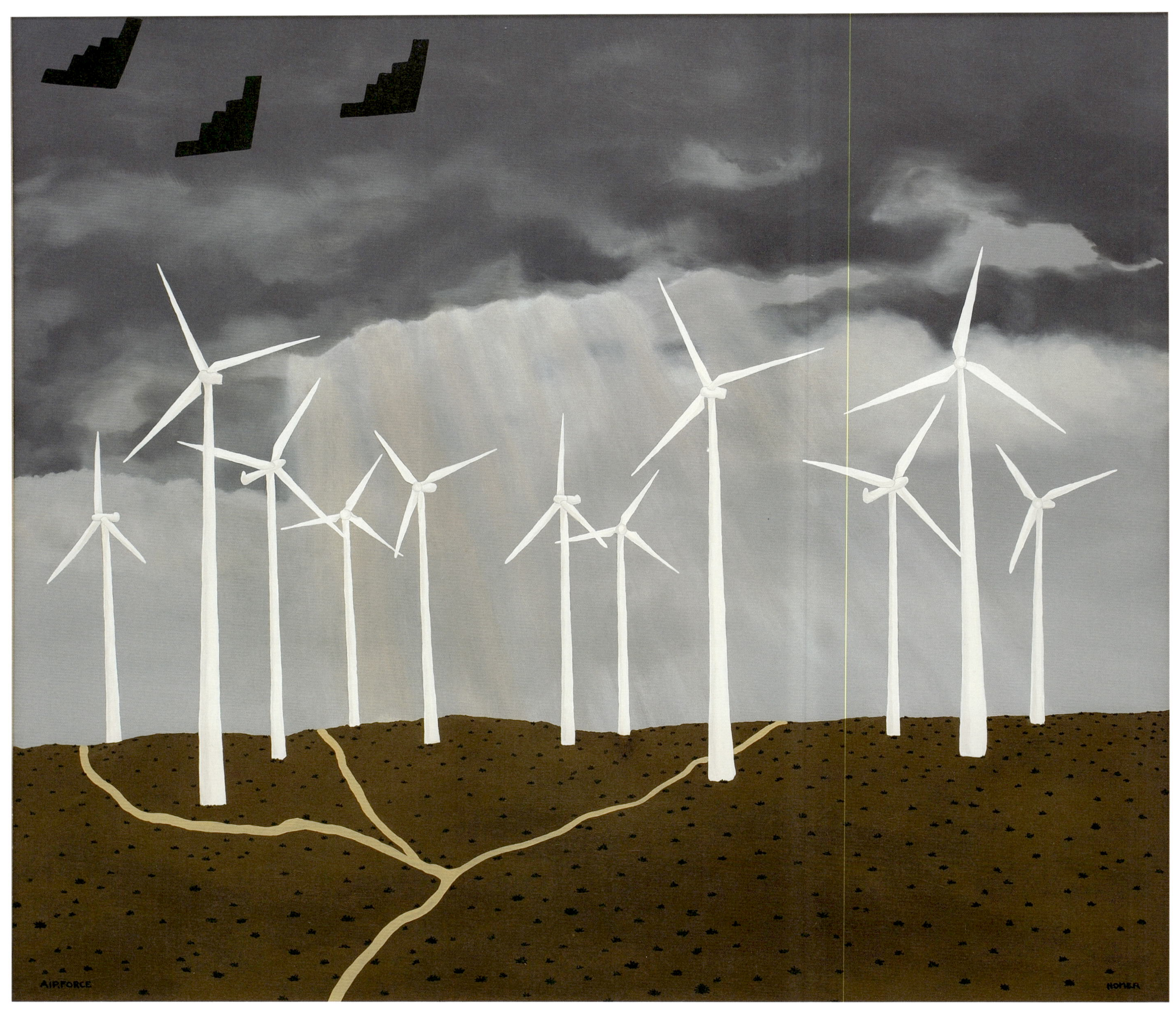

12. *Airforce*, 2014
Oil on canvas, 48 × 54 in. (121.9 × 137.2 cm)

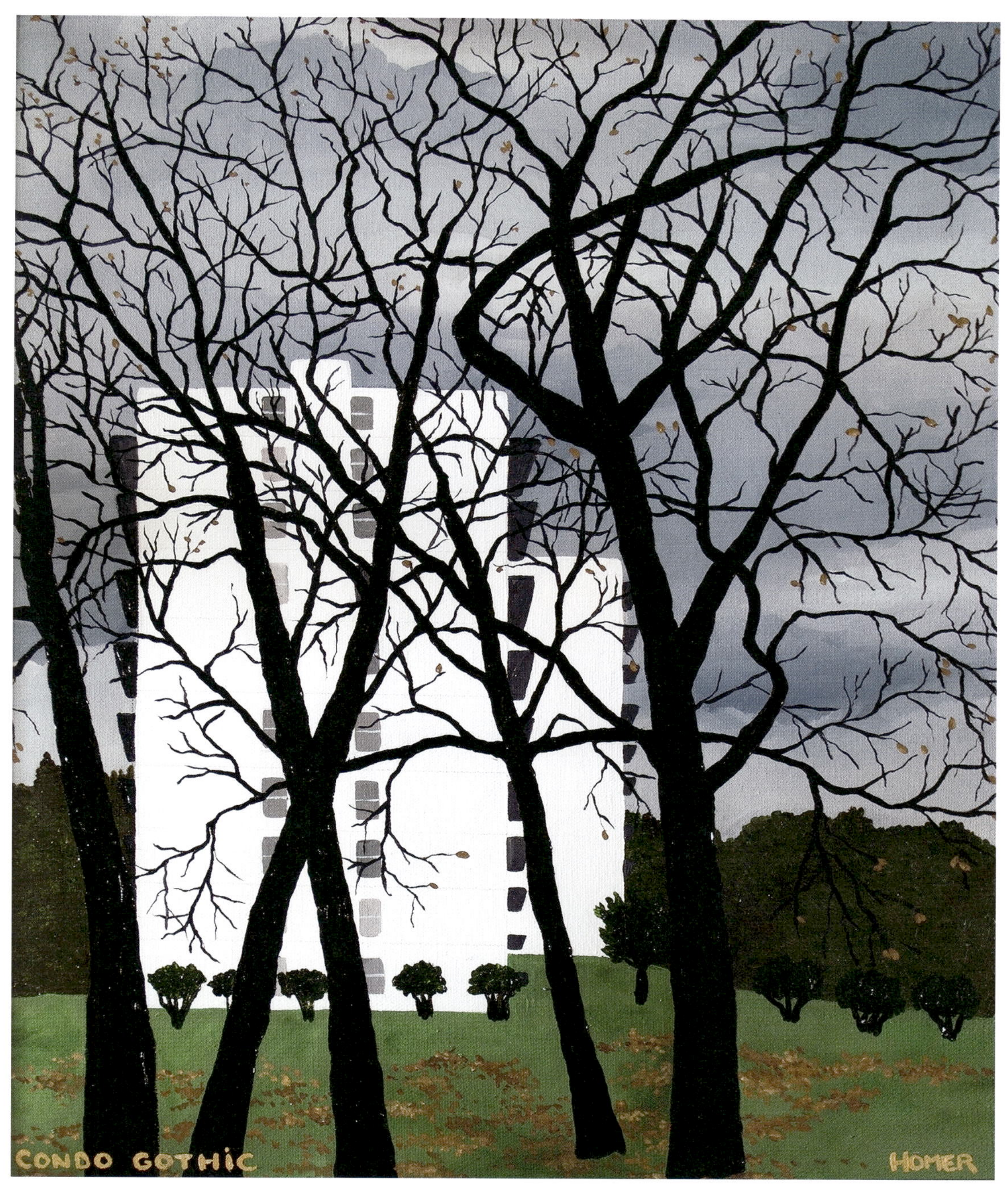

13. *Condo Gothic*, 2004
Oil on canvas, 18 × 14 in. (45.7 × 35.6 cm)

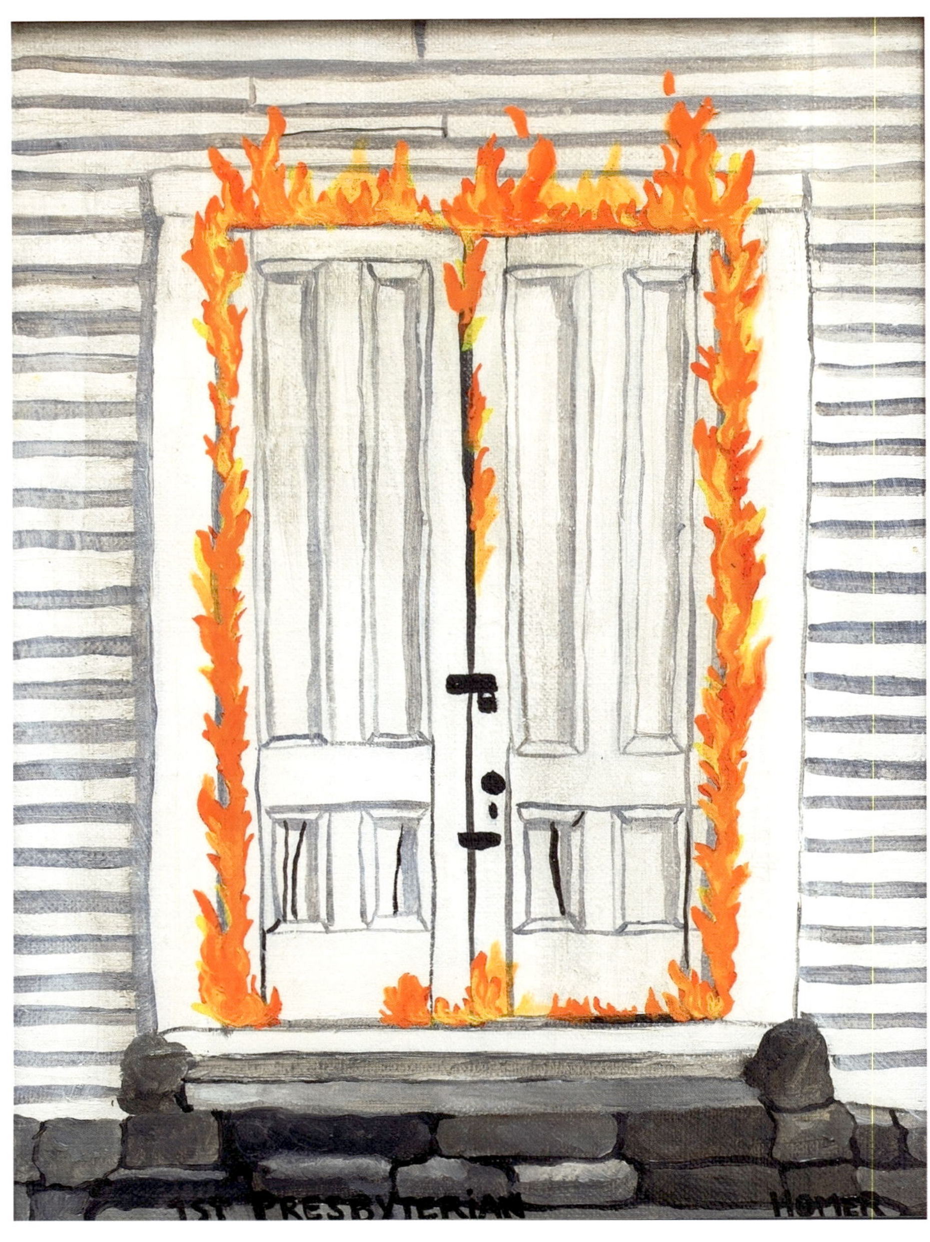

14. *1st Presbyterian*, 1994
Oil on canvas, 10 × 7½ in. (25.4 × 19.1 cm)

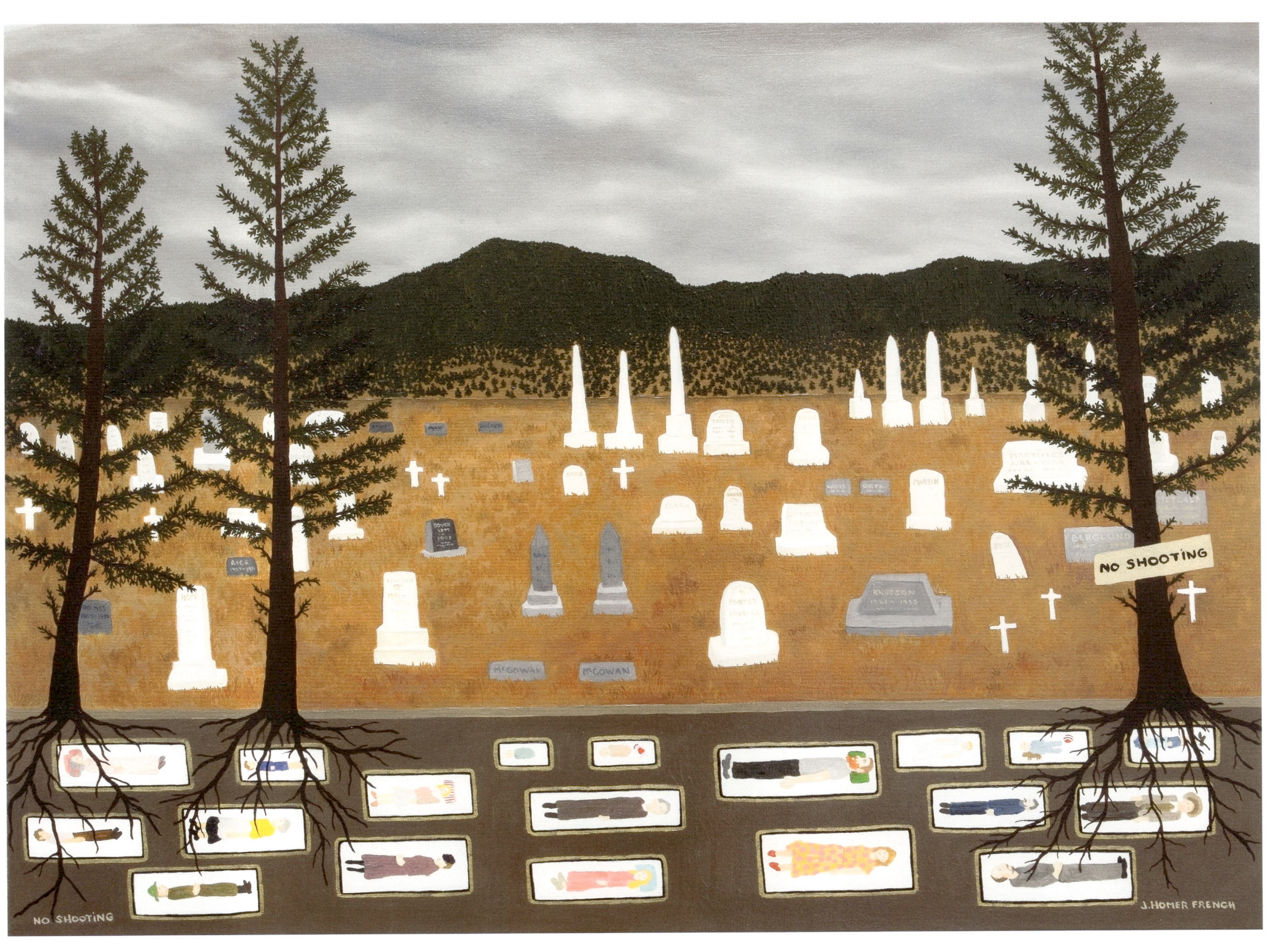

15. *No Shooting*, 2020
Oil on canvas, 30 × 40 in. (76.2 × 101.6 cm)

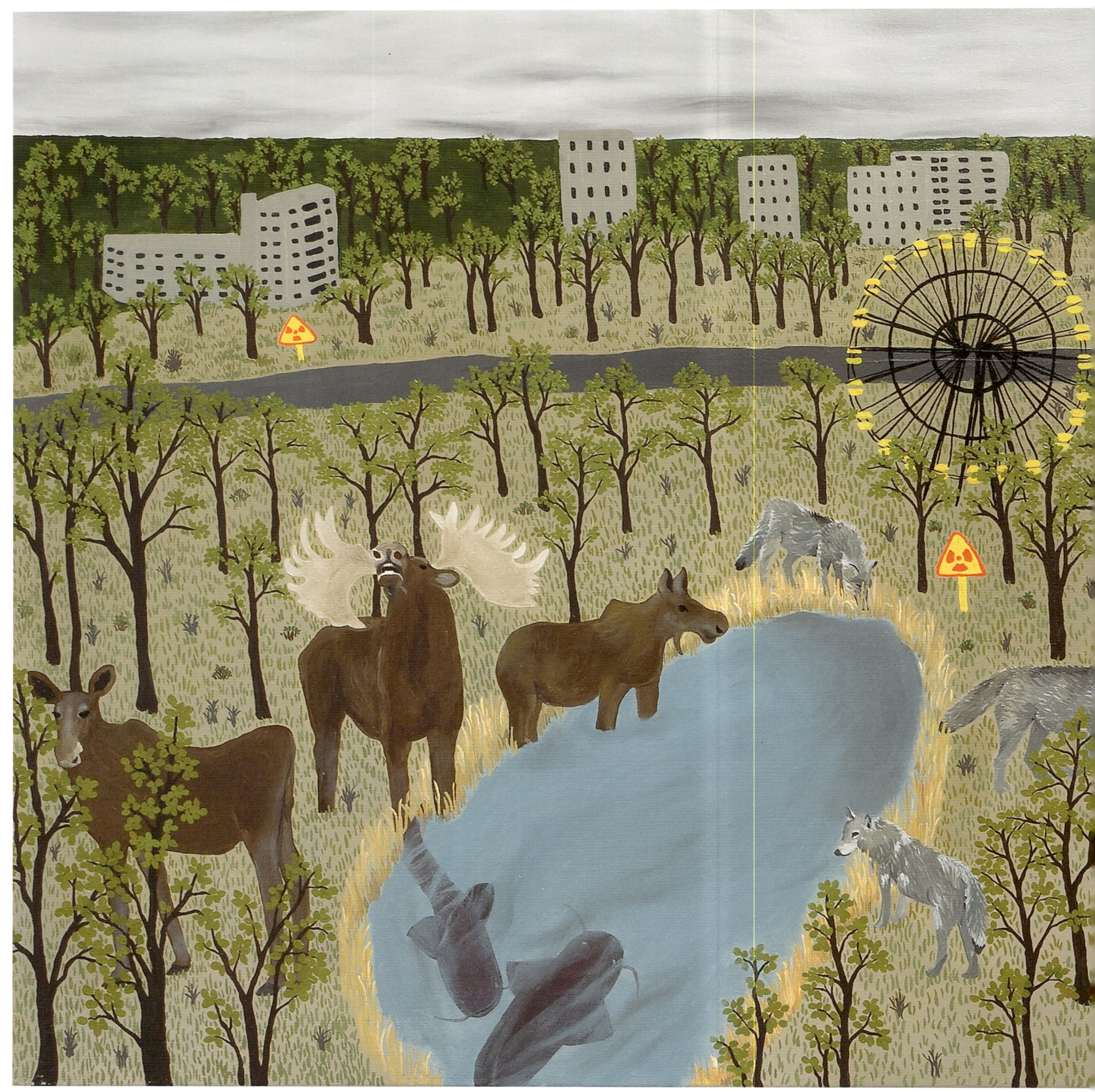

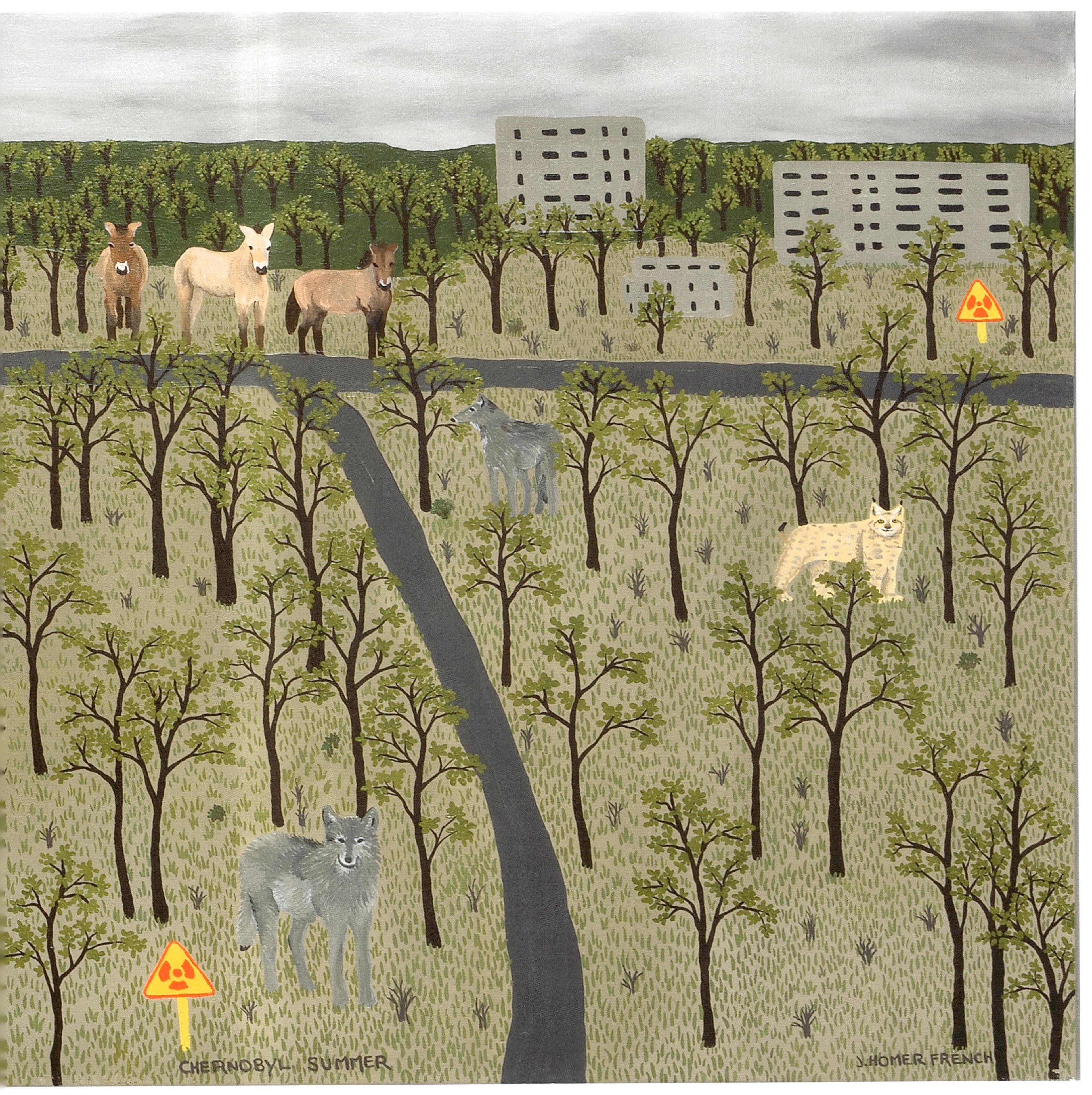

16. *Chernobyl Summer*, 2018
Oil on canvas, 24 × 48 in. (61 × 121.9 cm)

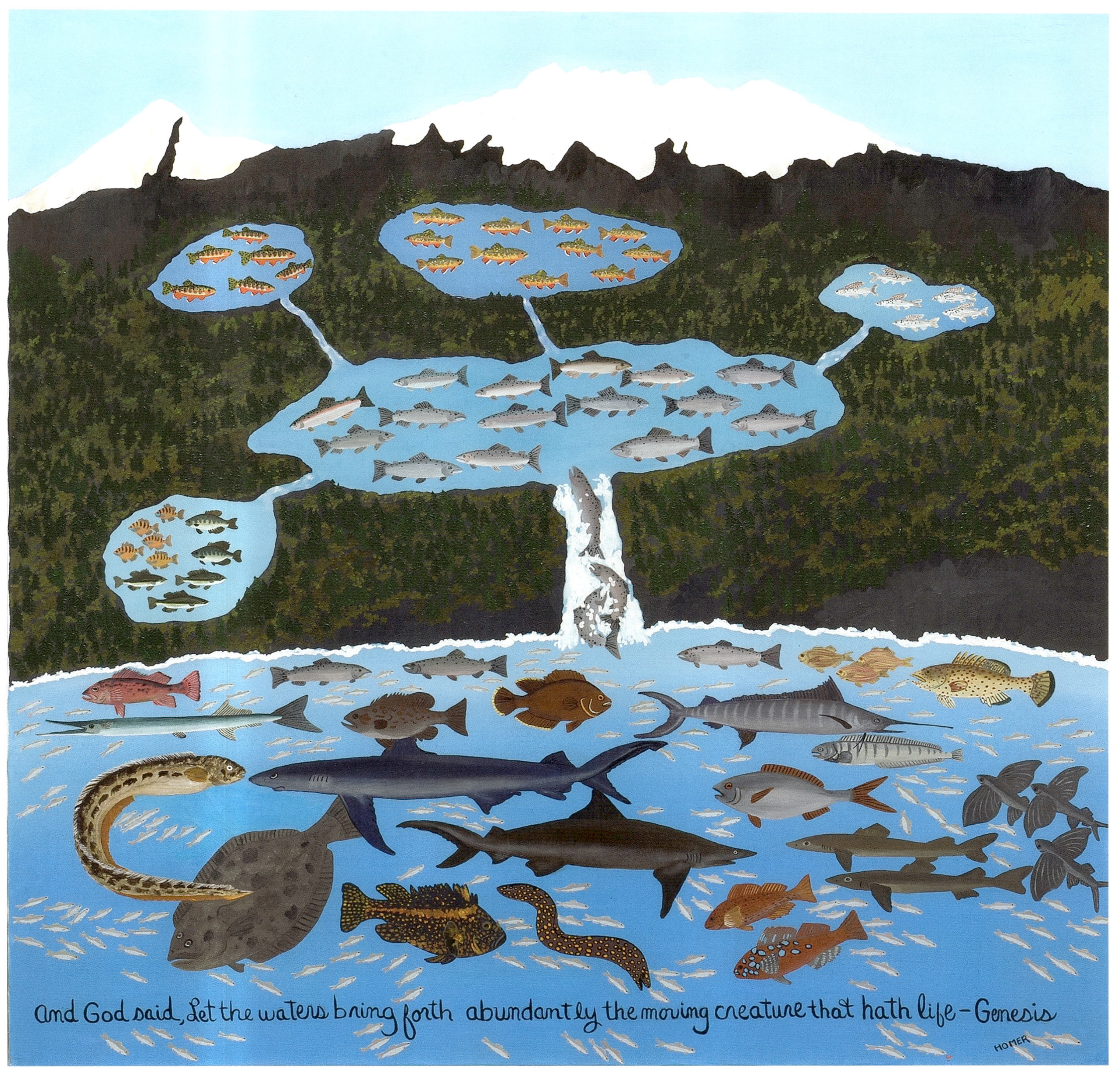

17. *Genesis*, 2017
Oil on canvas, 40 × 40 in. (101.6 × 101.6 cm)

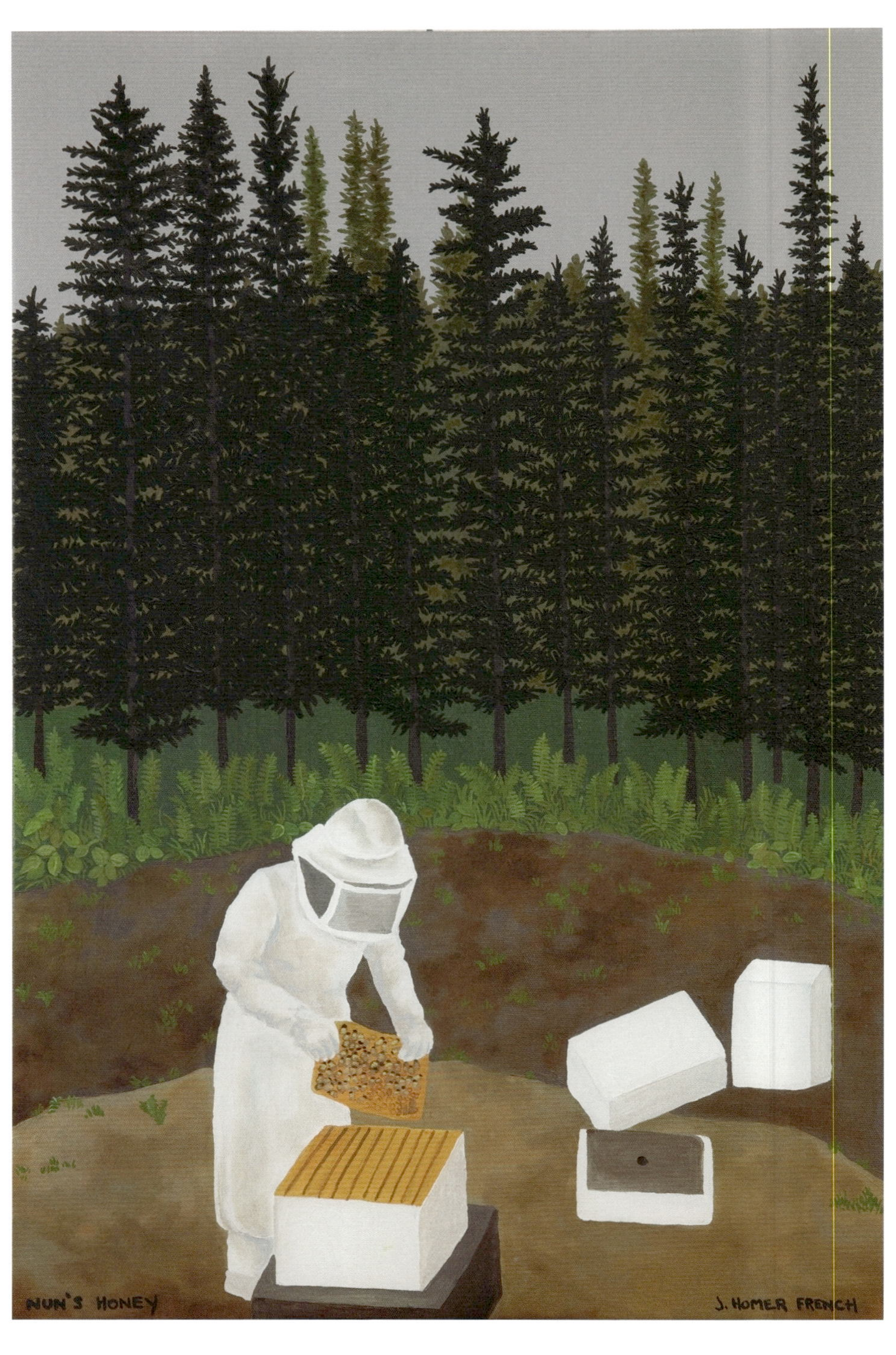

18. *Nun's Honey*, 2021
Oil on canvas, 20 × 16 in. (50.8 × 40.6 cm)

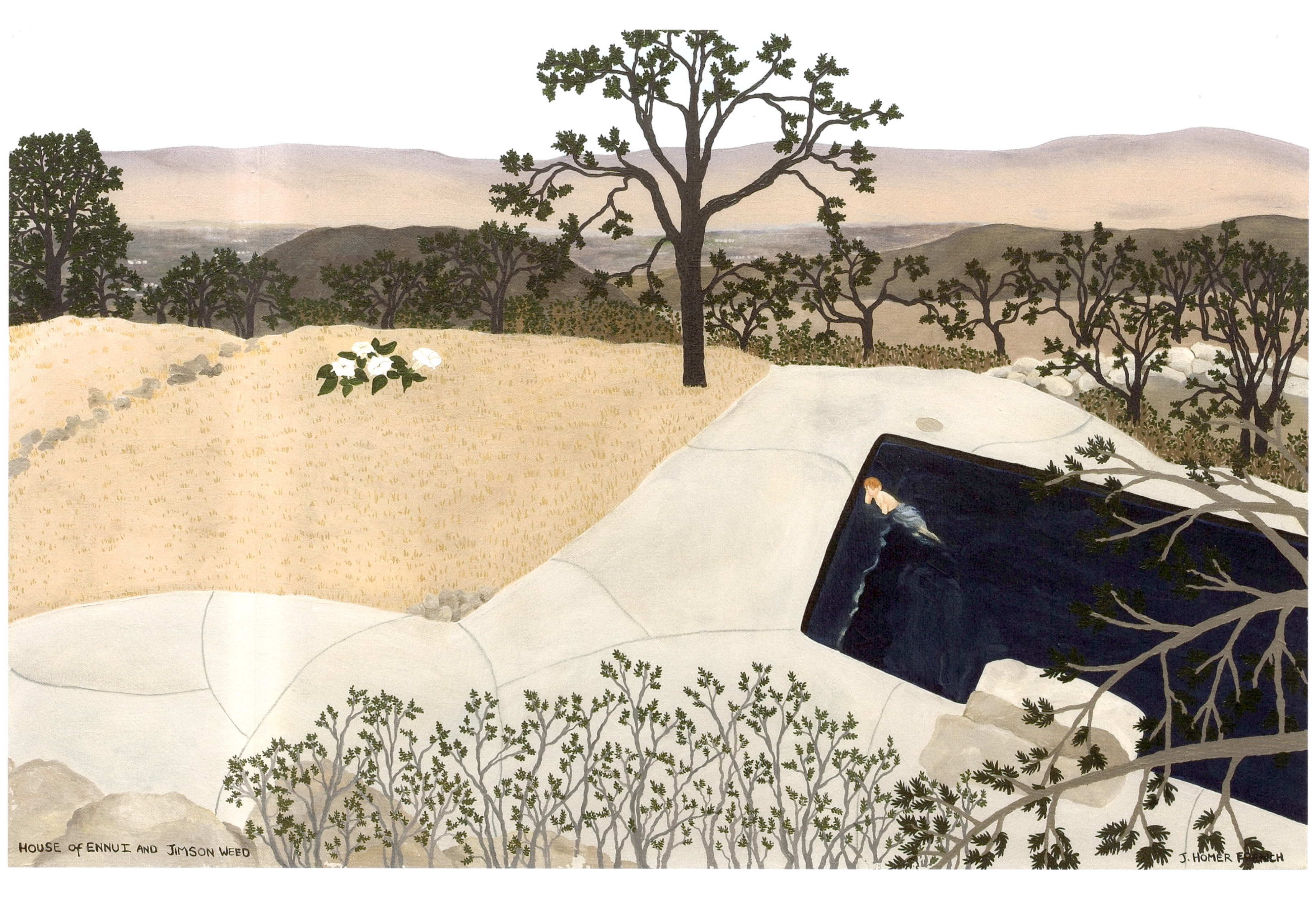

19. *House of Ennui and Jimson Weed*, 2018
Oil on canvas, 24 × 36 in. (61 × 91.4 cm)

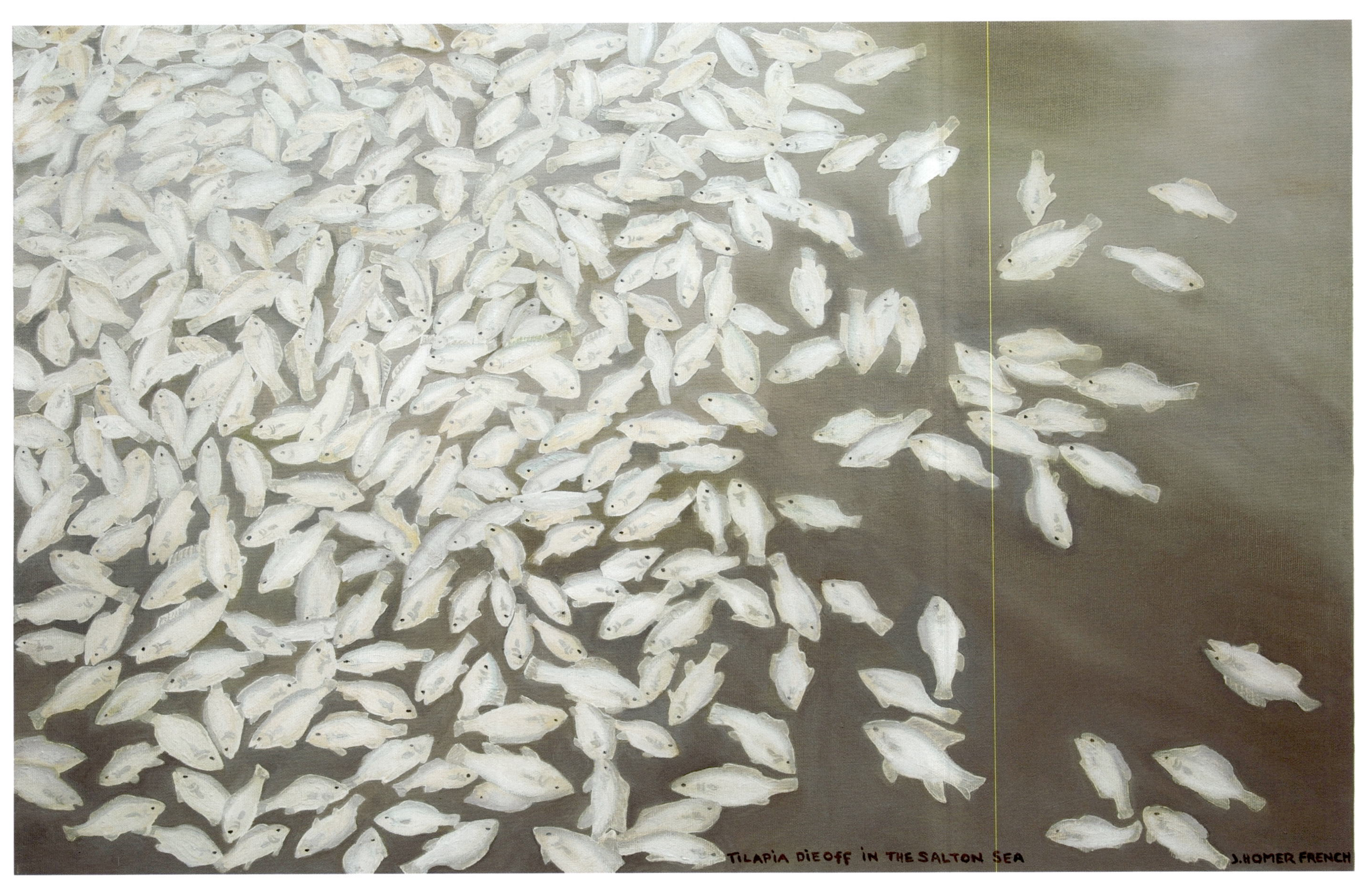

20. *Tilapia Dieoff in the Salton Sea*, 2022
Oil on canvas, 16 × 24 in. (40.6 × 61 cm)

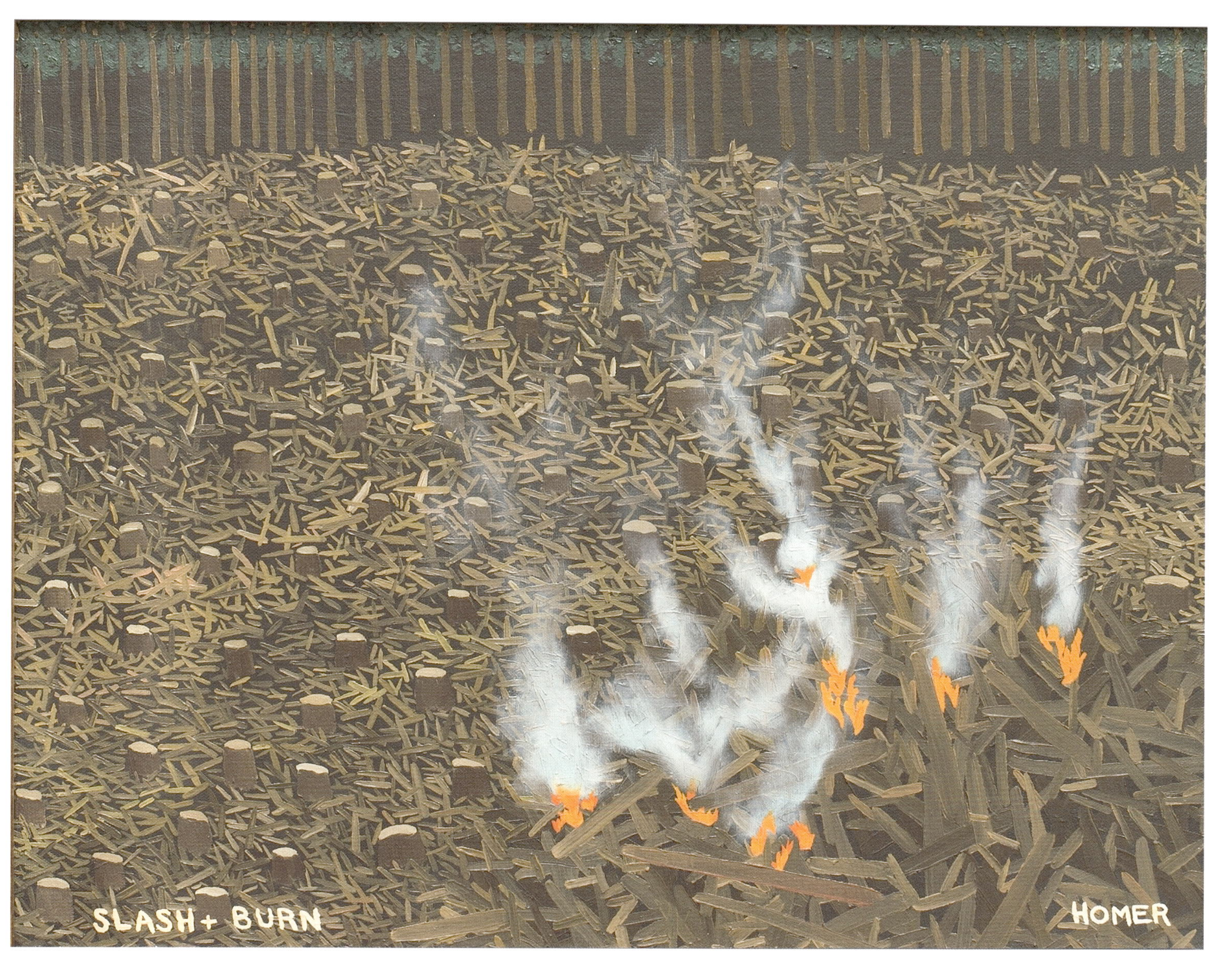

21. *Slash + Burn*, 2000
Oil on canvas, 16 × 20 in. (40.6 × 50.8 cm)

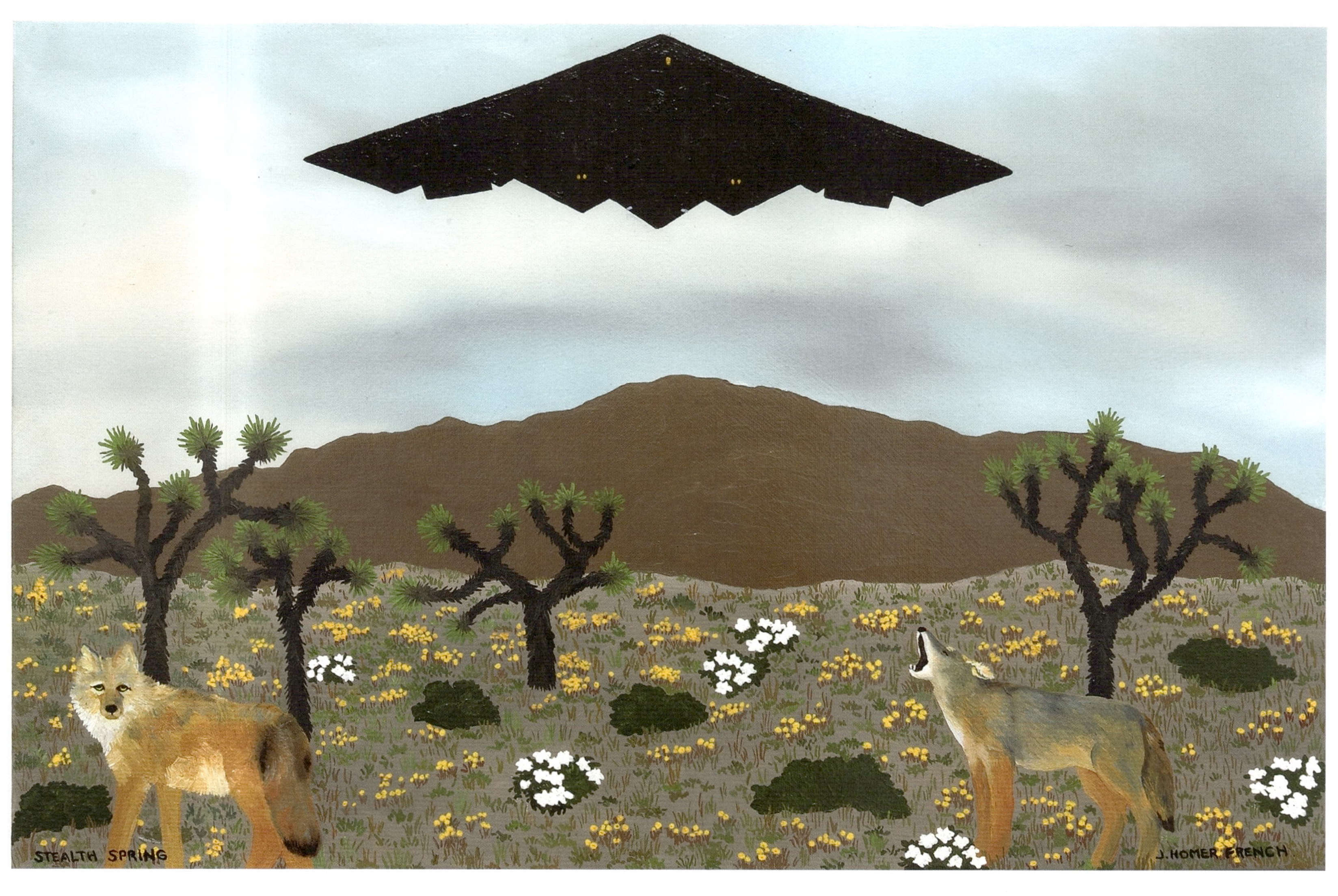

22. *Stealth Spring*, 2020
Oil on canvas, 16 × 24 in. (40.6 × 61 cm)

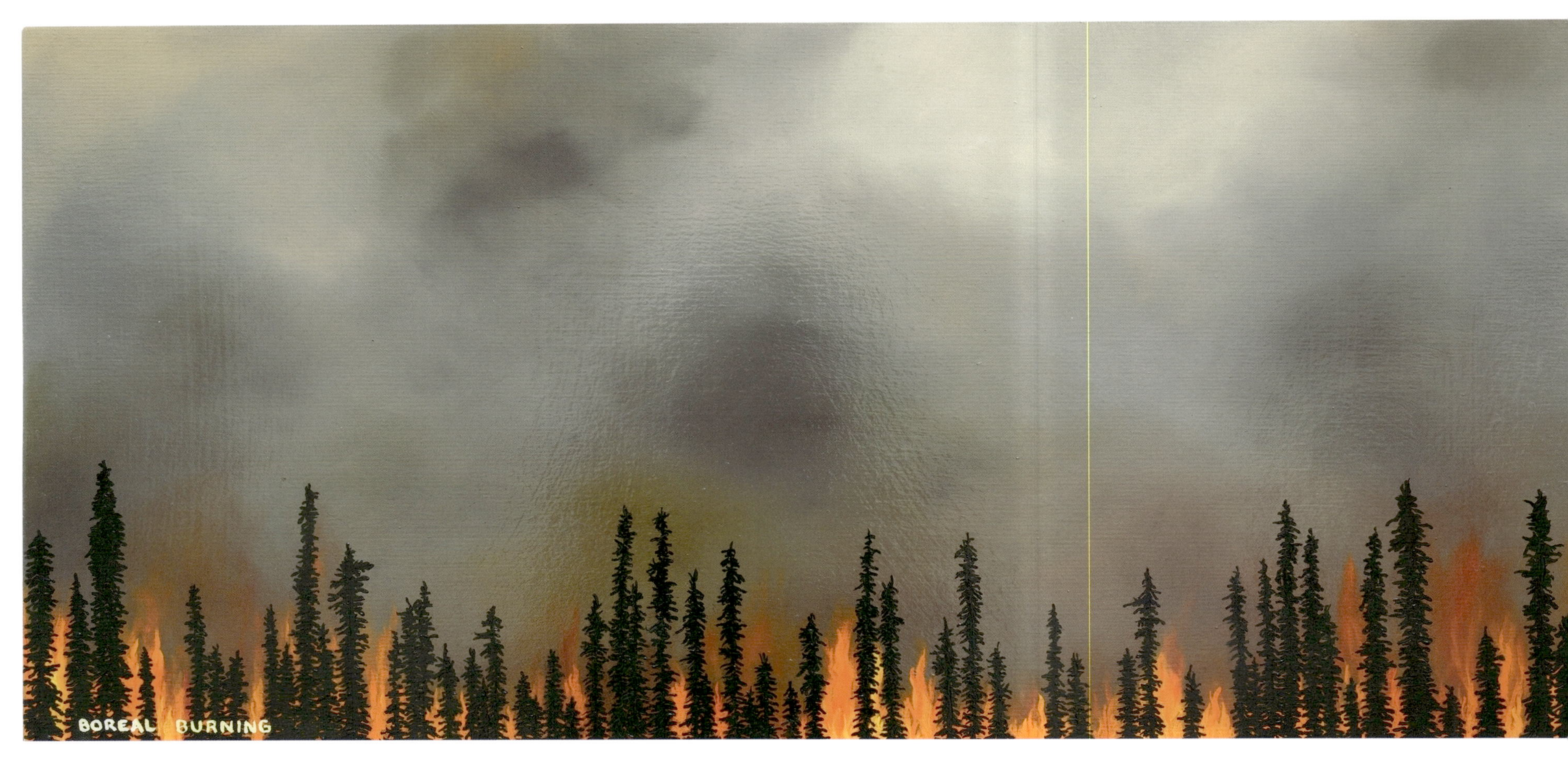
BOREAL BURNING

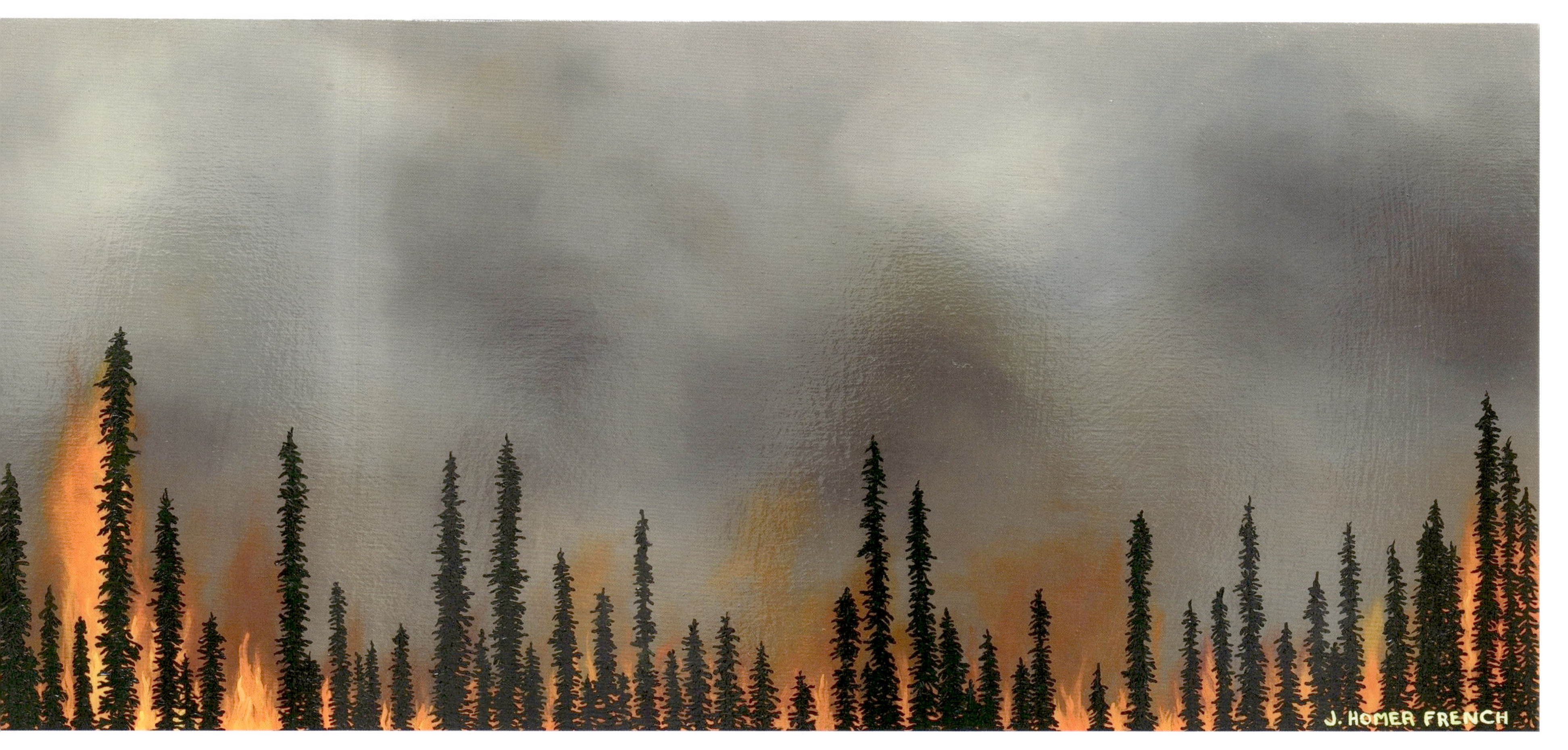

23. *Boreal Burning*, 2022
Oil on canvas, 14 × 60 in. (35.6 × 152.4 cm)

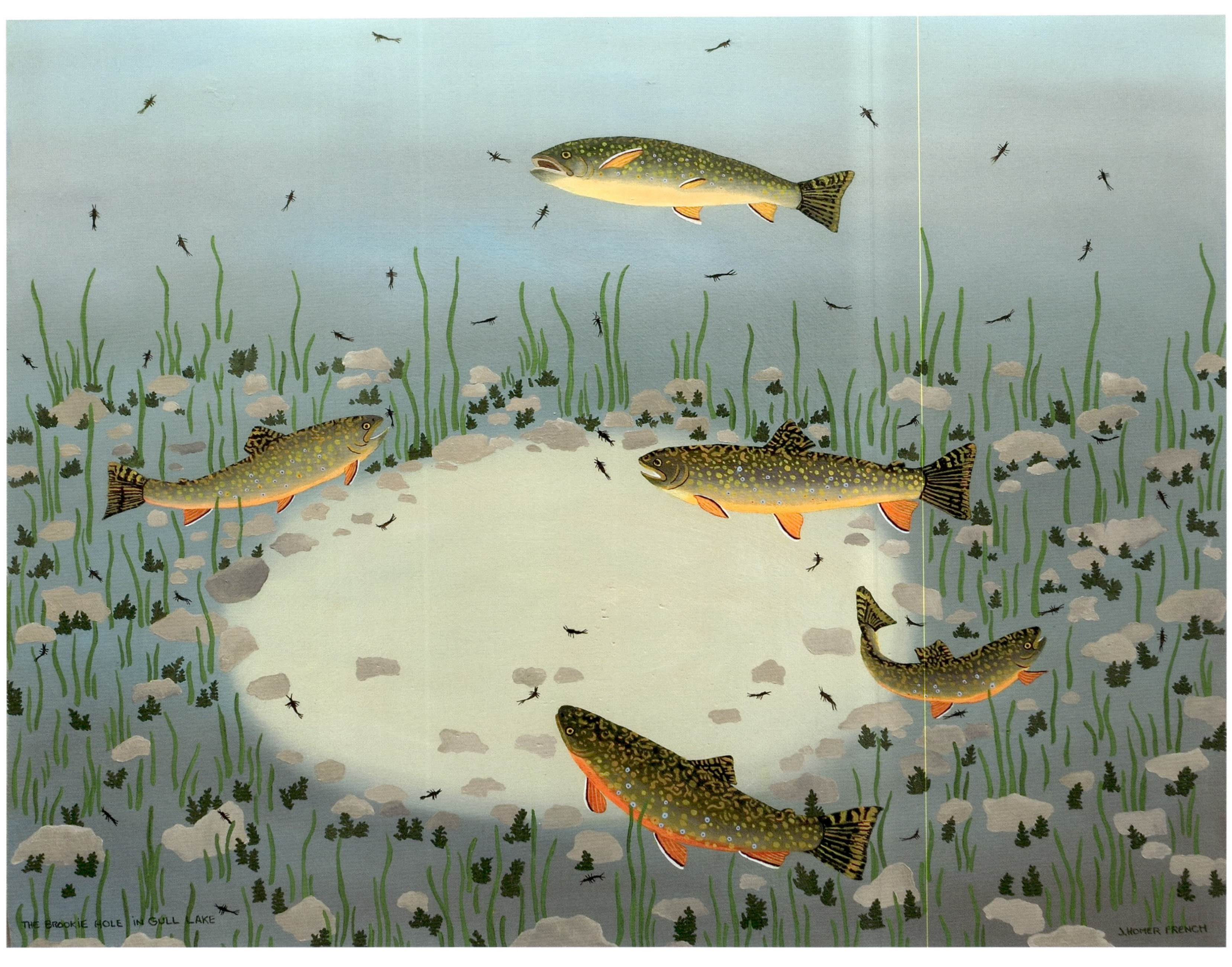

24. *The Brookie Hole in Gull Lake*, 2020
Oil on plywood, 24 × 30 in. (61 × 76.2 cm)

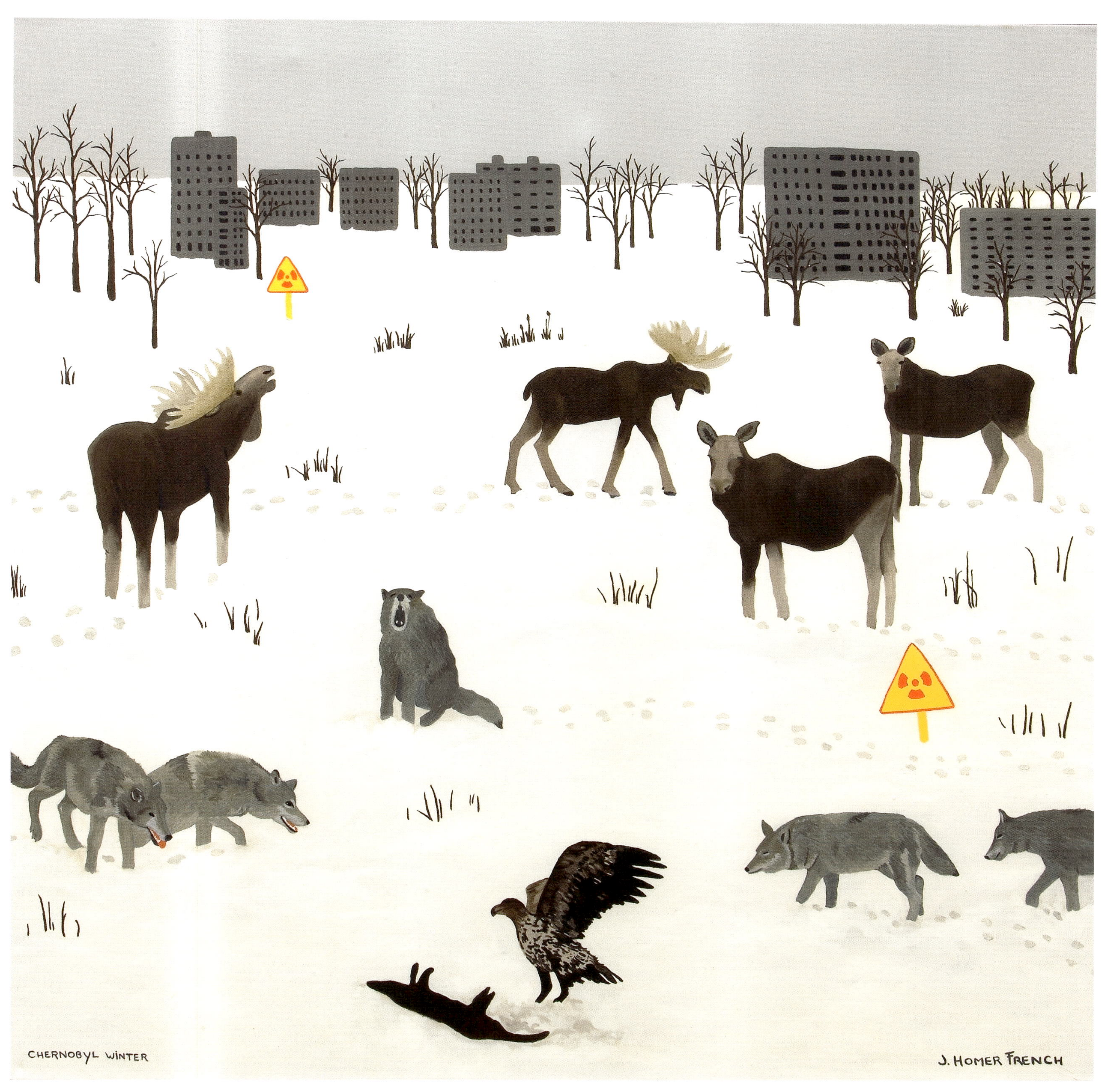

25. *Chernobyl Winter*, 2018
Oil on canvas, 36 × 26 in. (91.4 × 66 cm)

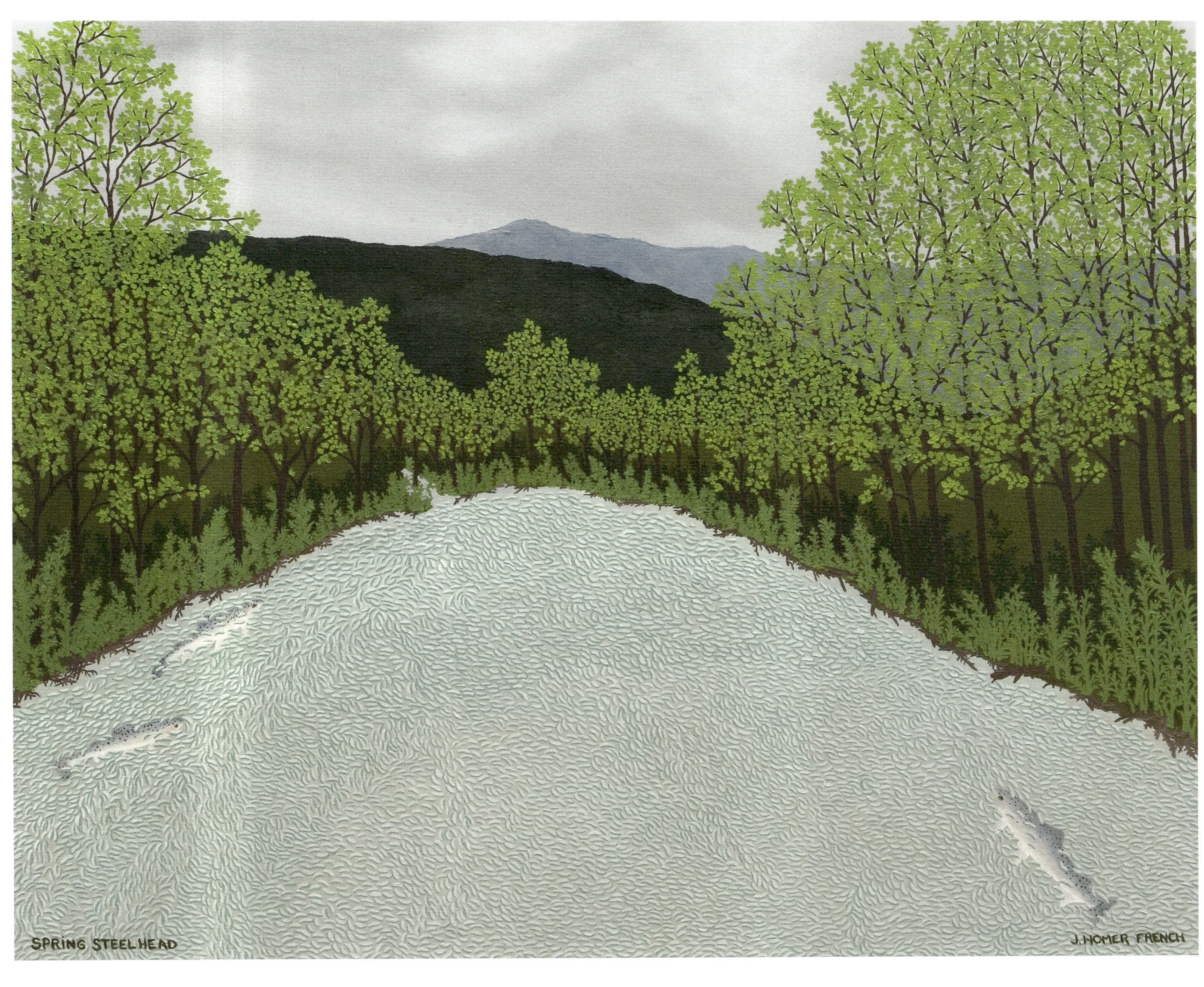

26. *Spring Steelhead*, 2019
Oil on canvas, 26 × 32 in. (66 × 81.3 cm)

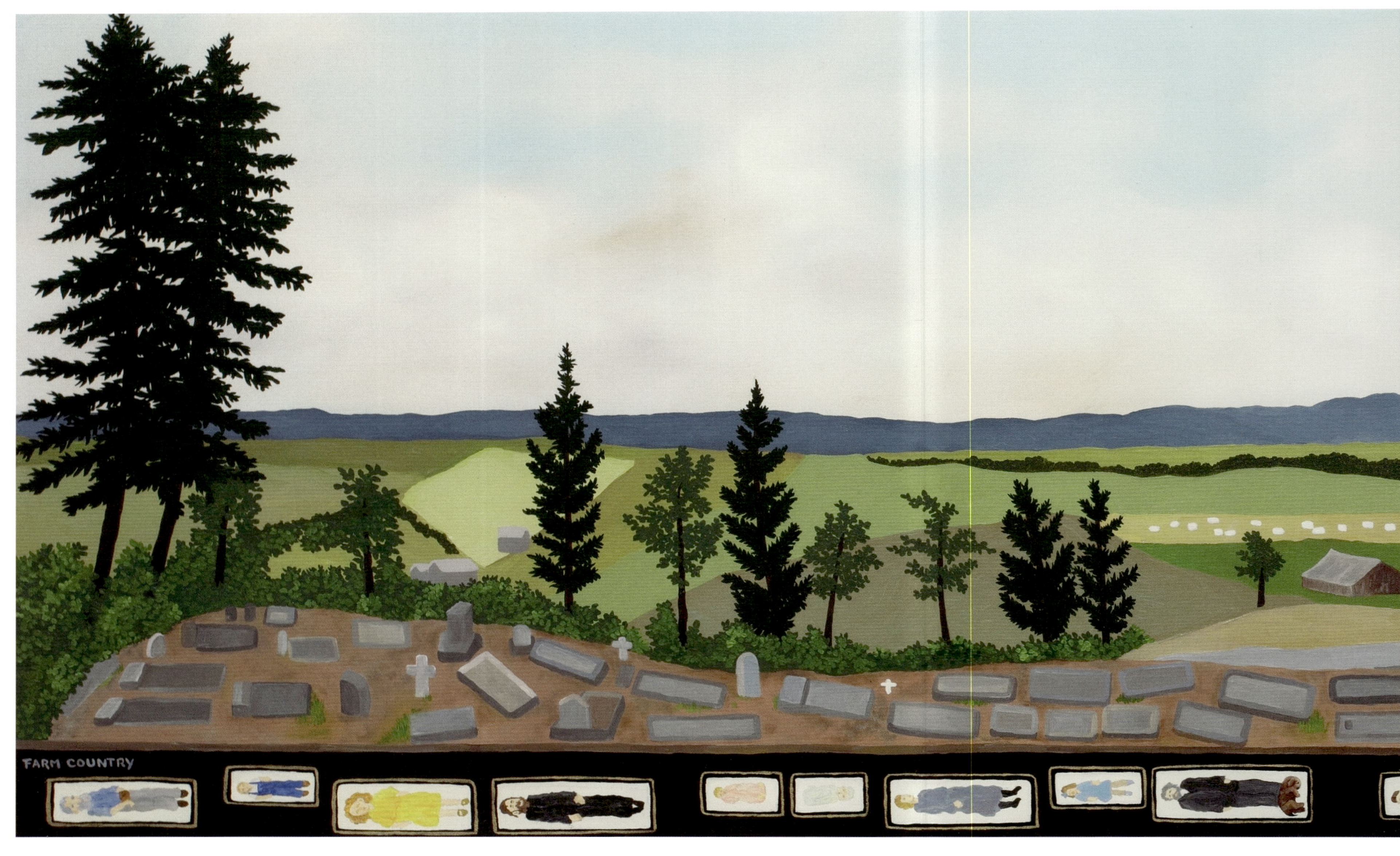
FARM COUNTRY

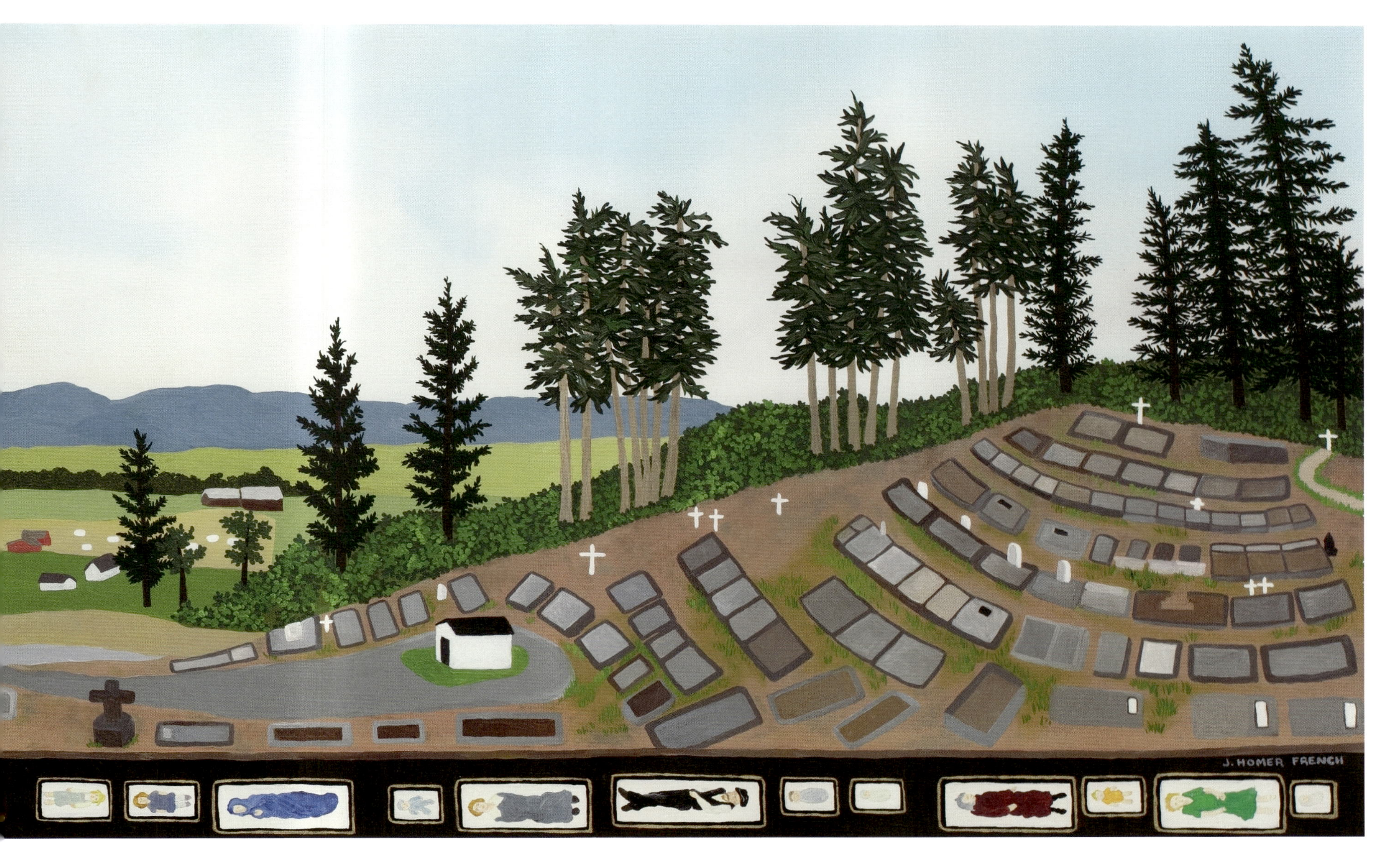

27. *Farm Country*, 2021
Oil on canvas, 18 × 60 in. (45.7 × 152.4 cm)

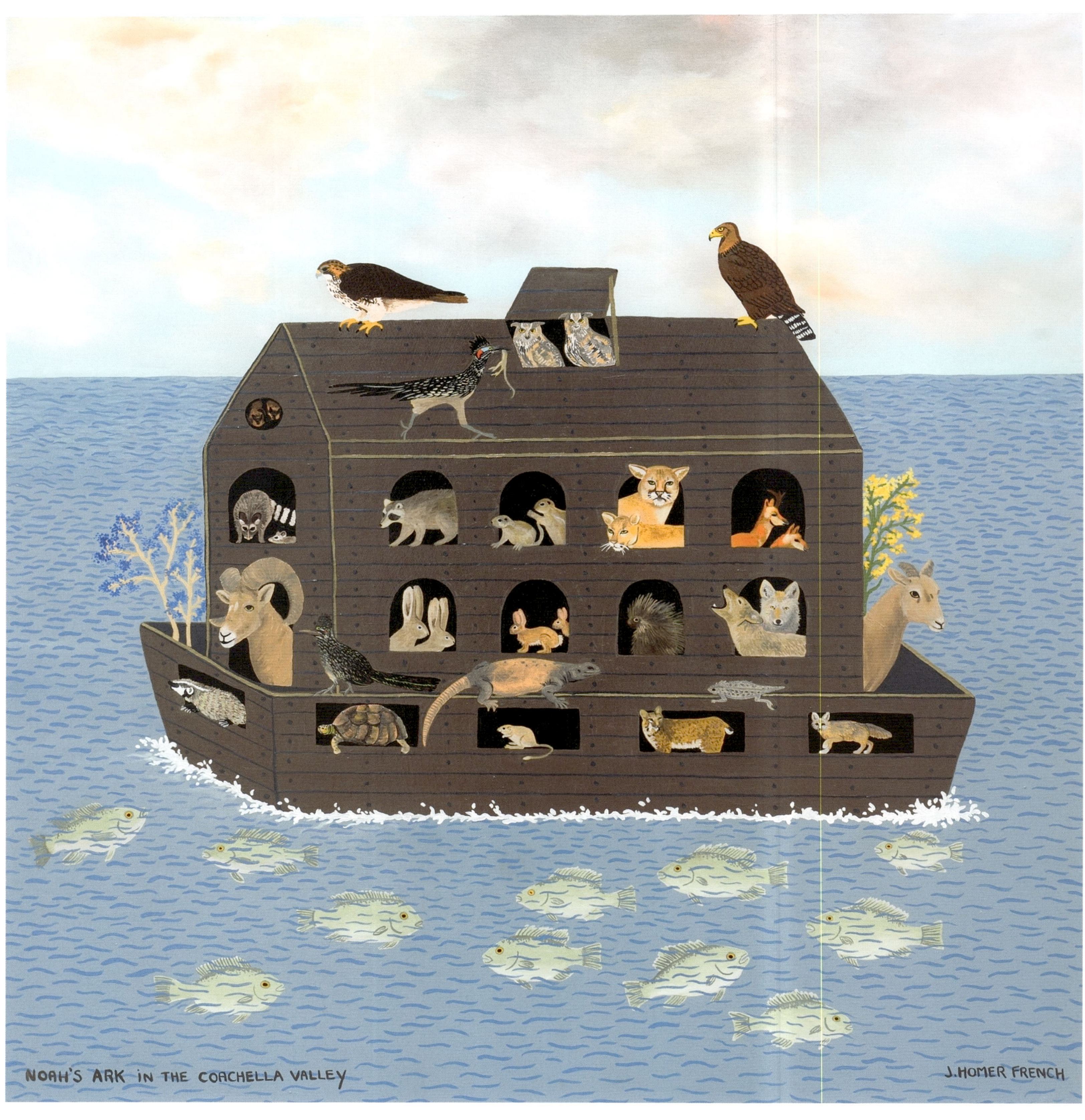

28. *Noah's Ark in the Coachella Valley*, 2016
Oil on plywood, 35½ × 35½ in. (90.2 × 90.2 cm)

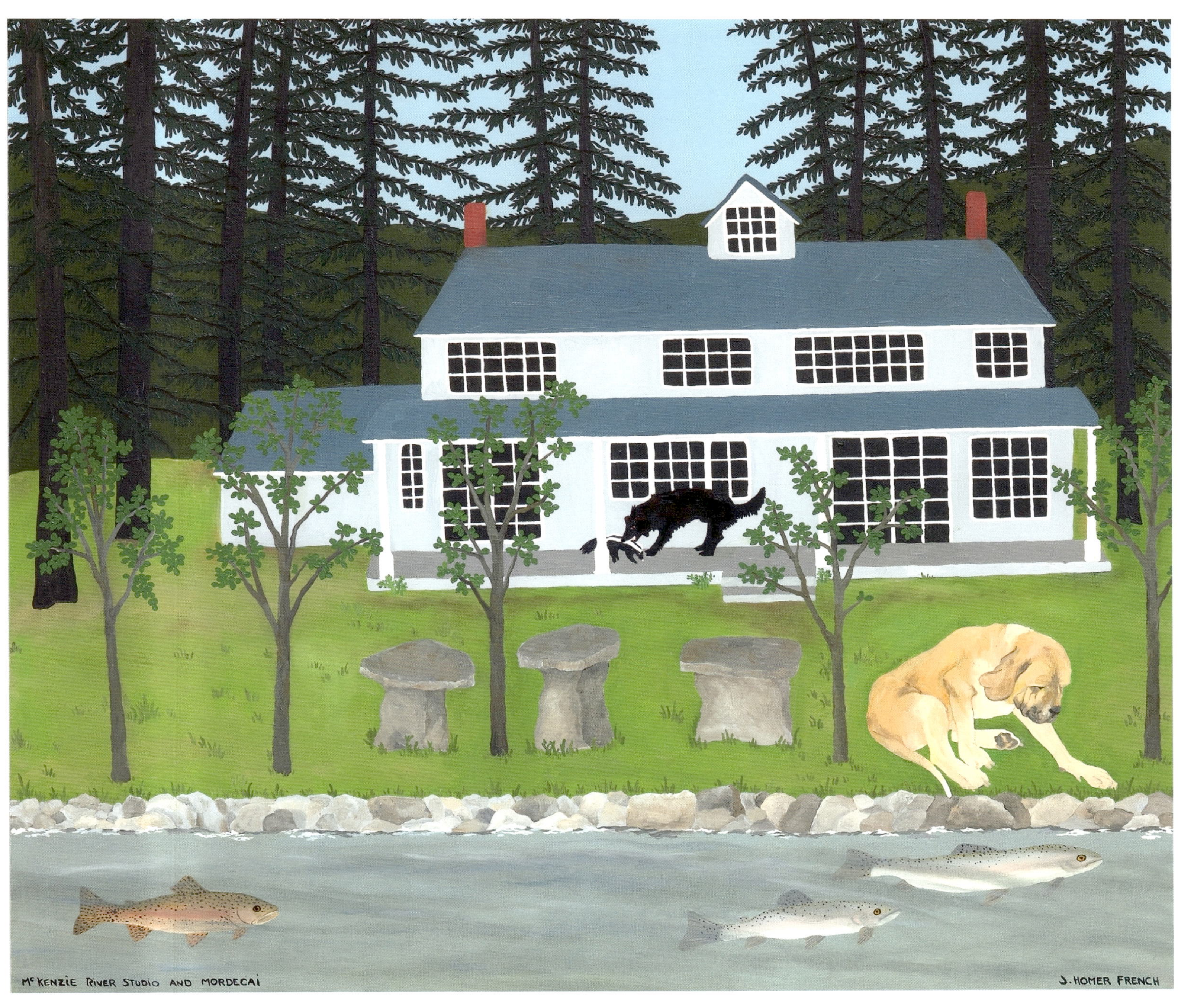

29. *McKenzie River Studio and Mordecai*, 2021
Oil on canvas, 26 × 30 in. (66 × 76.2 cm)

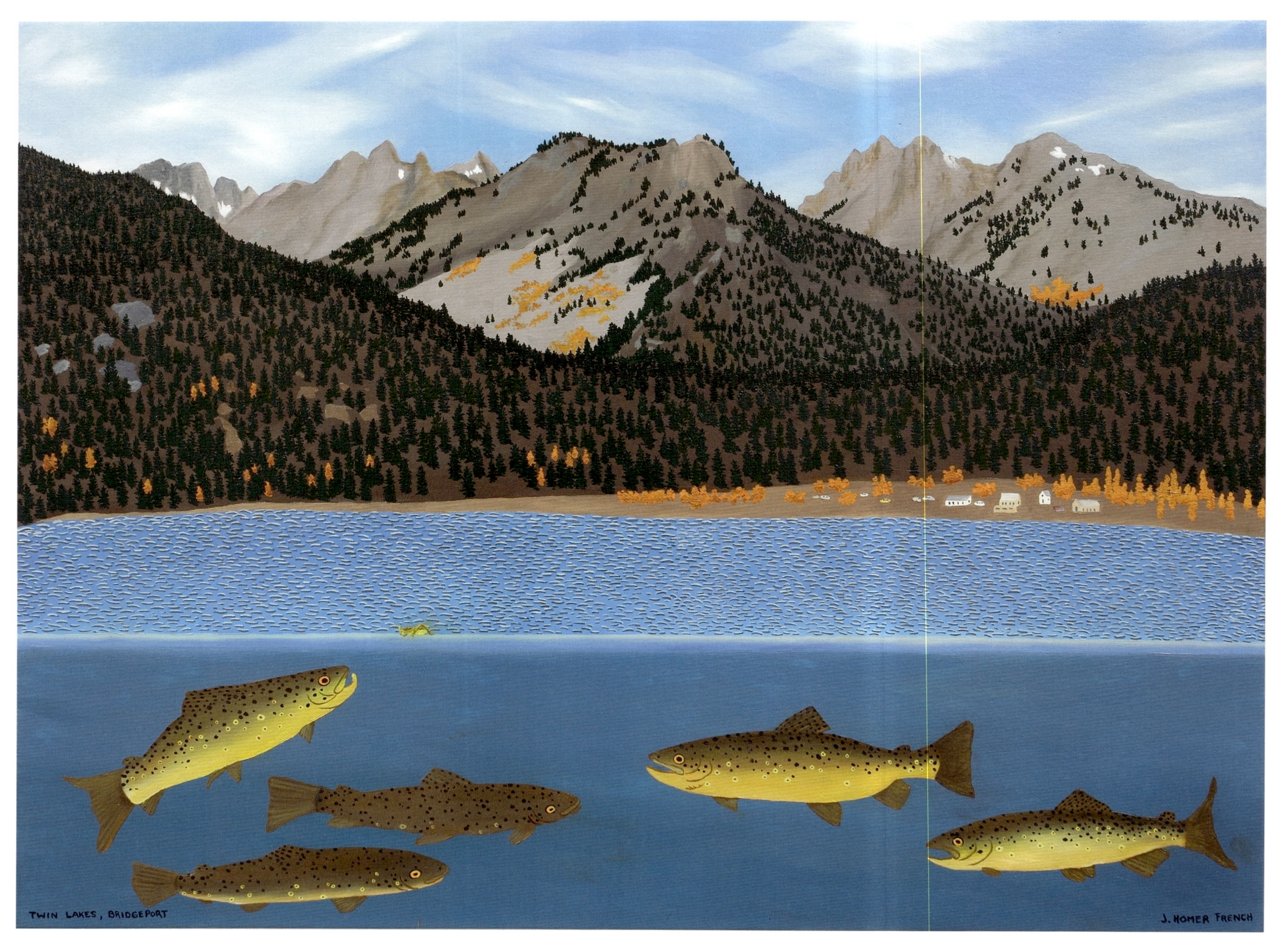

30. *Twin Lakes, Bridgeport*, 2022
Oil on canvas, 30 × 40 in. (76.2 × 101.6 cm)

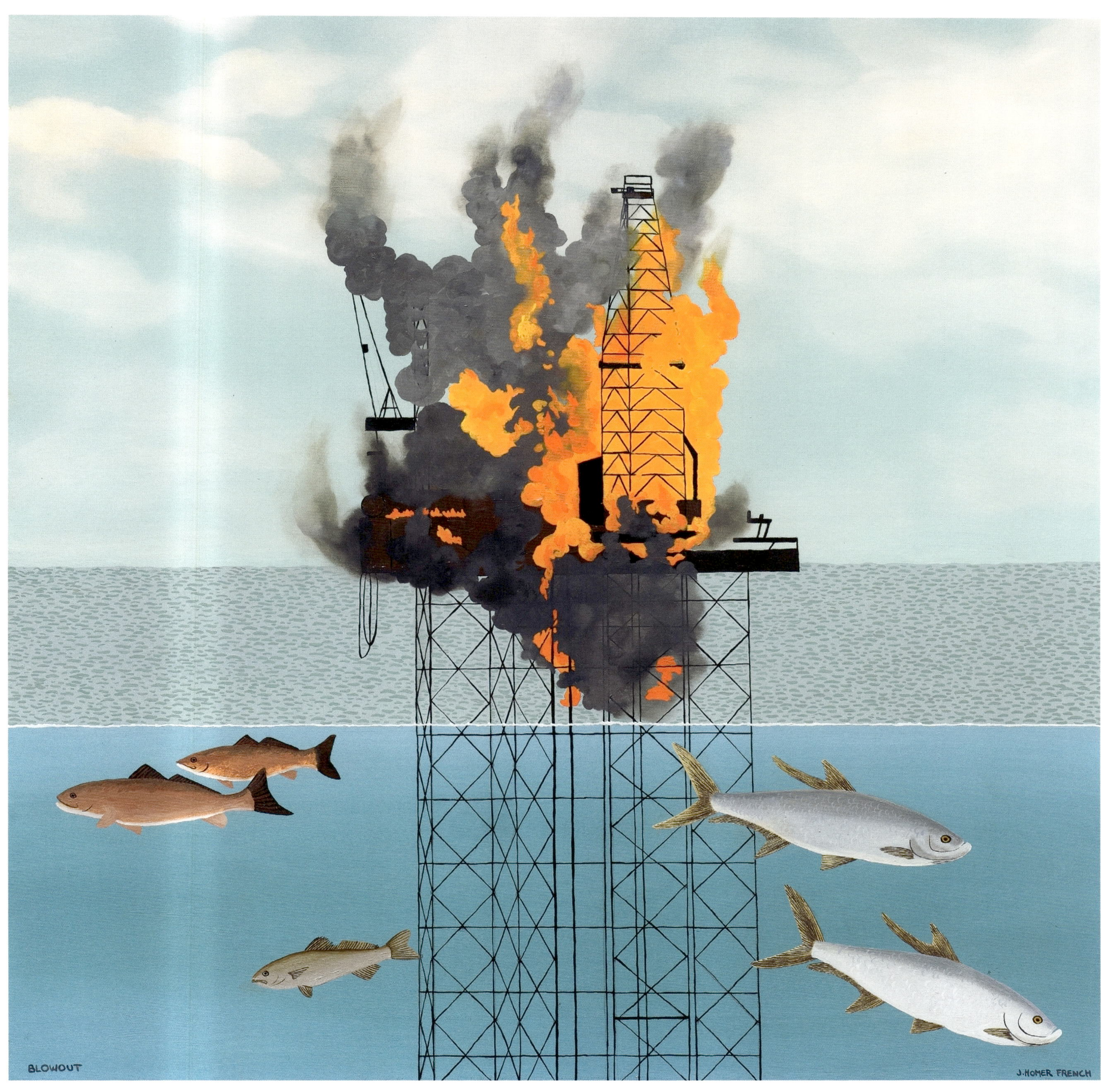

31. *Blowout*, 2020
Oil on canvas, 36 × 36 in. (91.4 × 91.4 cm)

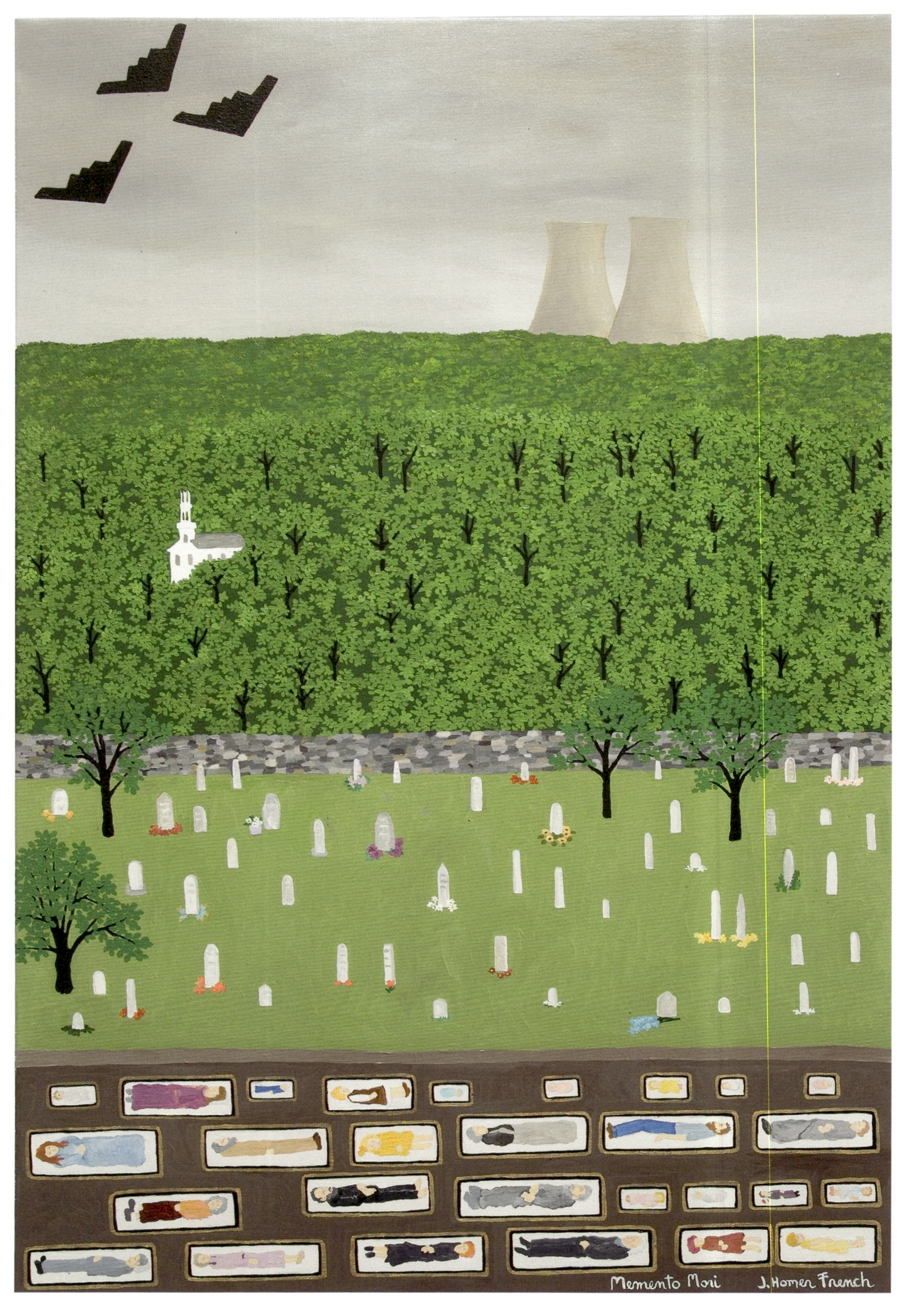

32. *Memento Mori*, 2022
Oil on canvas, 36 × 24 in. (91.4 × 61 cm)

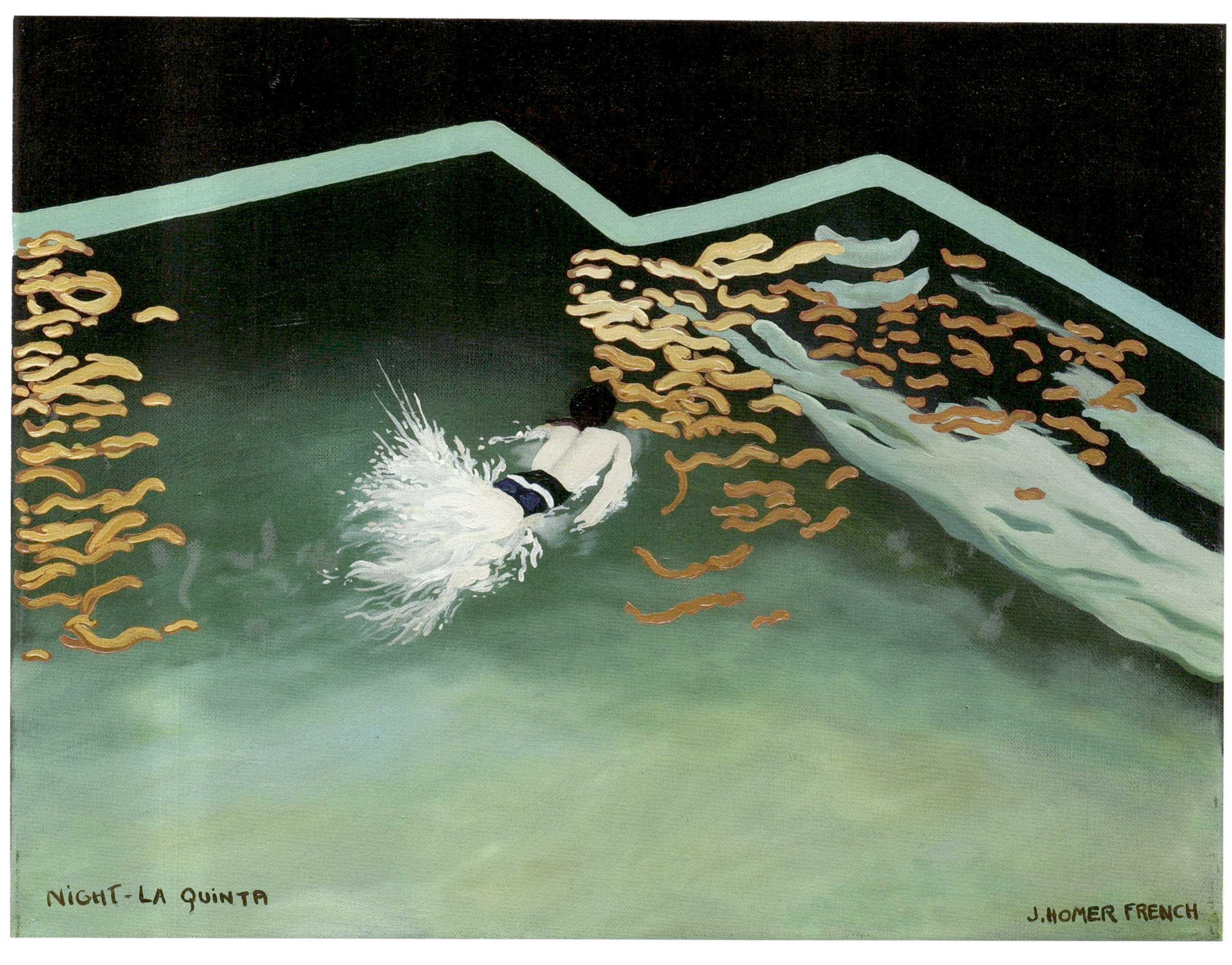

33. *Night–La Quinta*, 2017
Oil on canvas, 16 × 20 in. (40.6 × 50.8 cm)

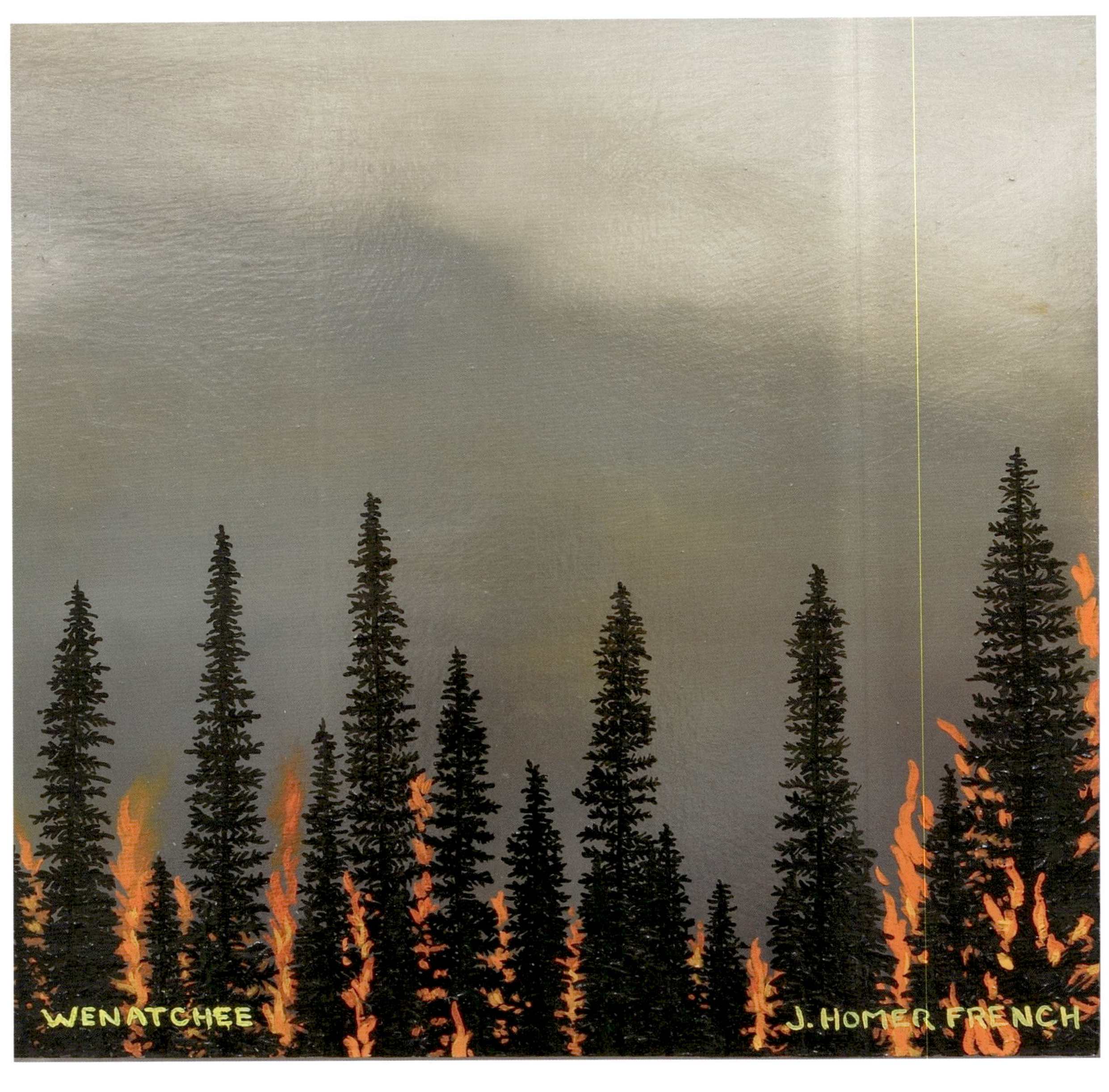

34. *Wenatchee*, 2019
Oil on plywood, 12 × 12 in. (30.5 × 30.5 cm)

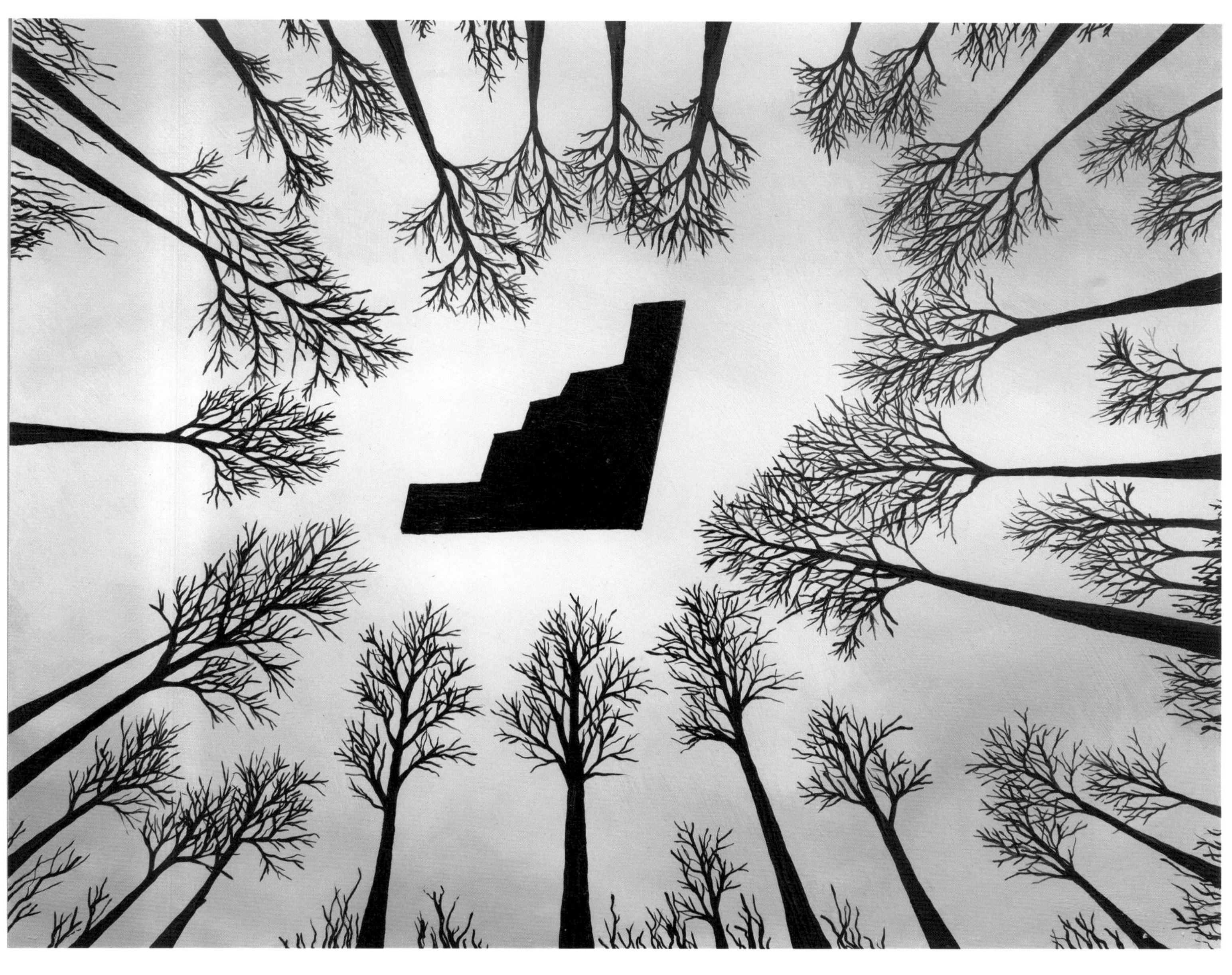

35. *High Above*, 2008
Oil on zinc plate, 16 × 20 in. (40.6 × 50.8 cm)

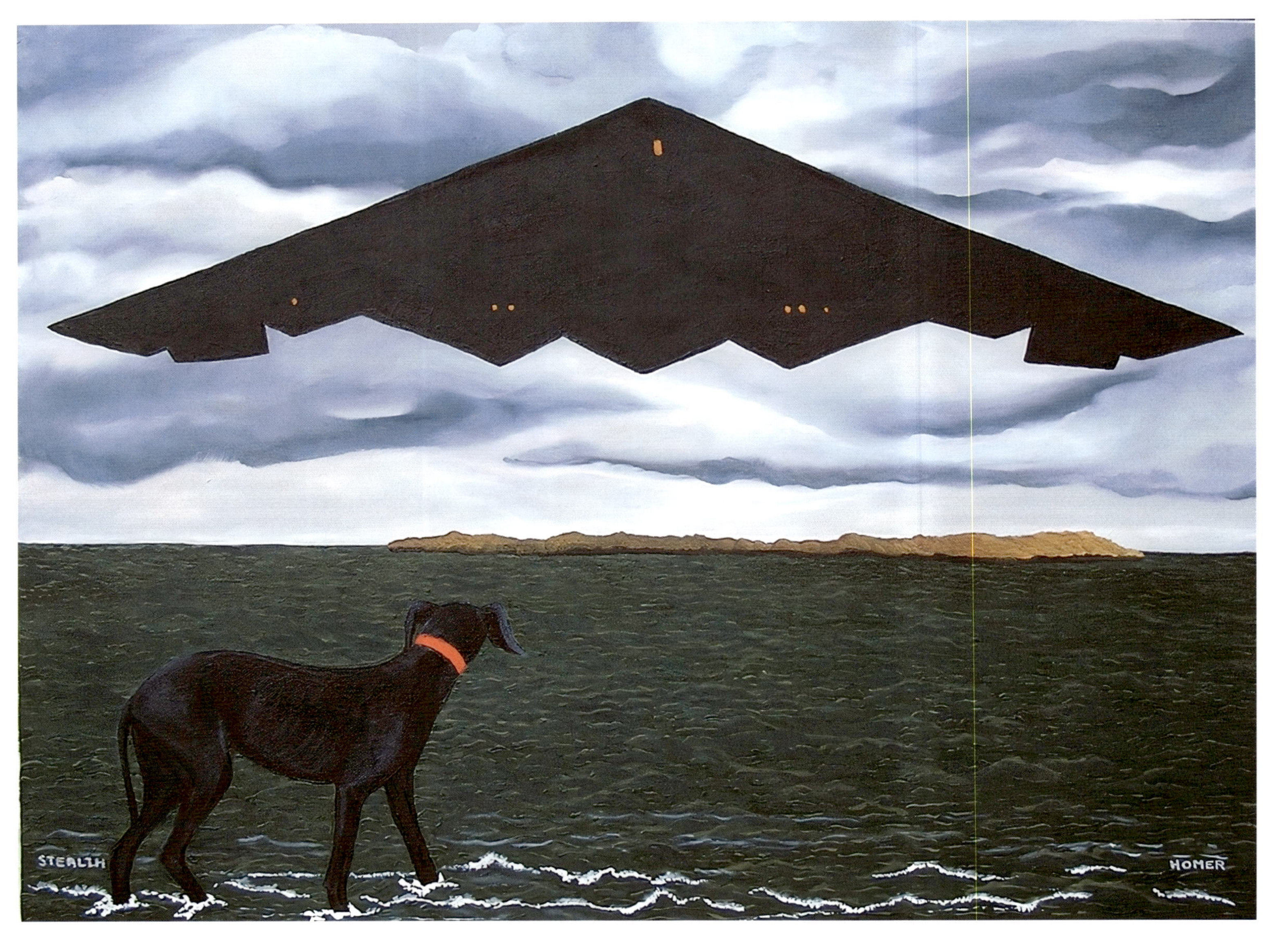

36. *Stealth*, 2004
Oil on canvas, 18 × 24 in. (45.7 × 61 cm)

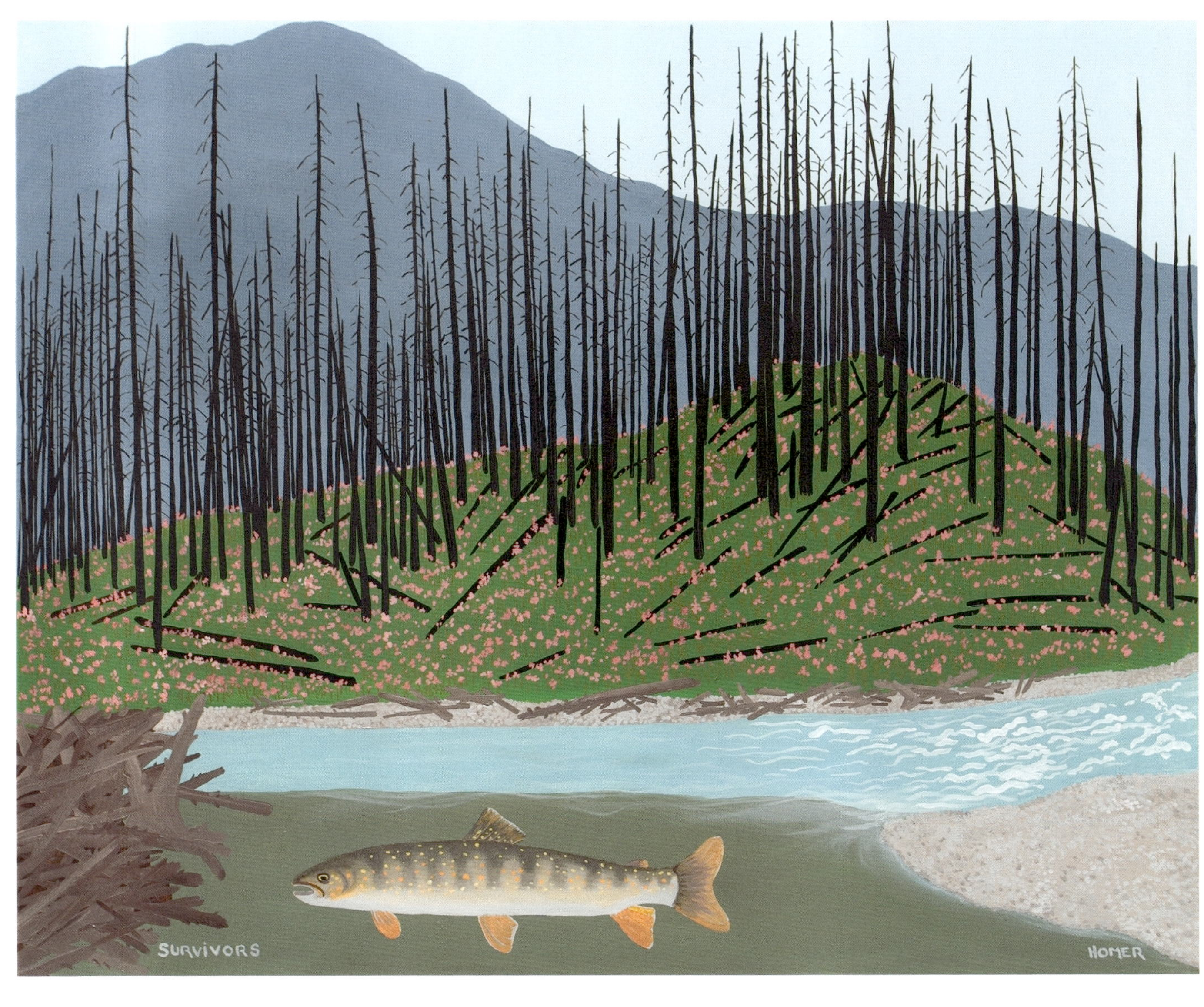

37. *Survivors*, 2009
Oil on canvas, 20 × 24 in. (50.8 × 61 cm)

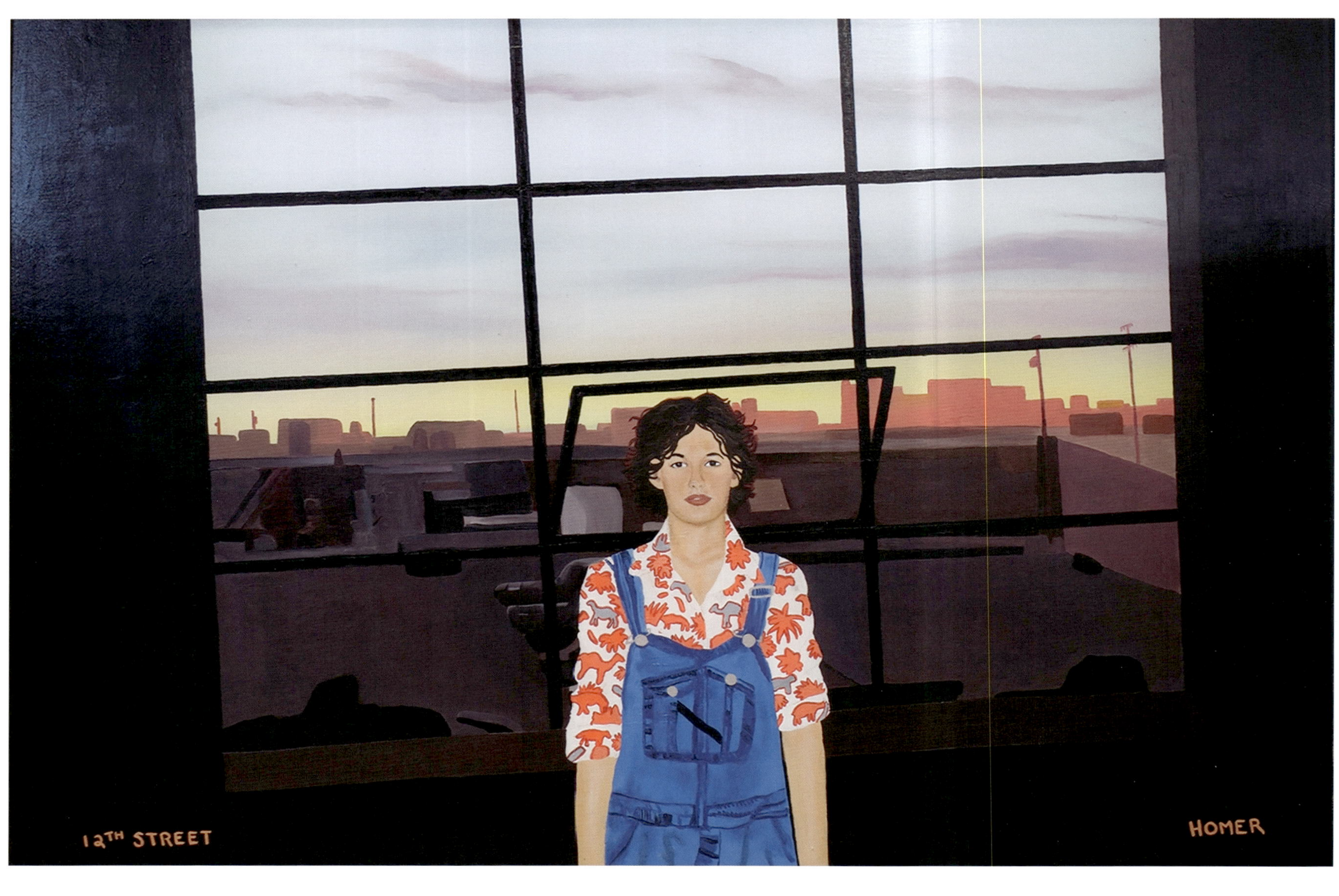

38. *12th Street*, 1998
Oil on masonite, 25 × 37 in. (63.5 × 94 cm)

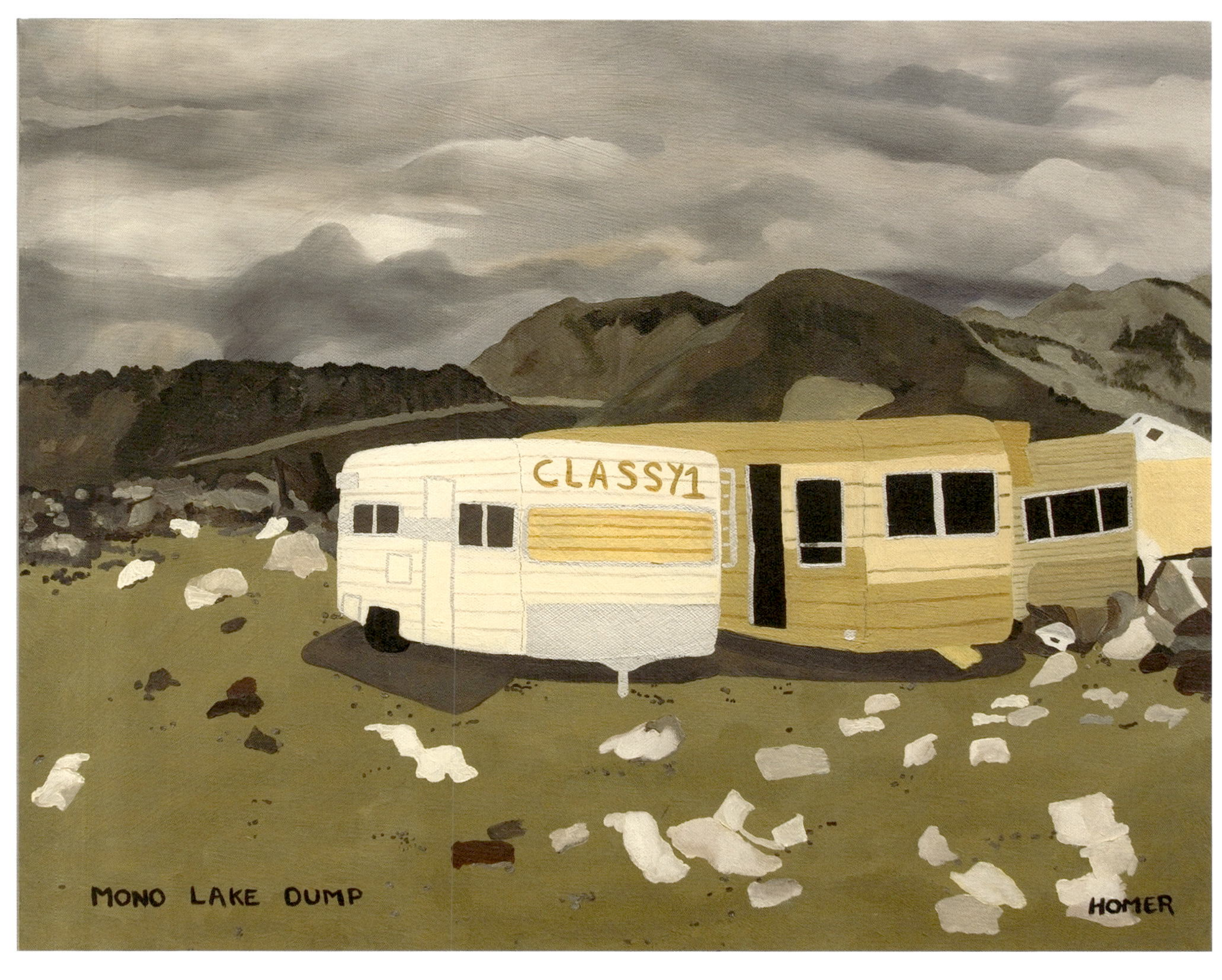

39. *Mono Lake Dump*, 1998
Oil on canvas, 16 × 20 in. (40.6 × 50.8 cm)

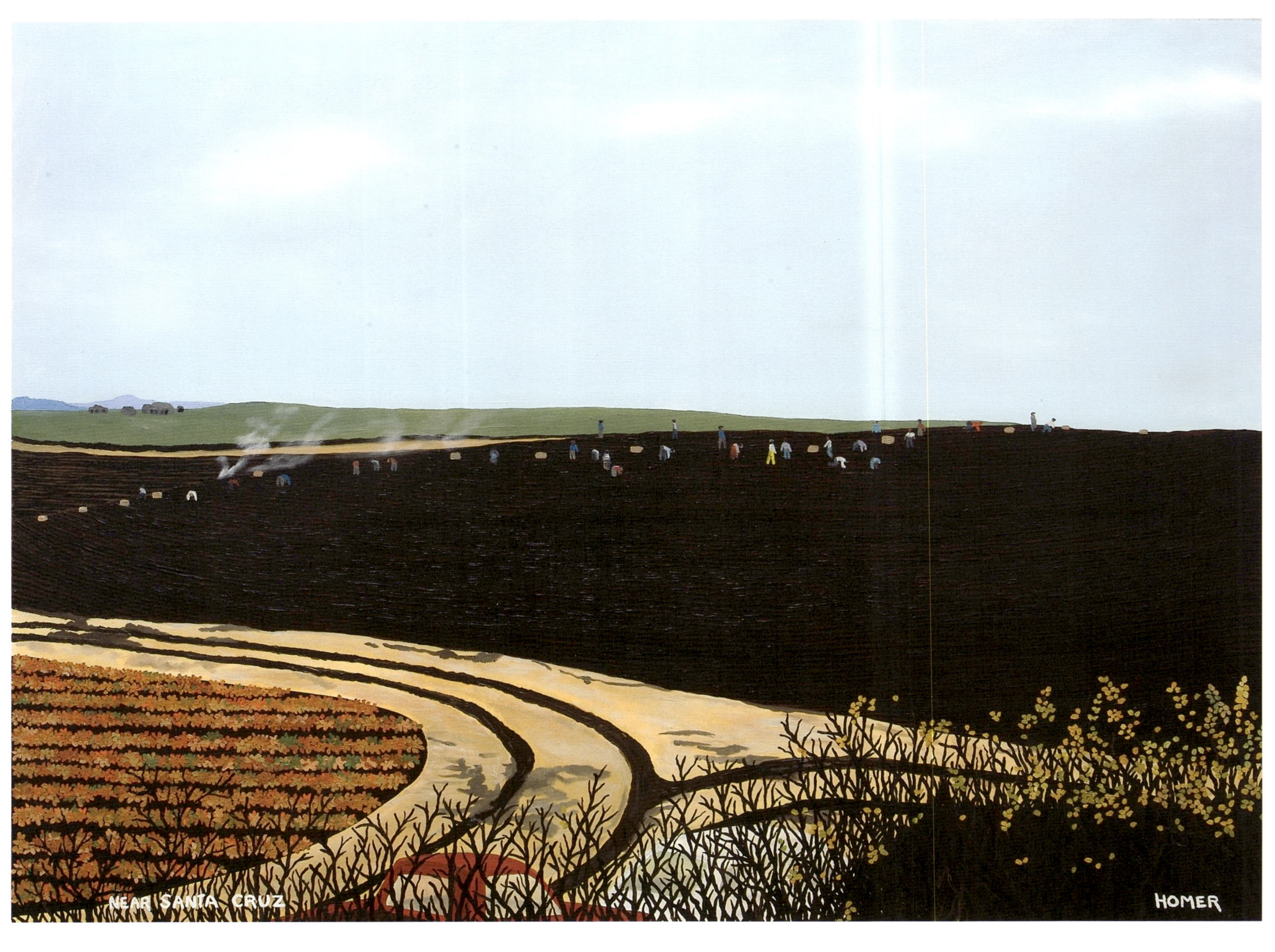

40. *Near Santa Cruz*, 1998
Oil on canvas, 30 × 40 in. (76.2 × 101.6 cm)

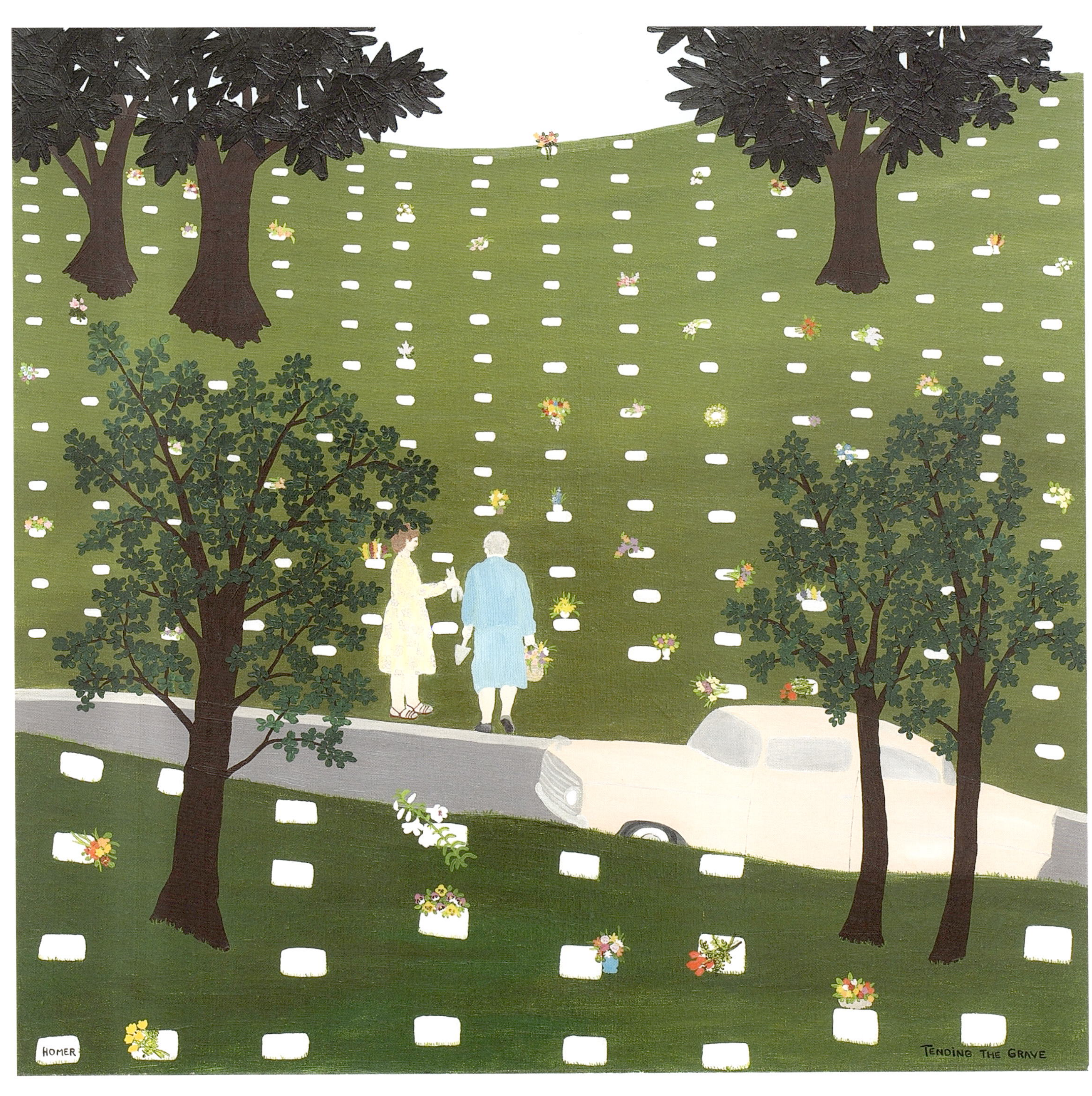

41. *Tending the Grave*, 1999
Oil on canvas, 36 × 36 in. (91.4 × 91.4 cm)

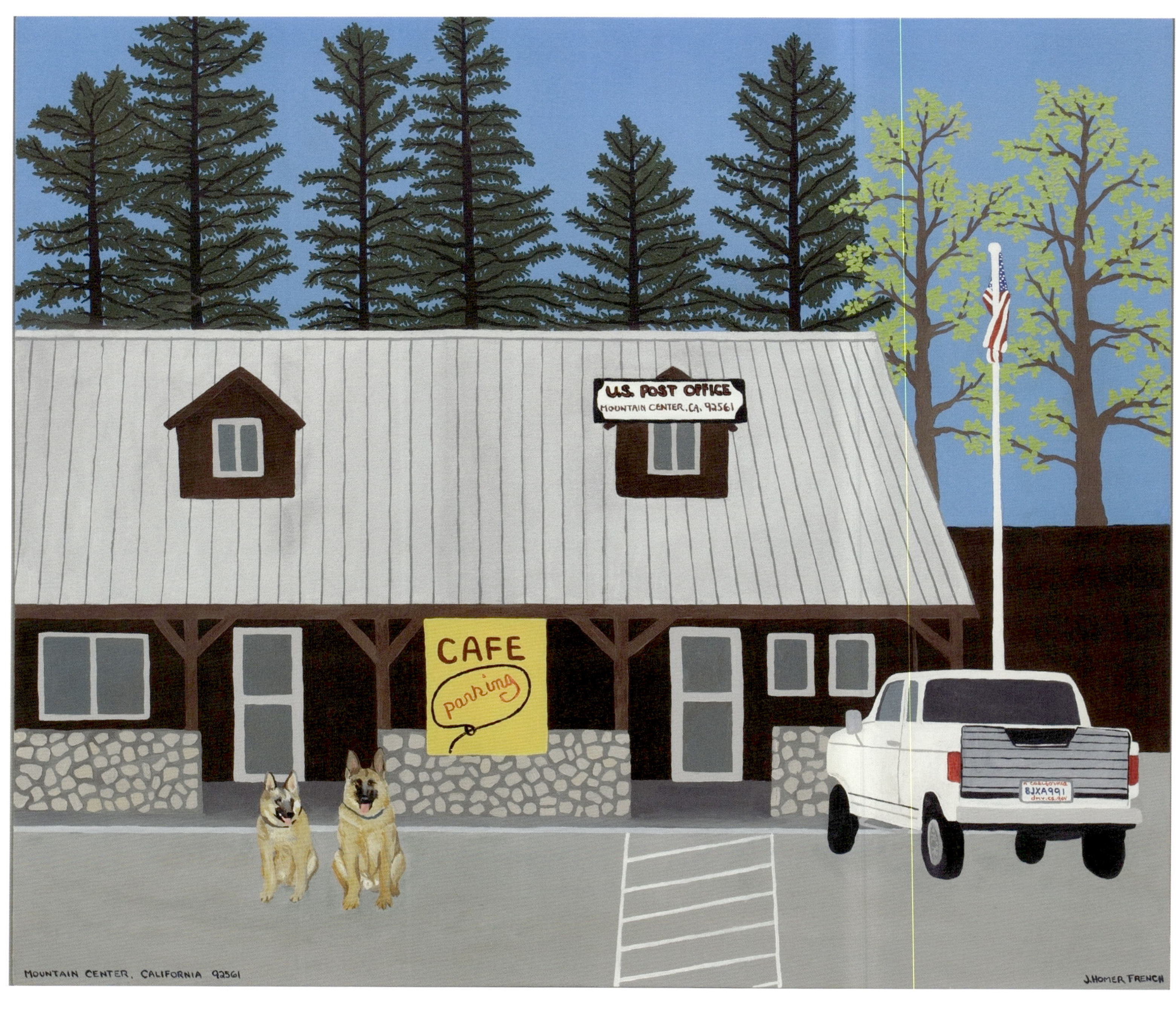

42. *Mountain Center, California 92561*, 2021
Oil on canvas, 26 × 30 in. (66 × 76.2 cm)

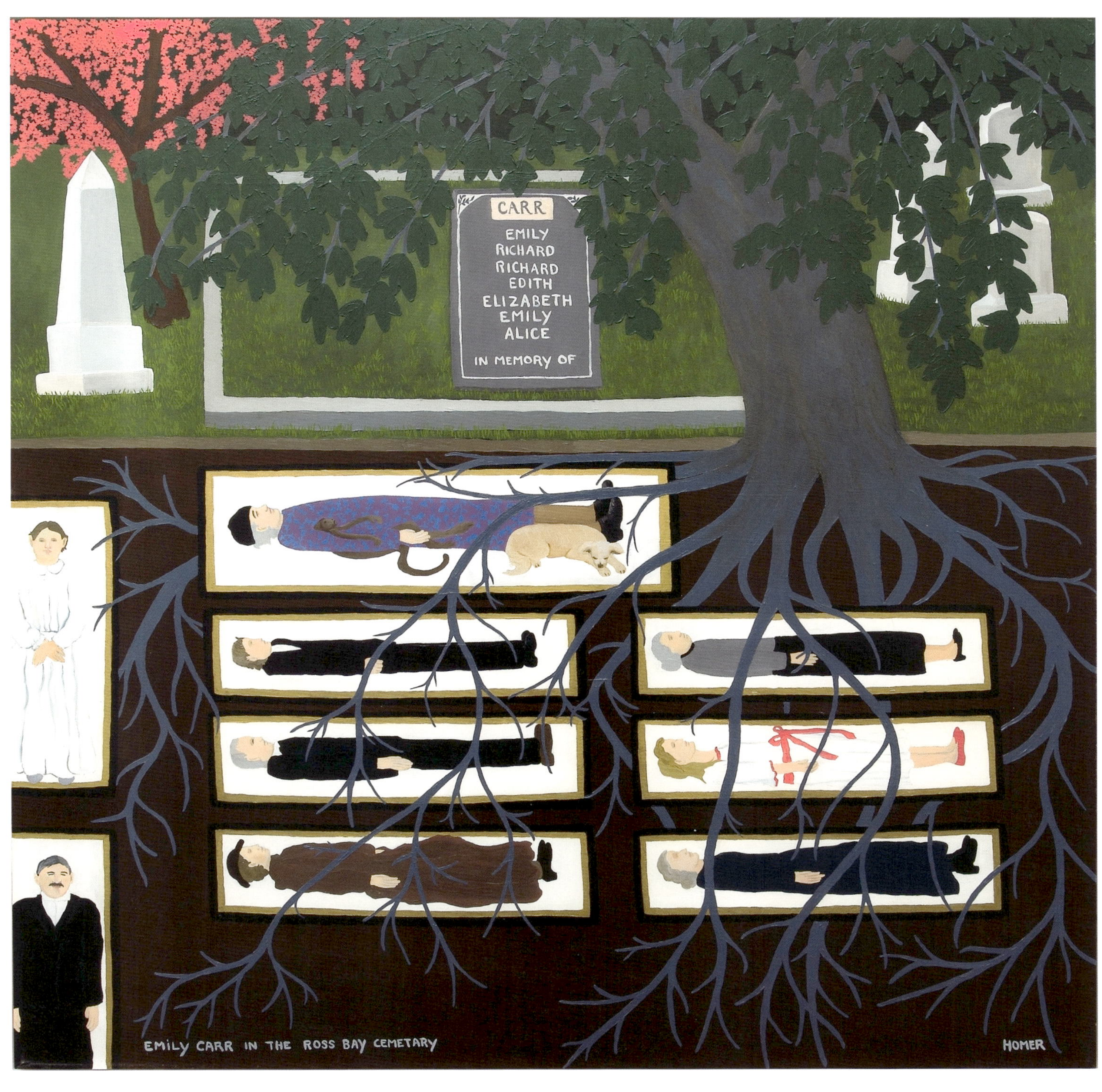

43. *Emily Carr in the Ross Bay Cemetery*, 2000
Oil on canvas, 36 × 36 in. (91.4 × 91.4 cm)

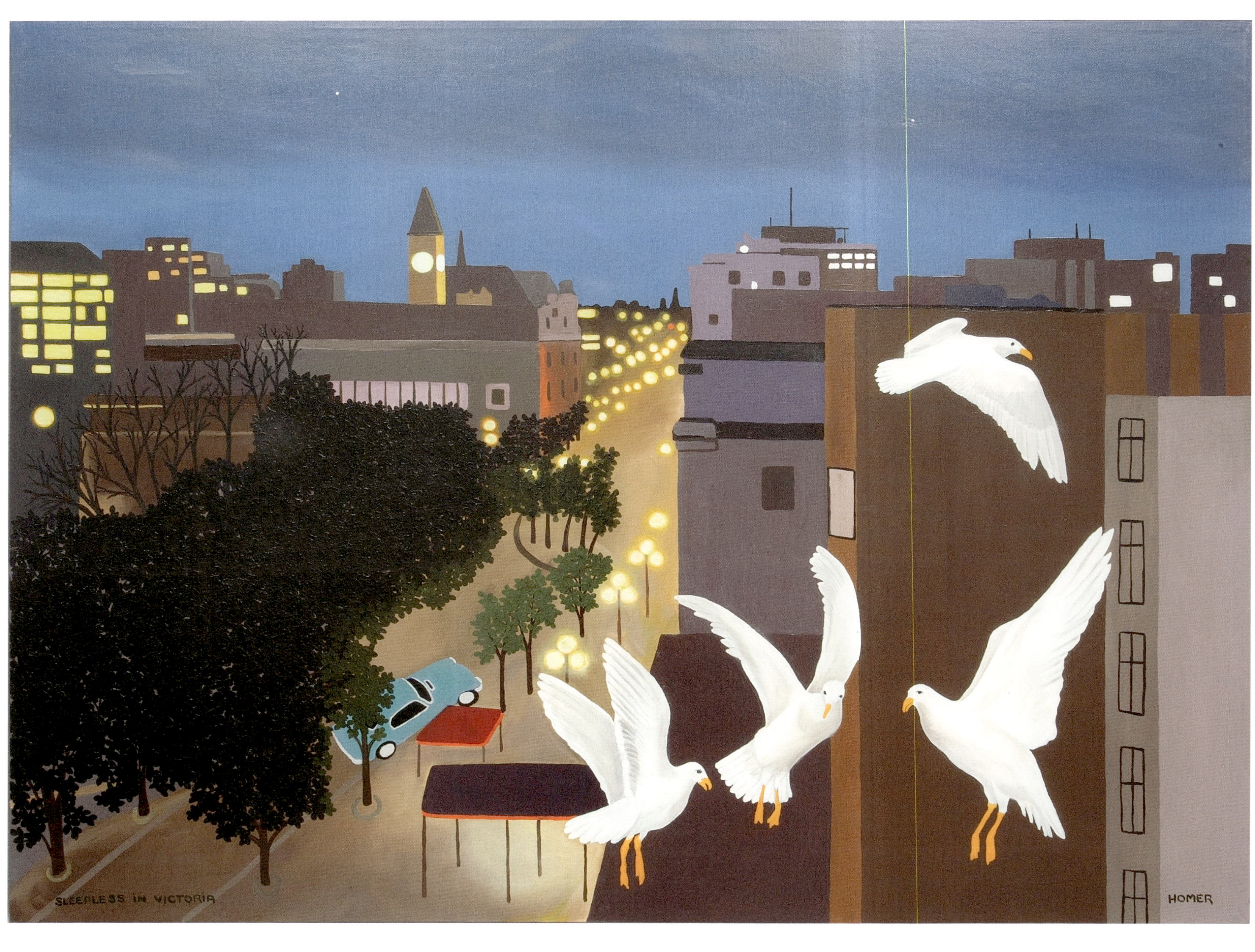

44. *Sleepless in Victoria*, 2008
Oil on canvas, 30 × 40 in. (76.2 × 101.6 cm)

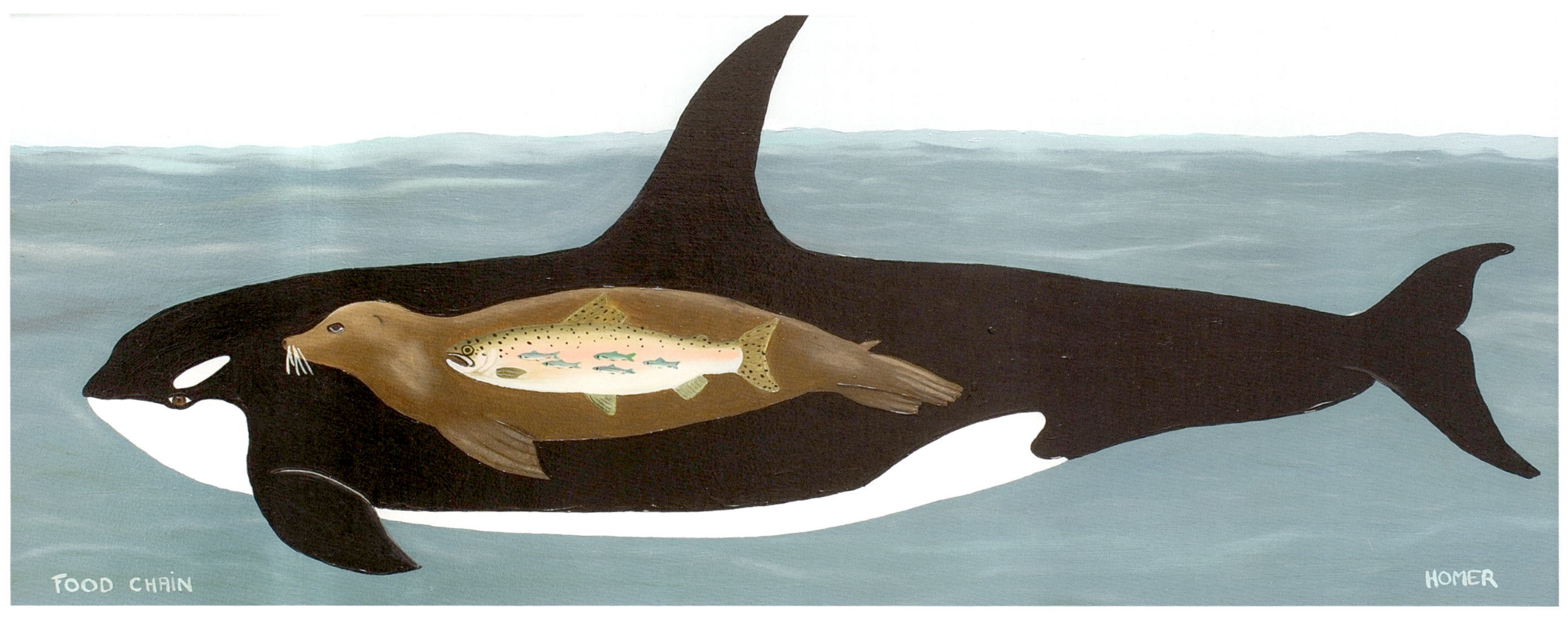

45. *Food Chain*, 2005
Oil on canvas, 12 × 28 in. (30.5 × 71.1 cm)

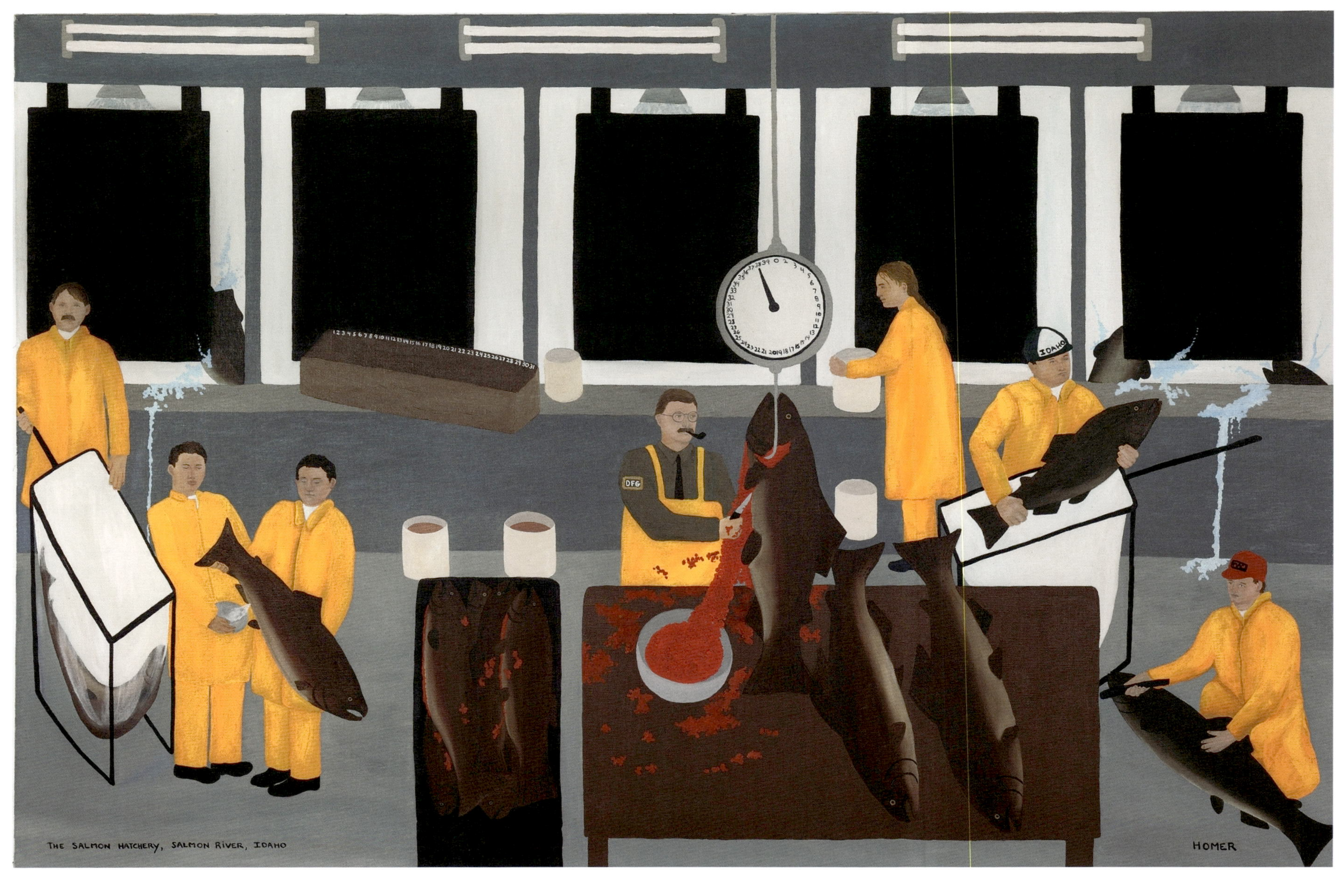

46. *The Salmon Hatchery, Salmon River, Idaho*, 1989
Oil on canvas, 40 × 60 in. (101.6 × 152.4 cm)

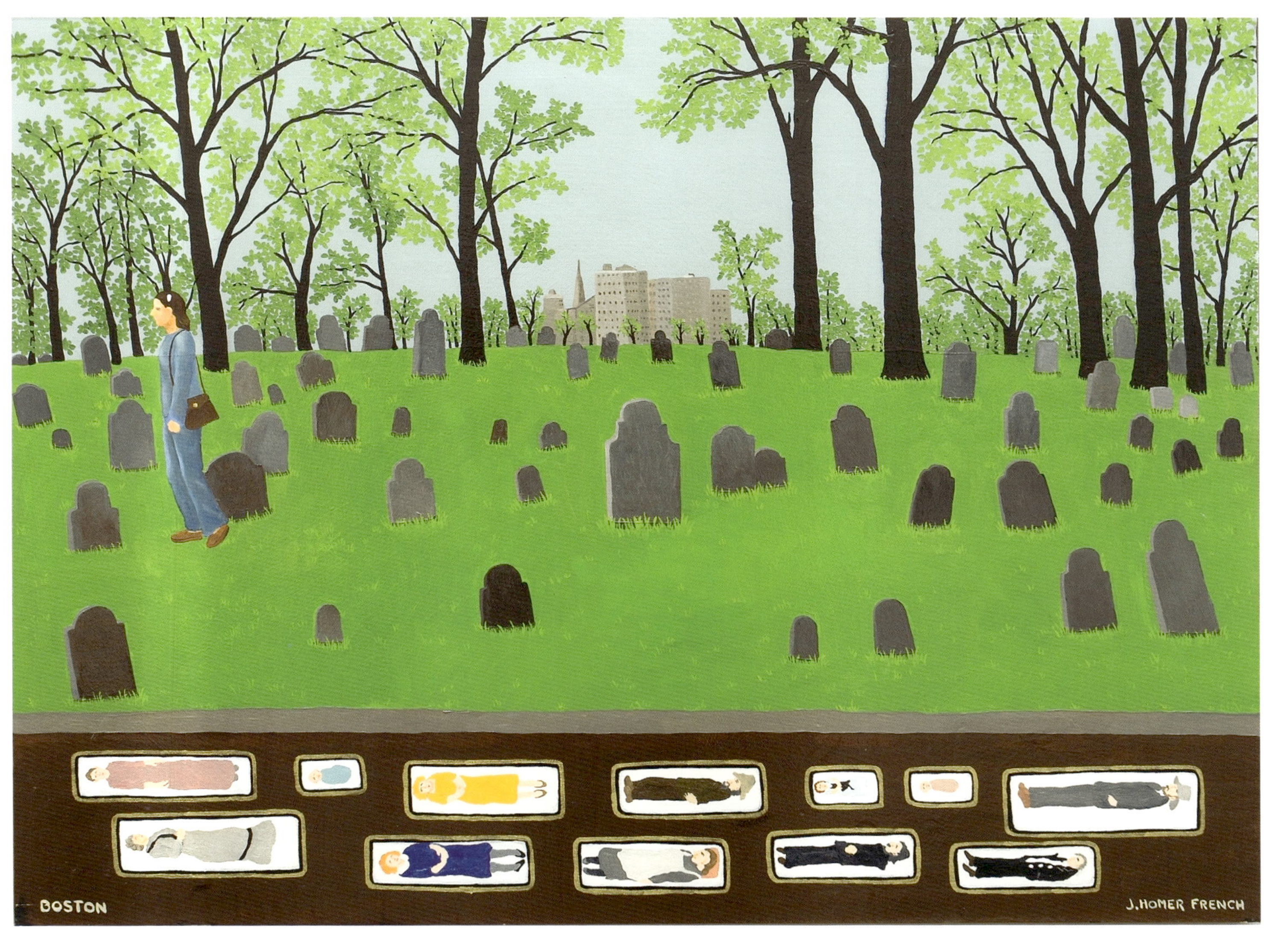

47. *Boston*, 2020
Oil on plywood, 24 × 32 in. (61 × 81.3 cm)

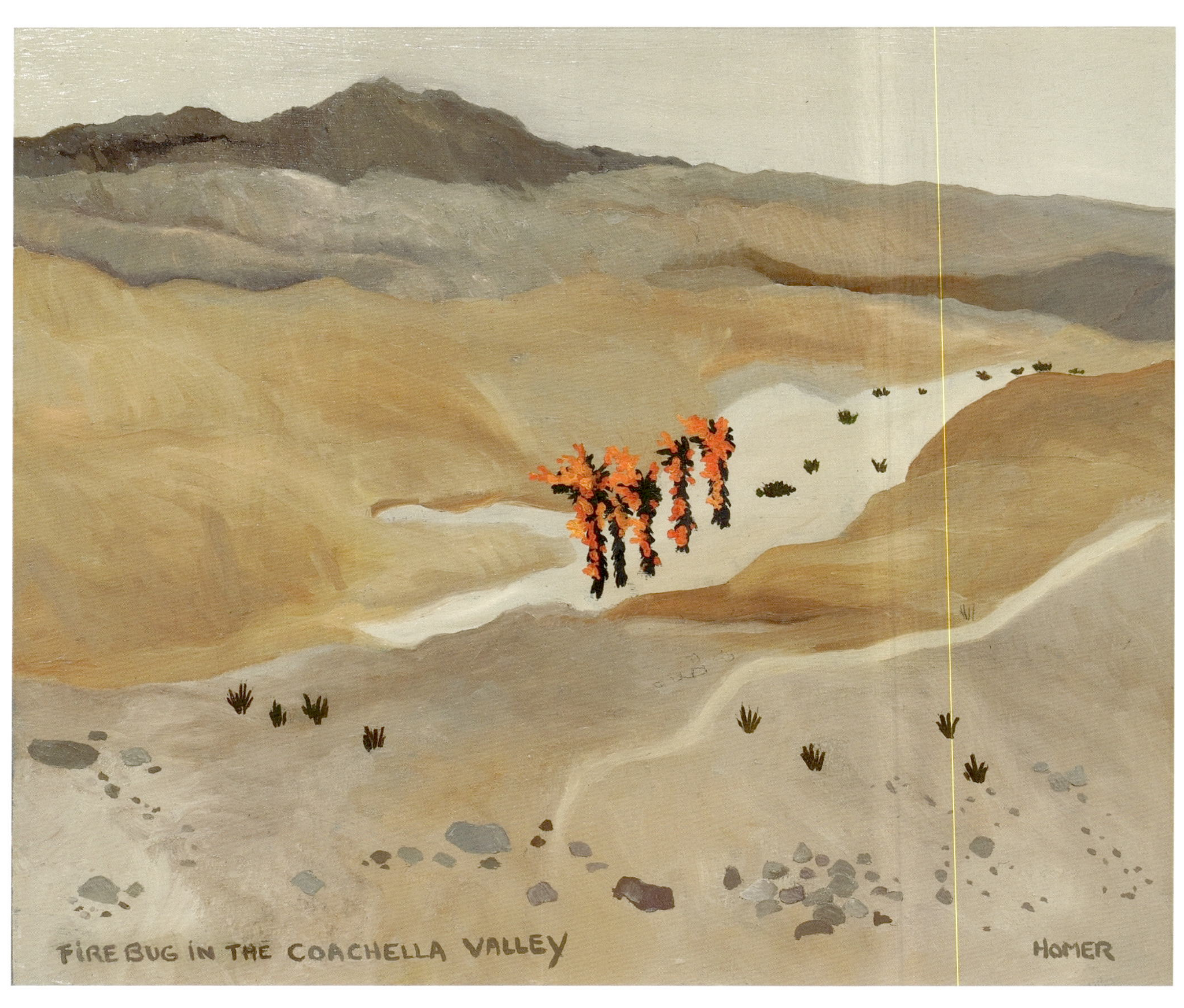

48. *Firebug in the Coachella Valley*, 2013
Oil on plywood, 11 × 13 in. (27.9 × 33 cm)

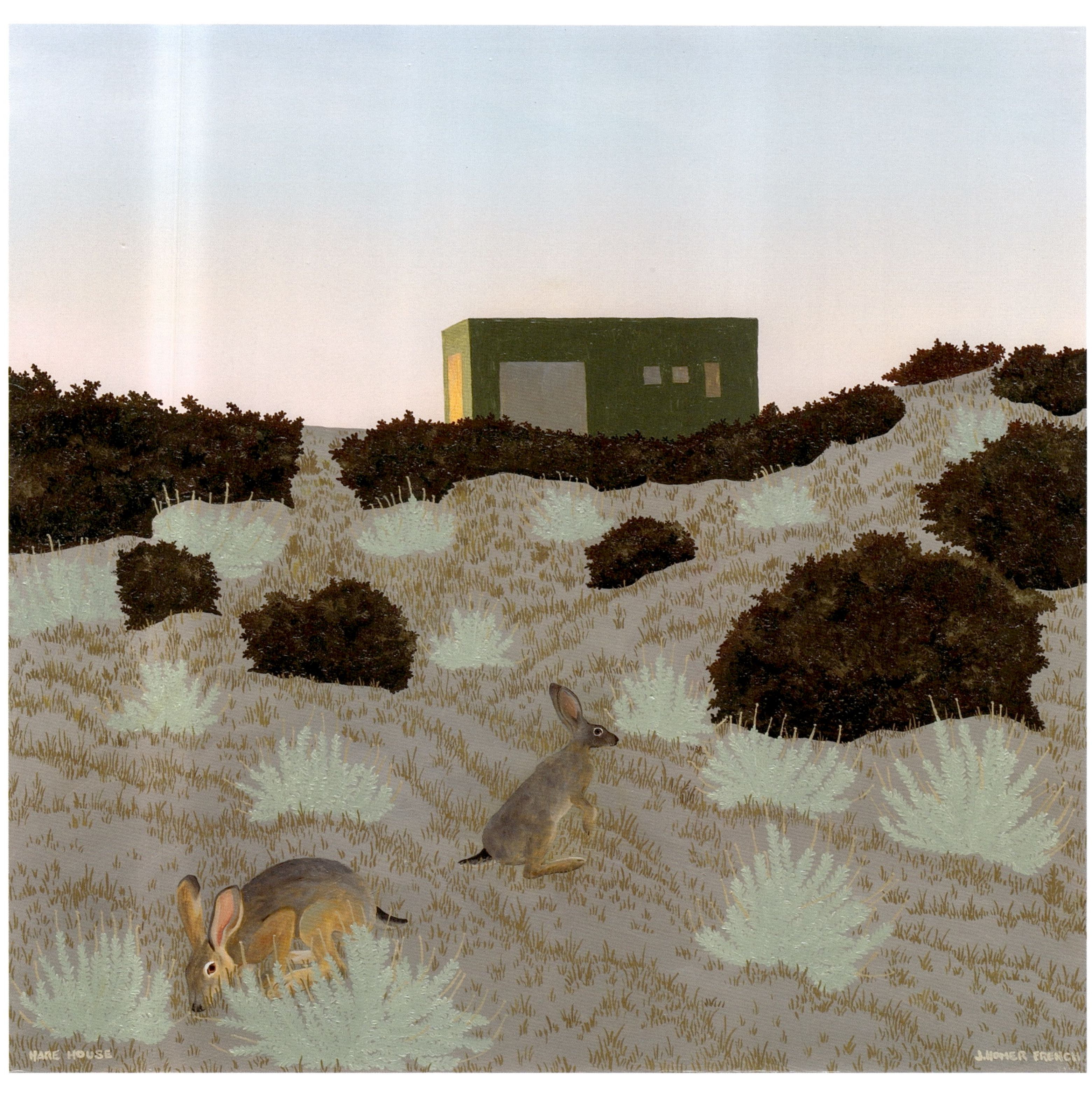

49. *Hare House*, 2020
Oil on plywood, 24 × 24 in. (61 × 61 cm)

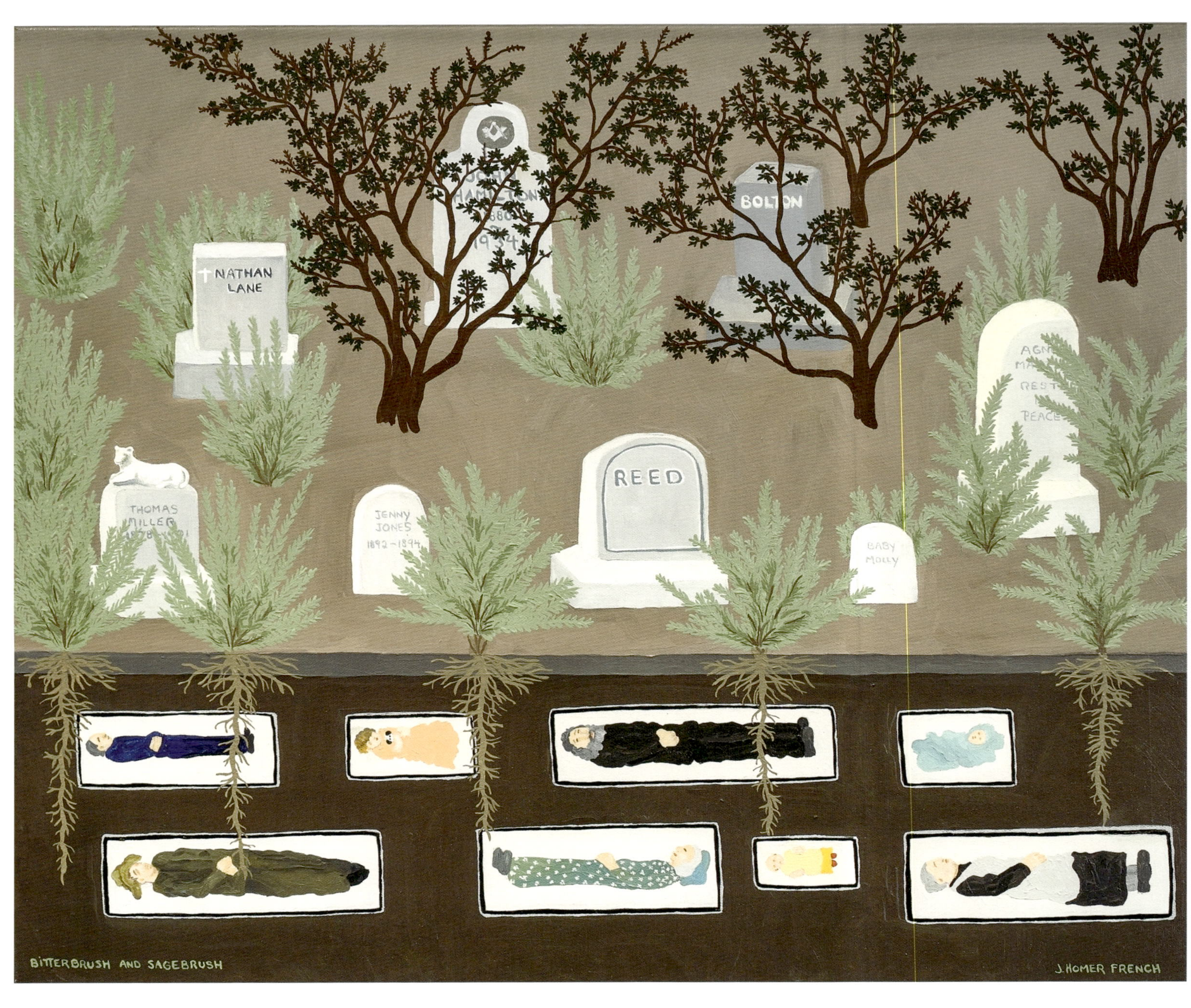

50. *Bitterbrush and Sagebrush*, 2020
Oil on canvas, 20 × 24 in. (50.8 × 61 cm)

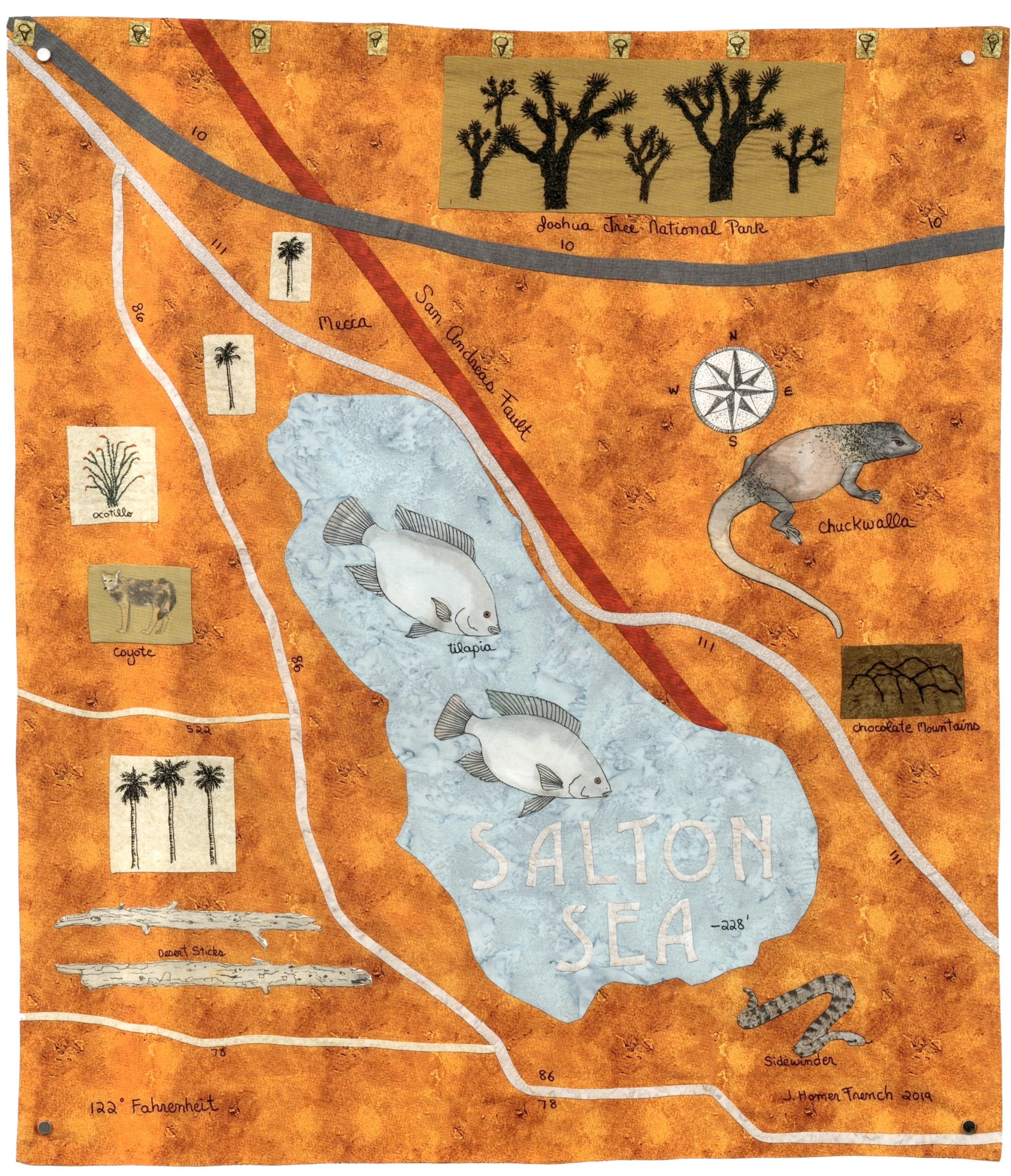

51. *122° Fahrenheit*, 2019
Fabric, thread, fabric paint and pens, 50 × 42 in. (127 × 106.7 cm)

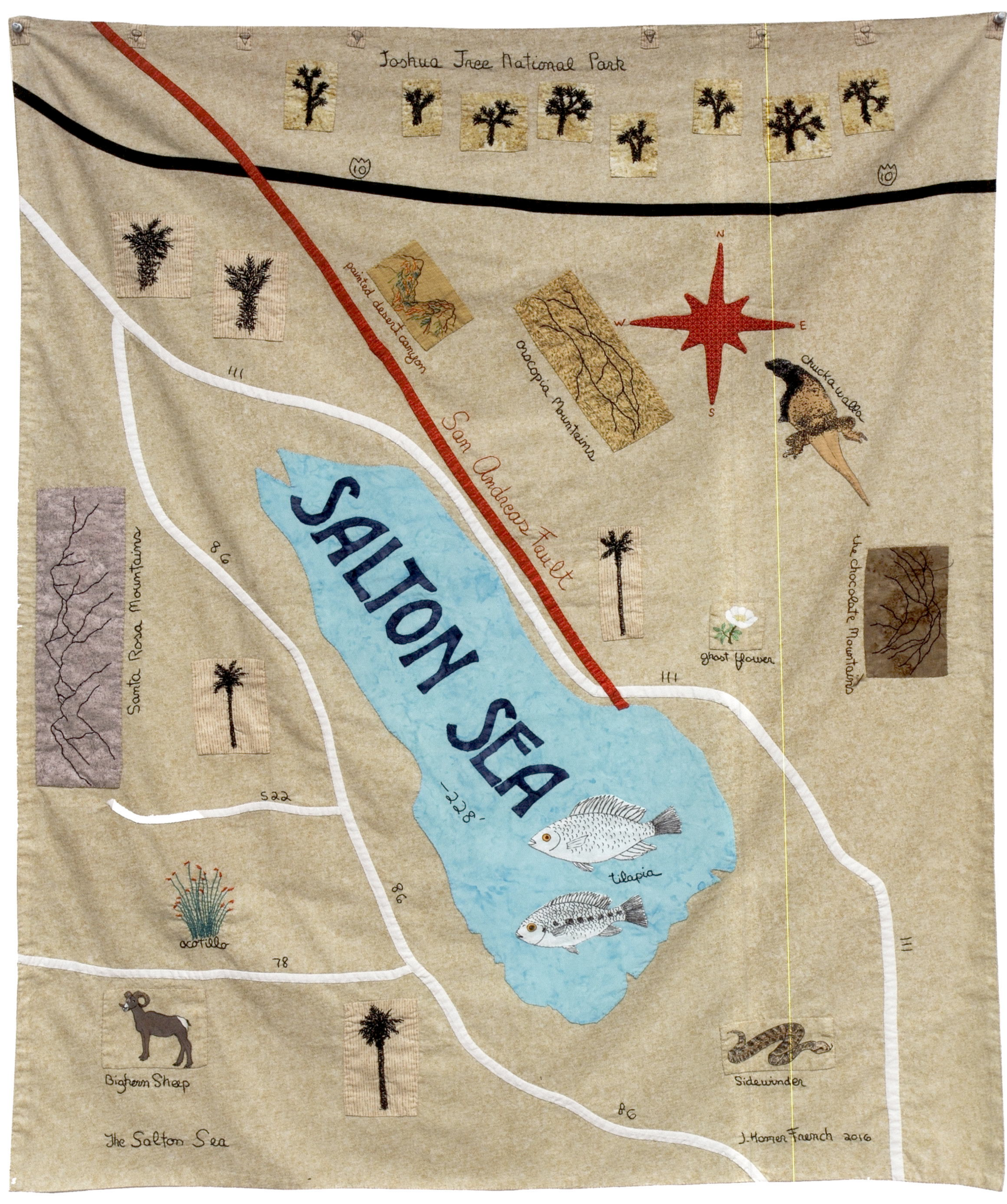

52. *The Salton Sea*, 2016
Fabric, fabric paint, thread and hardware, 51 × 40 in. (129.5 × 101.6 cm)

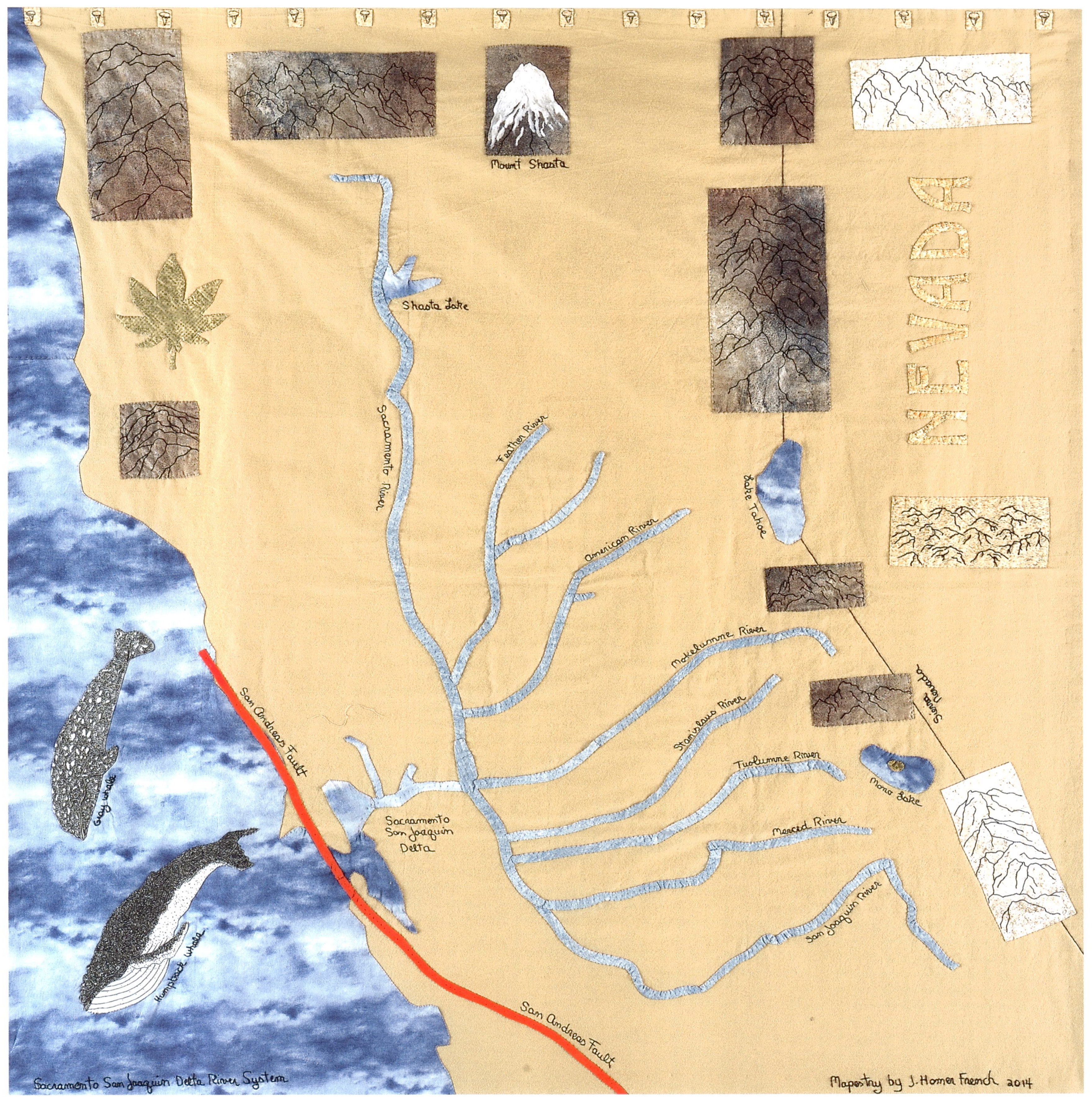

53. *Sacramento San Joaquin Delta River System*, 2014
Fabric, thread, fabric paint and pens, 53 × 51 in. (134.6 × 129.5 cm)

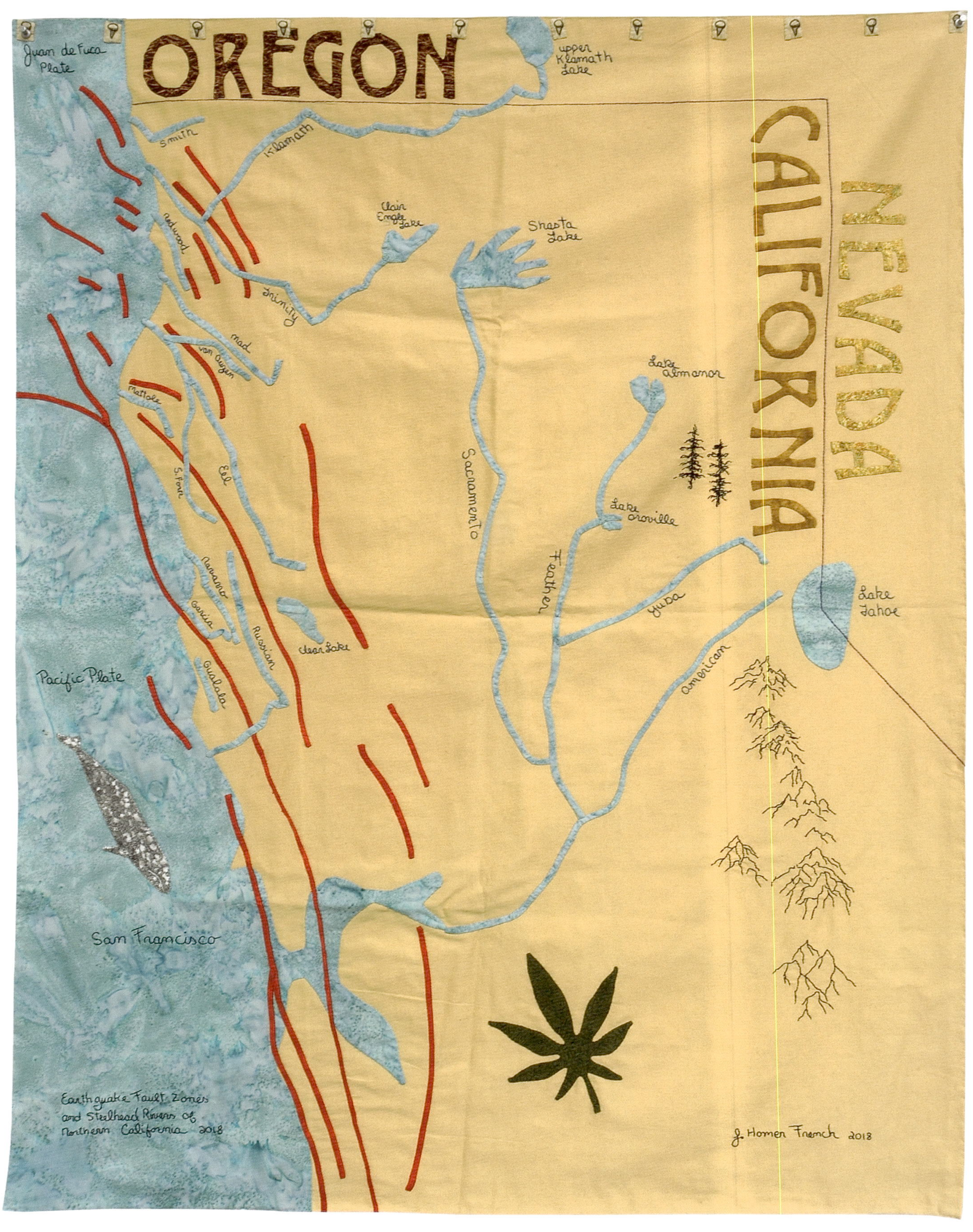

54. *Earthquake Fault Zones and Steelhead Rivers of Northern California*, 2018
Fabric, thread, fabric paint and pens, 52 × 41 in. (132.1 × 104.1 cm)

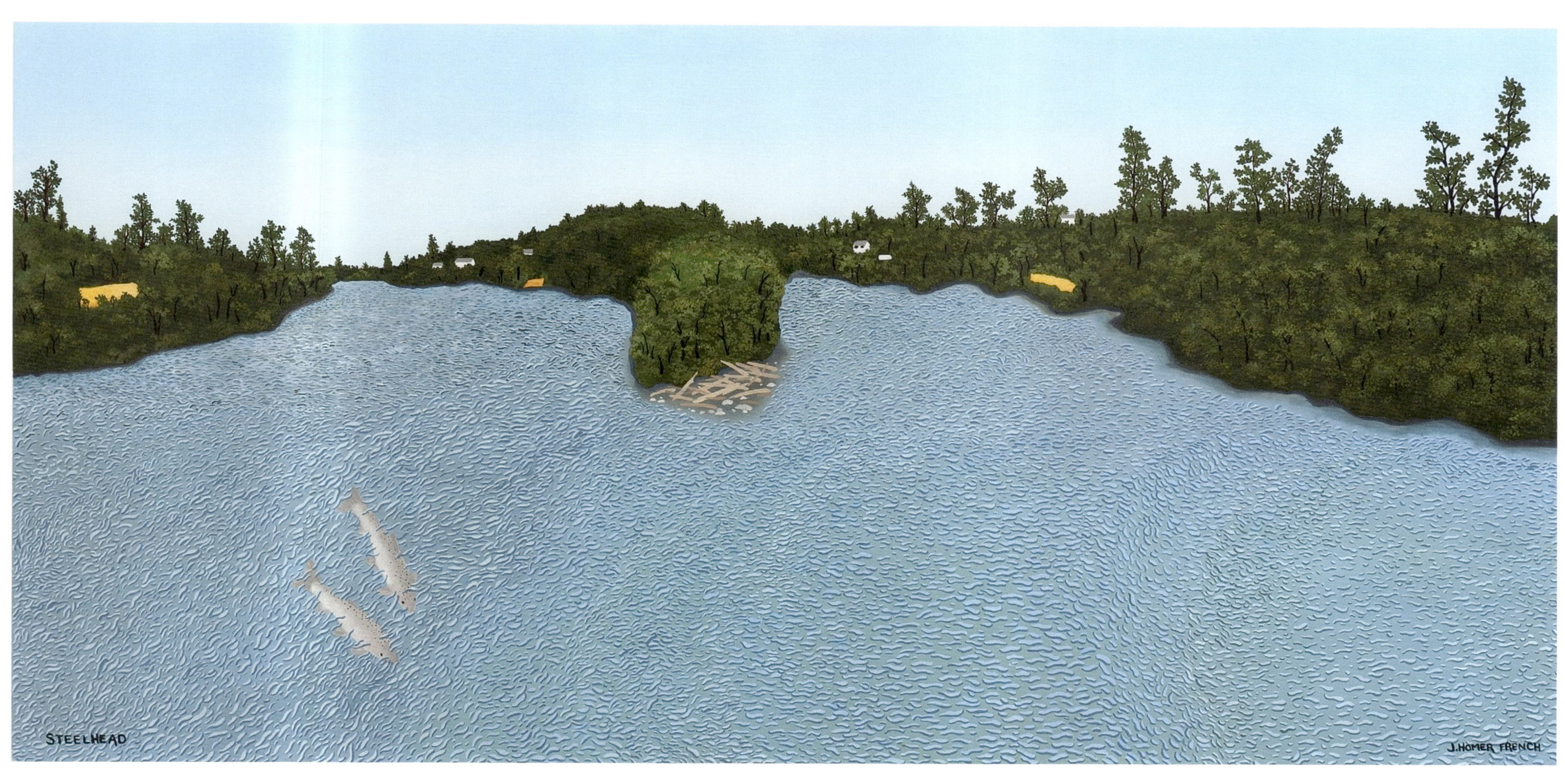

55. *Steelhead*, 2011
Oil on canvas, 24 × 48 in. (61 × 121.9 cm)

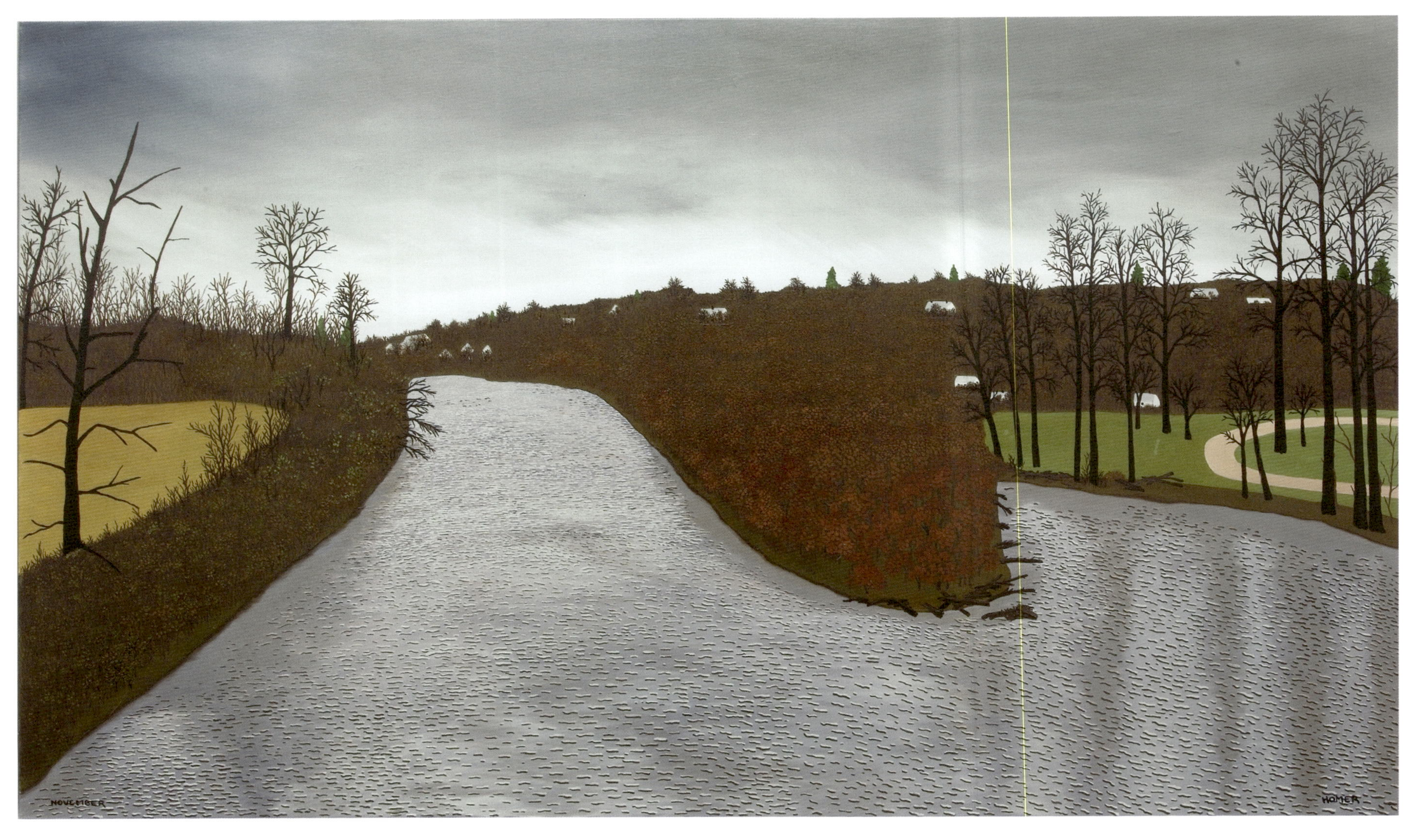

56. *November*, 2008
Oil on canvas, 36 × 60 in. (91.4 × 152.4 cm)

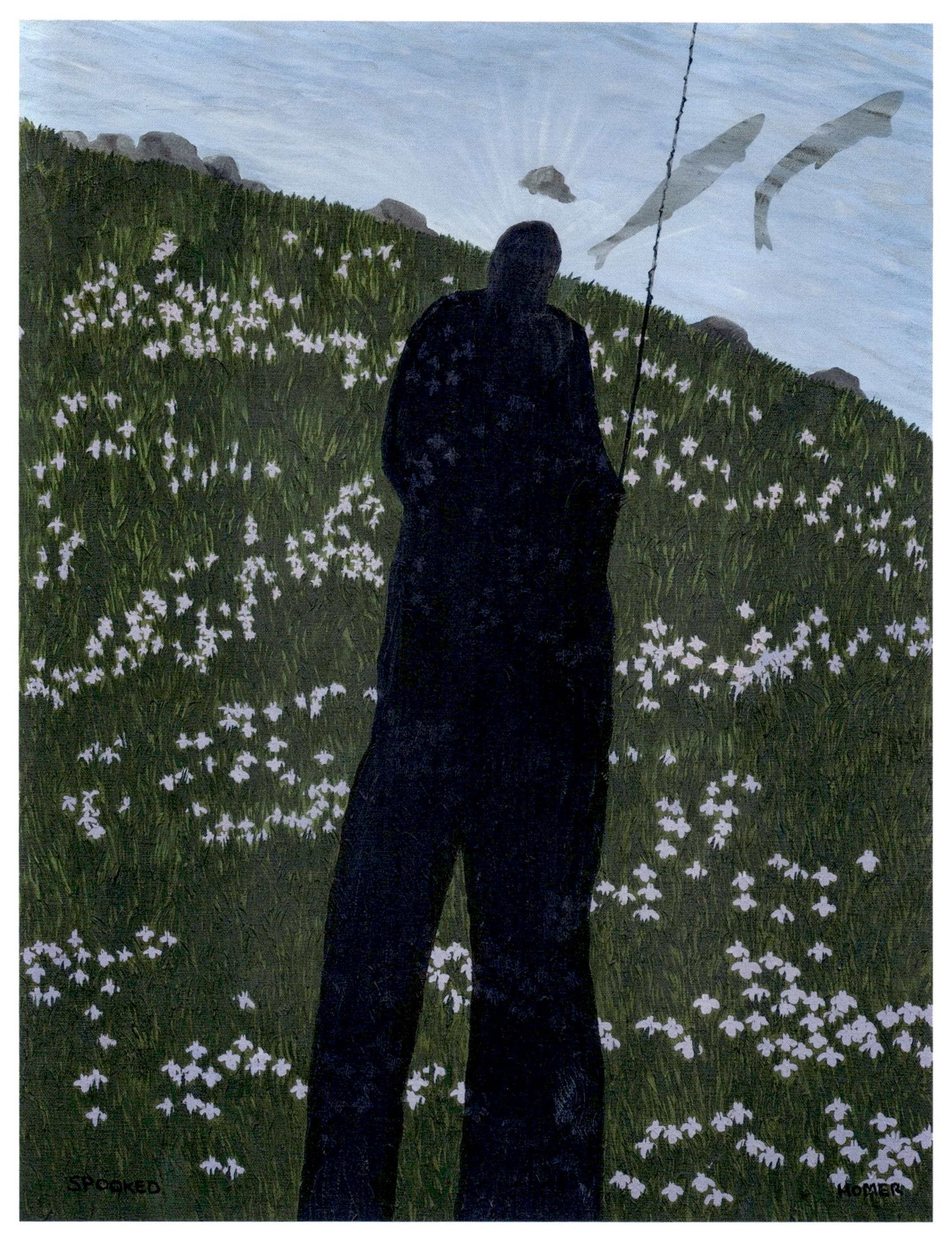

57. *Spooked*, 1999
Oil on canvas, 24 × 18 in. (61 × 45.7 cm)

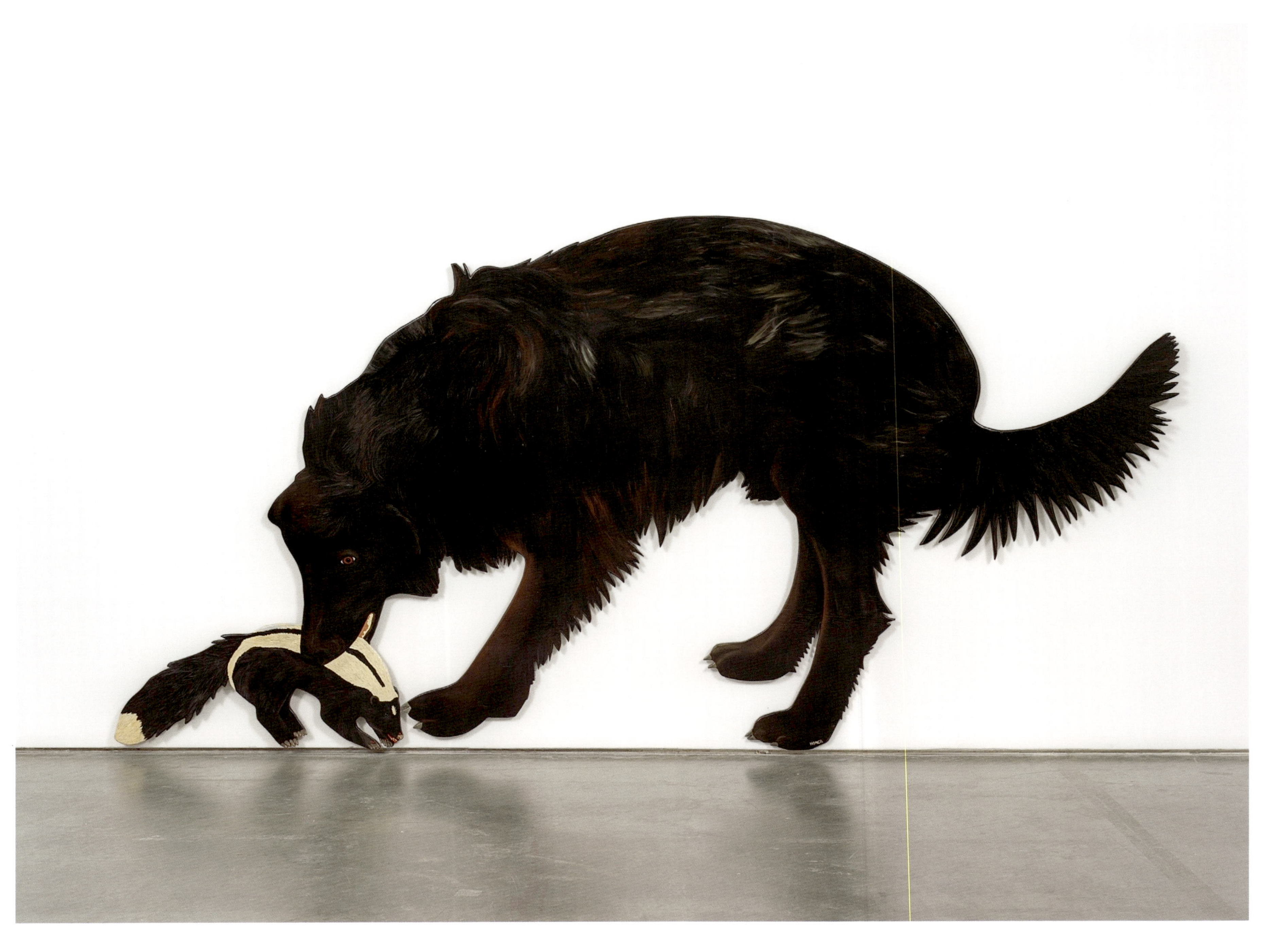

58. *Ezra and the Skunk*, 1988
Acrylic and oil on plywood, 44 × 87 in. (111.8 × 221 cm)

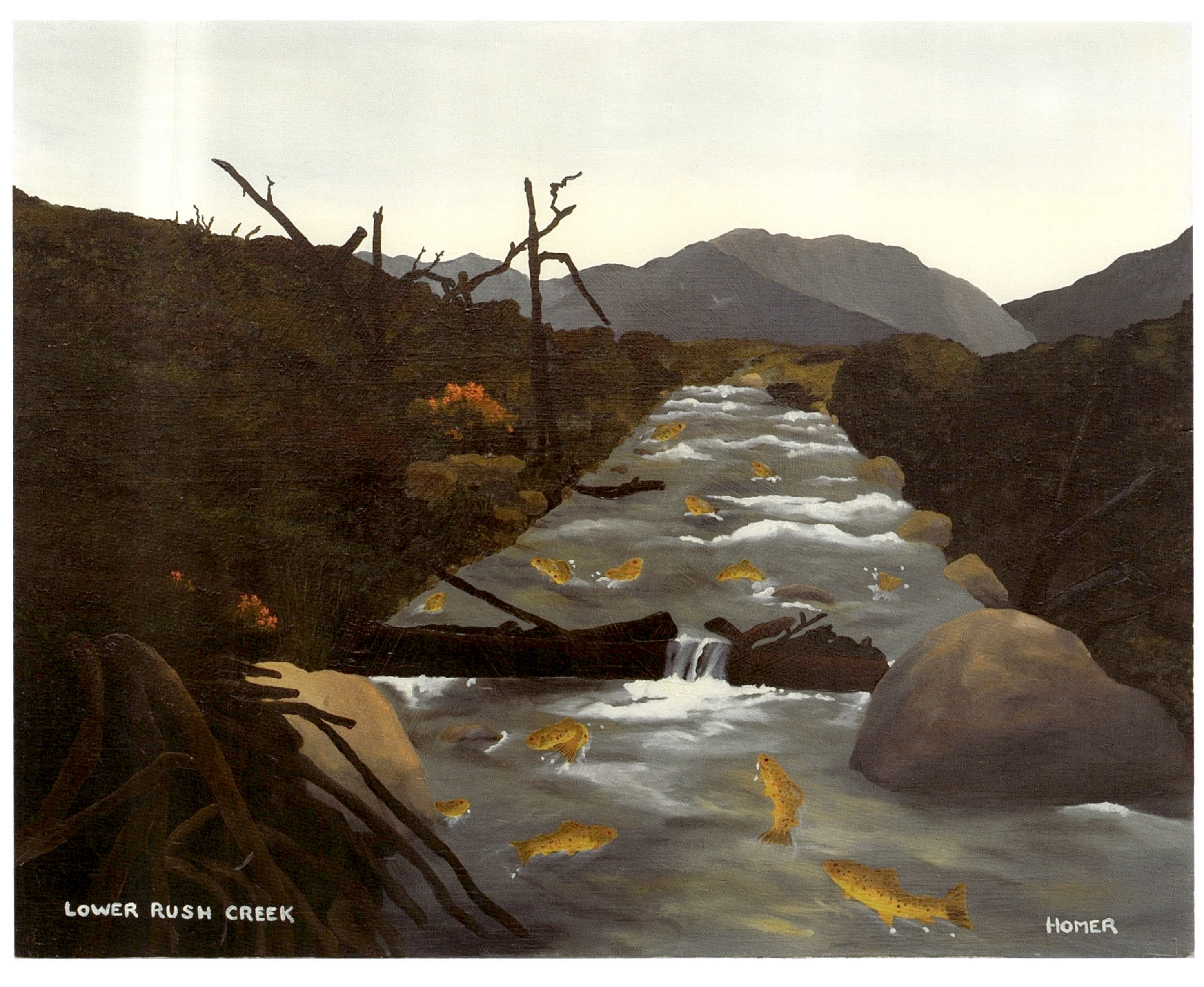

59. *Lower Rush Creek*, 1994
Oil on canvas, 24 × 30 in. (61 × 76.2 cm)

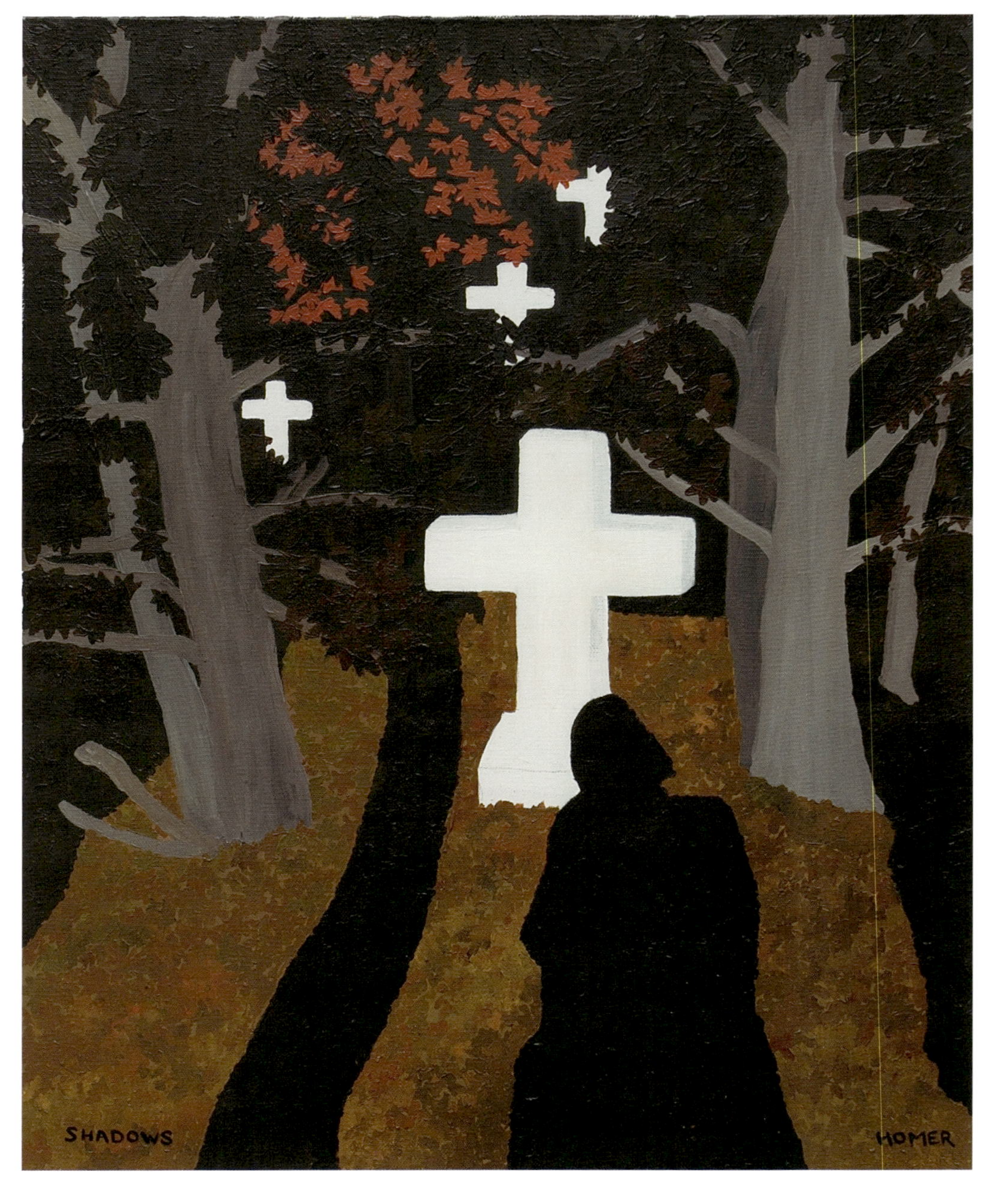

60. *Shadows*, 2002
Oil on canvas, 20 × 16 in. (50.8 × 40.6 cm)

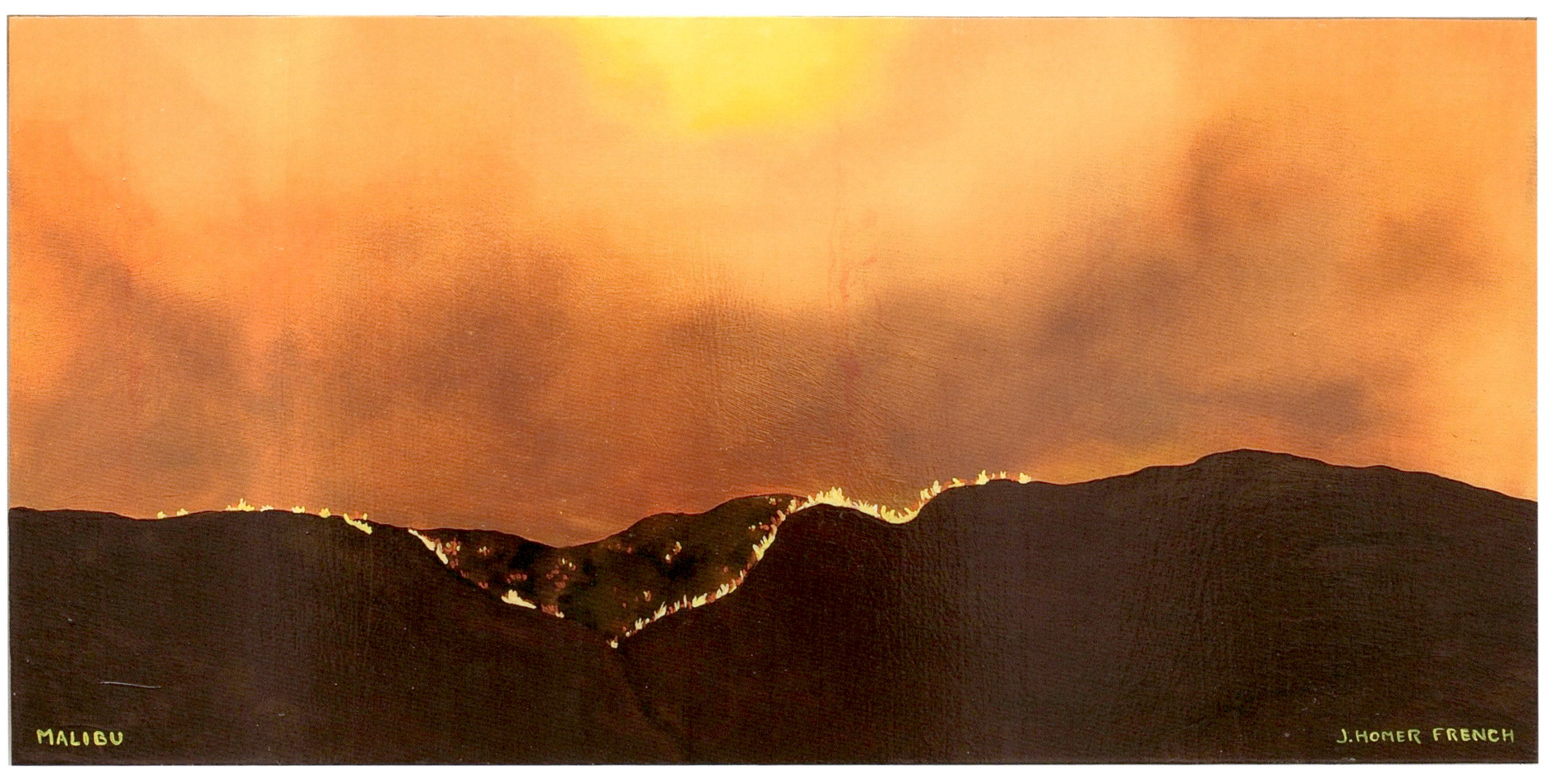

61. *Malibu*, 2019
Oil on plywood, 12 × 23½ in. (30.5 × 59.7 cm)

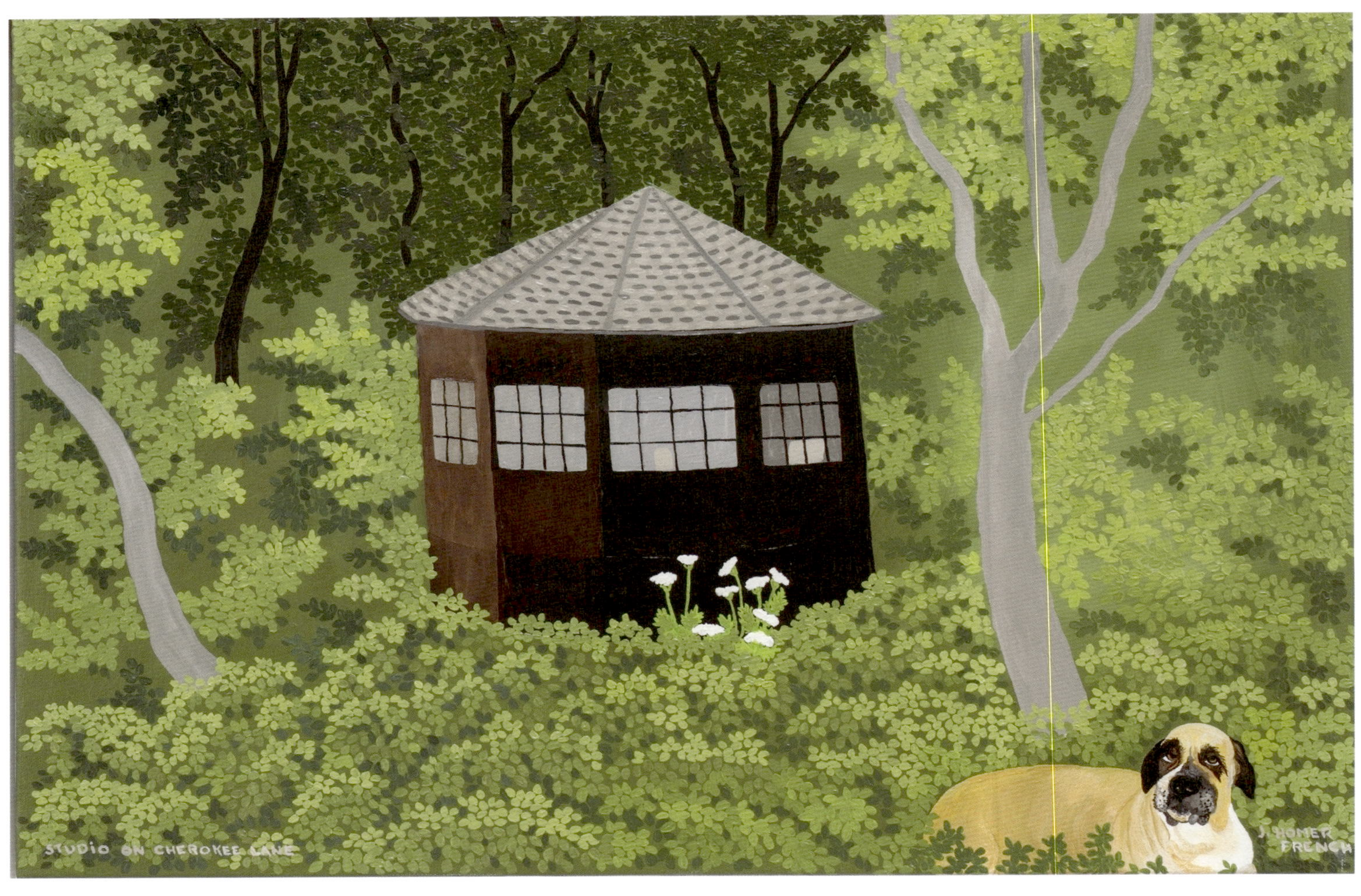

62. *Studio on Cherokee Lane*, 2020
Oil on canvas, 16 × 24 in. (40.6 × 61 cm)

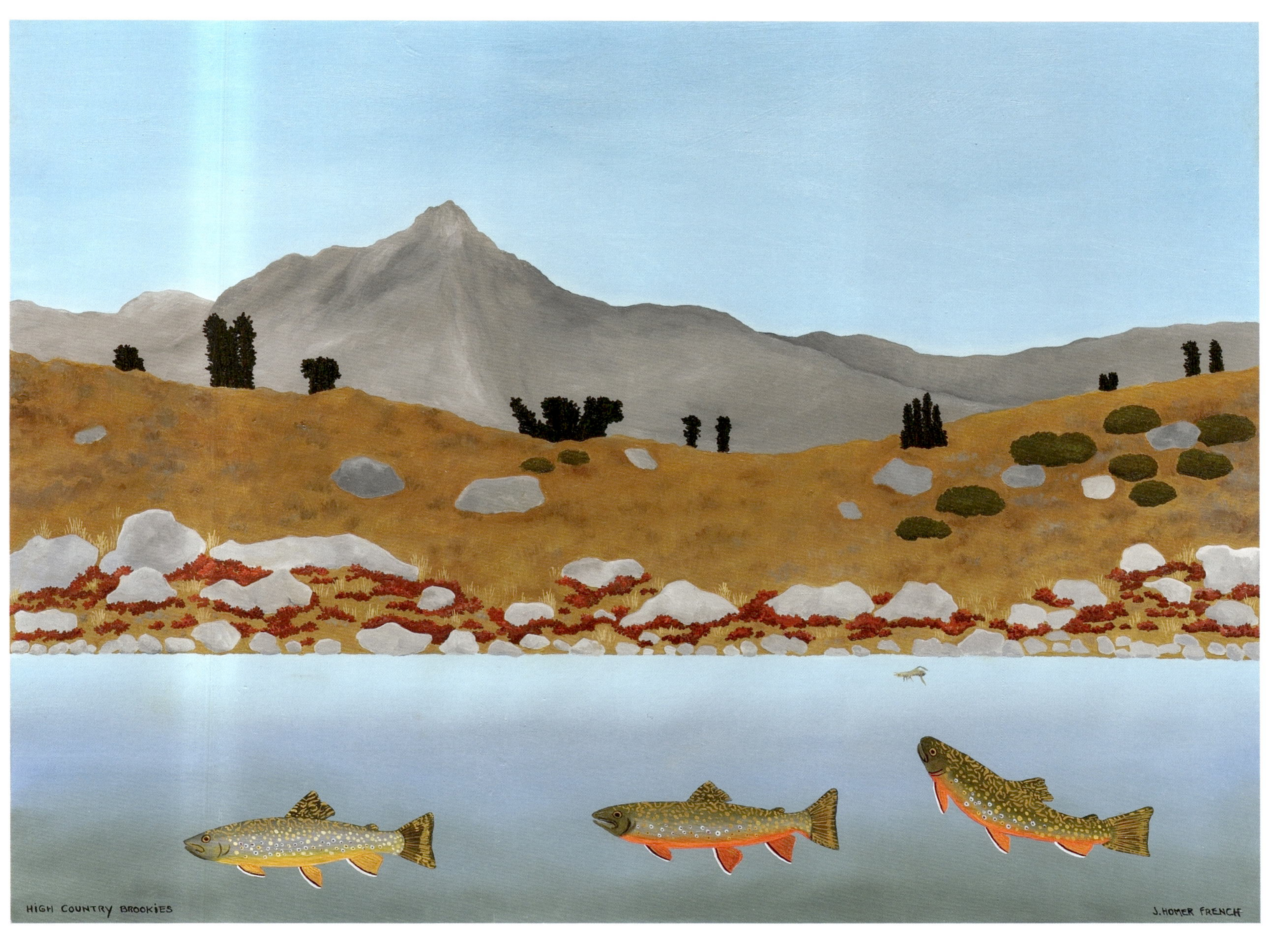

63. *High Country Brookies*, 2020
Oil on plywood, 24 × 32 in. (61 × 81.3 cm)

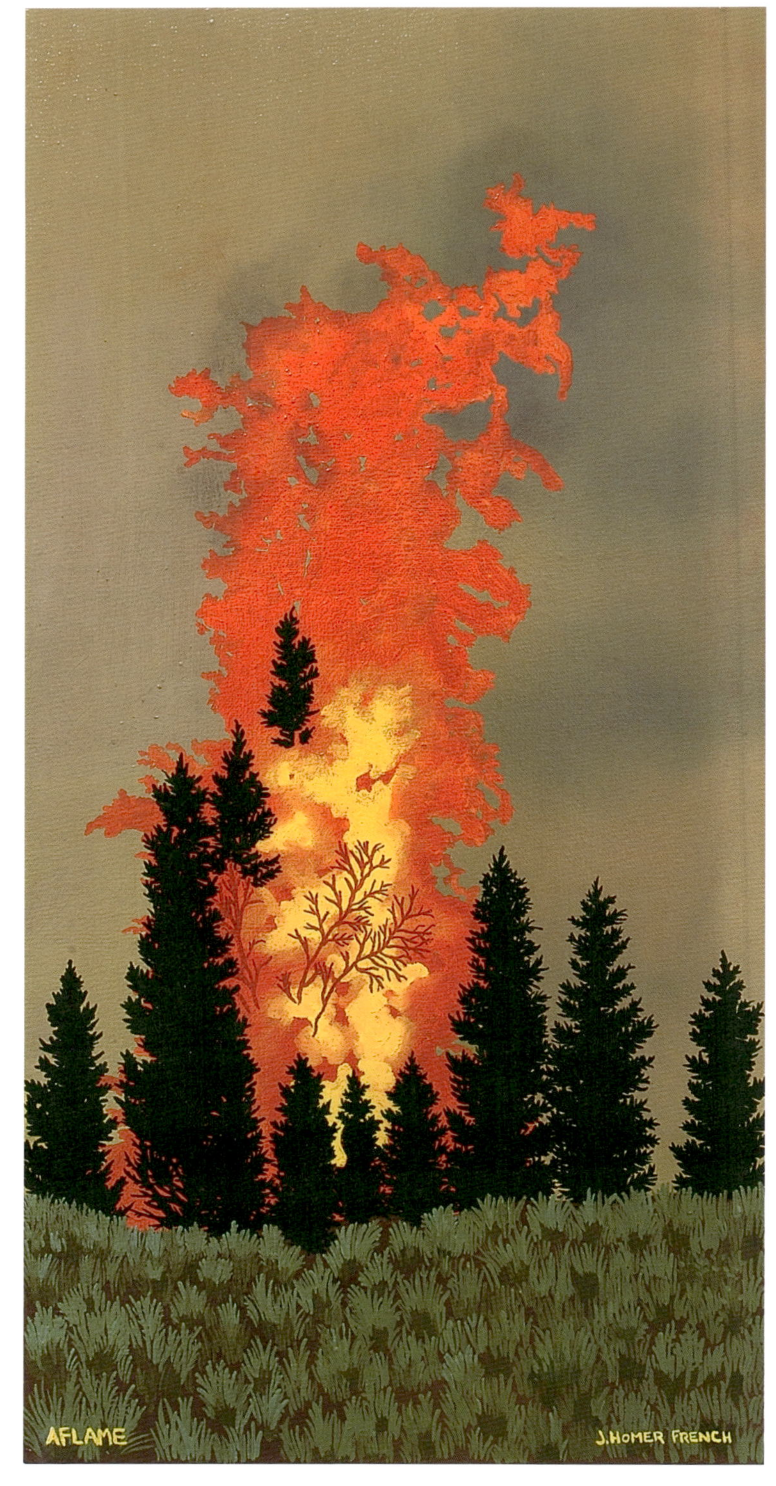

64. *Aflame*, 2020
Oil on canvas, 24 × 12 in. (61 × 30.5 cm)

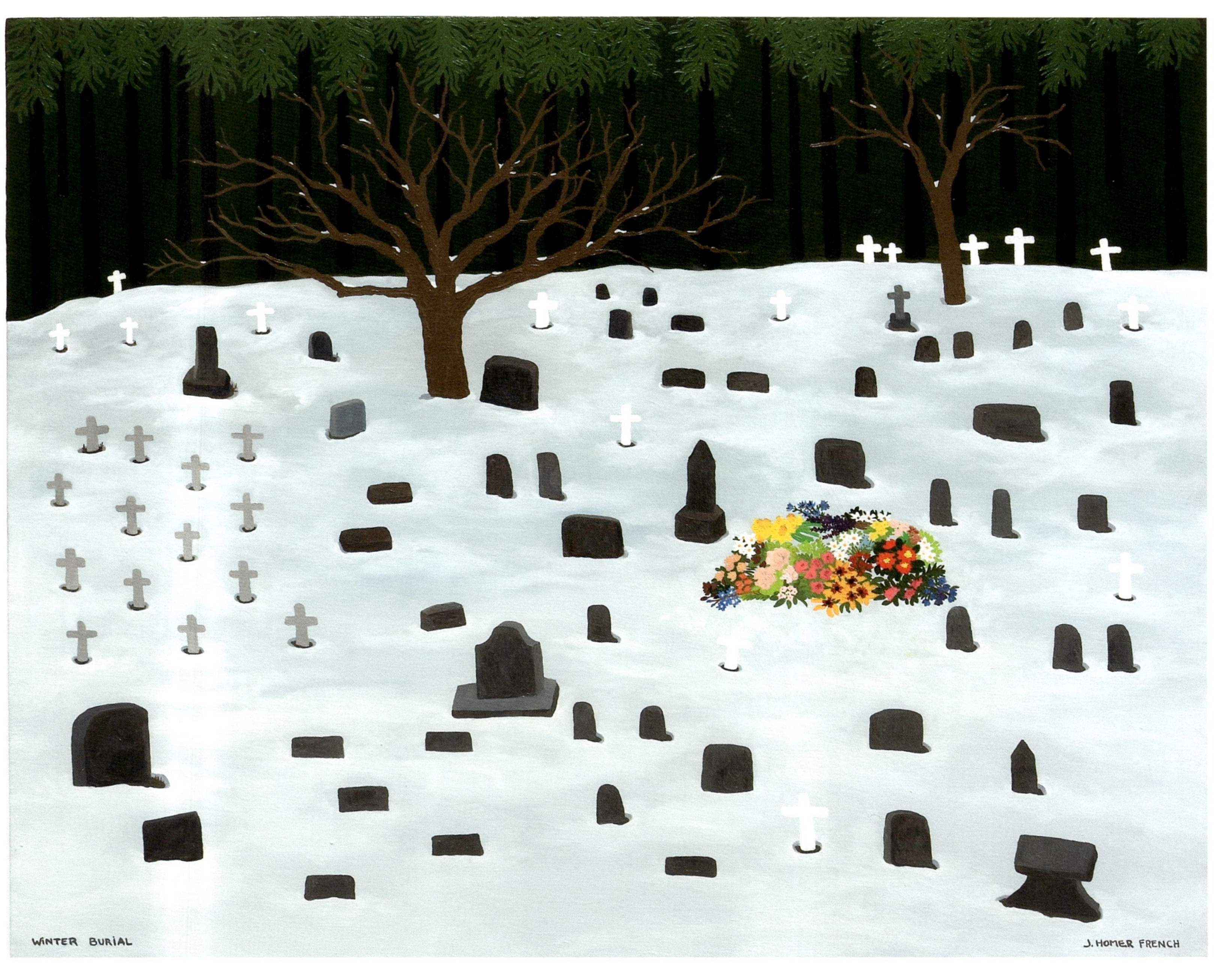

65. *Winter Burial*, 2020
Oil on canvas, 26 × 32 in. (66 × 81.3 cm)

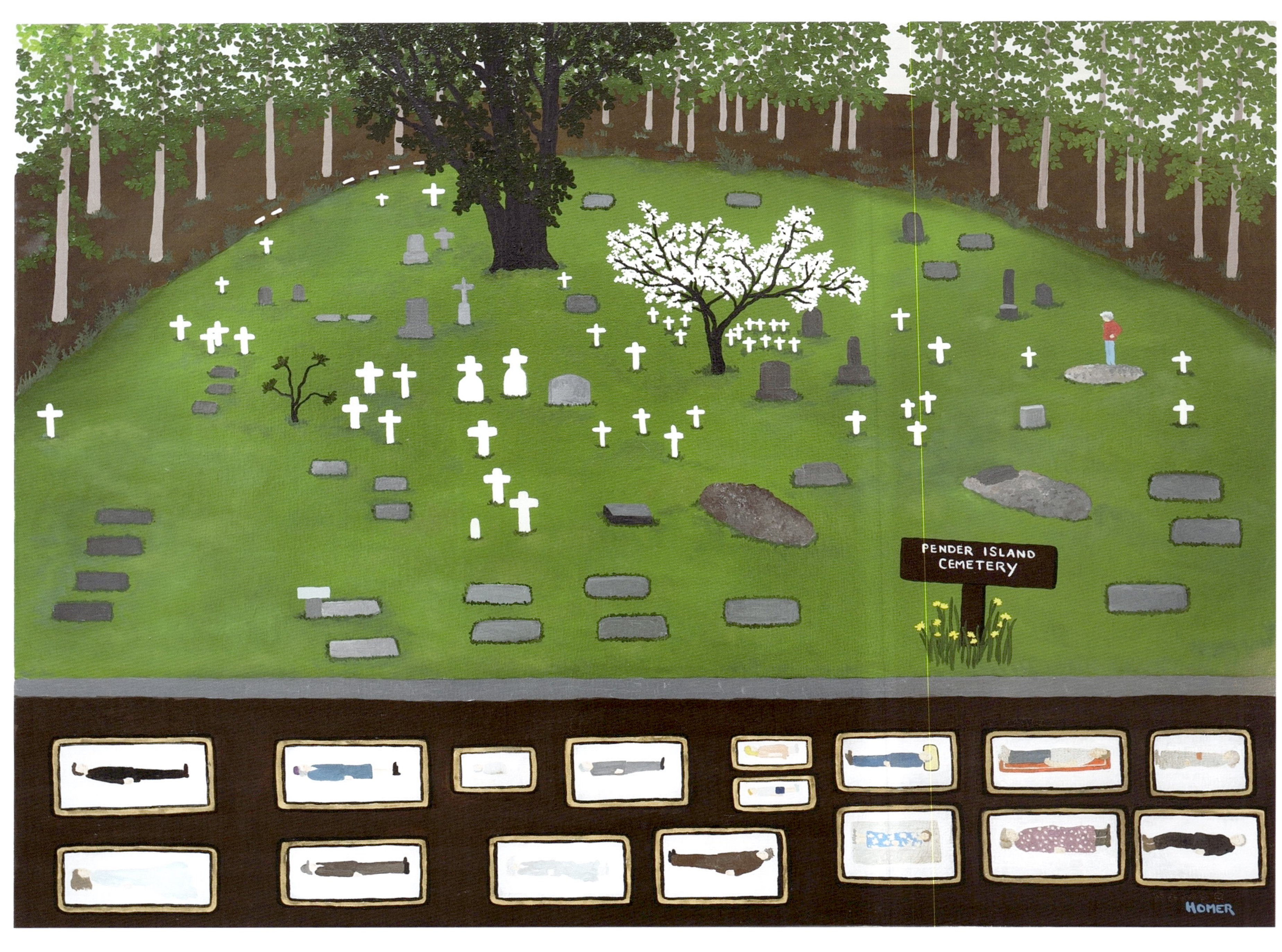

66. *Pender Island Cemetery*, 2014
Oil on canvas, 30 × 40 in. (76.2 × 101.6 cm)

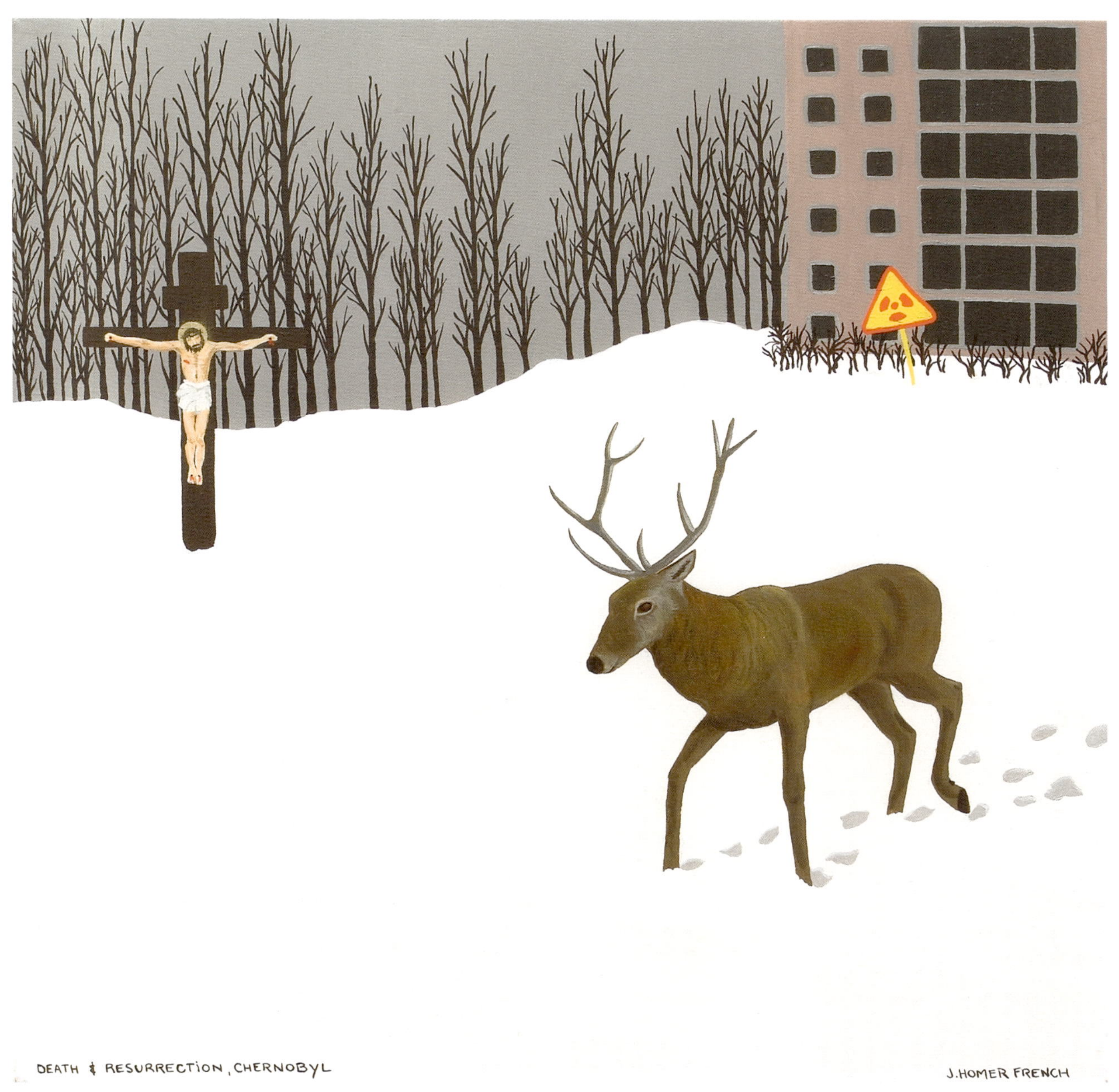

67. *Death & Resurrection, Chernobyl*, 2018
Oil on canvas, 24 × 24 in. (61 × 61 cm)

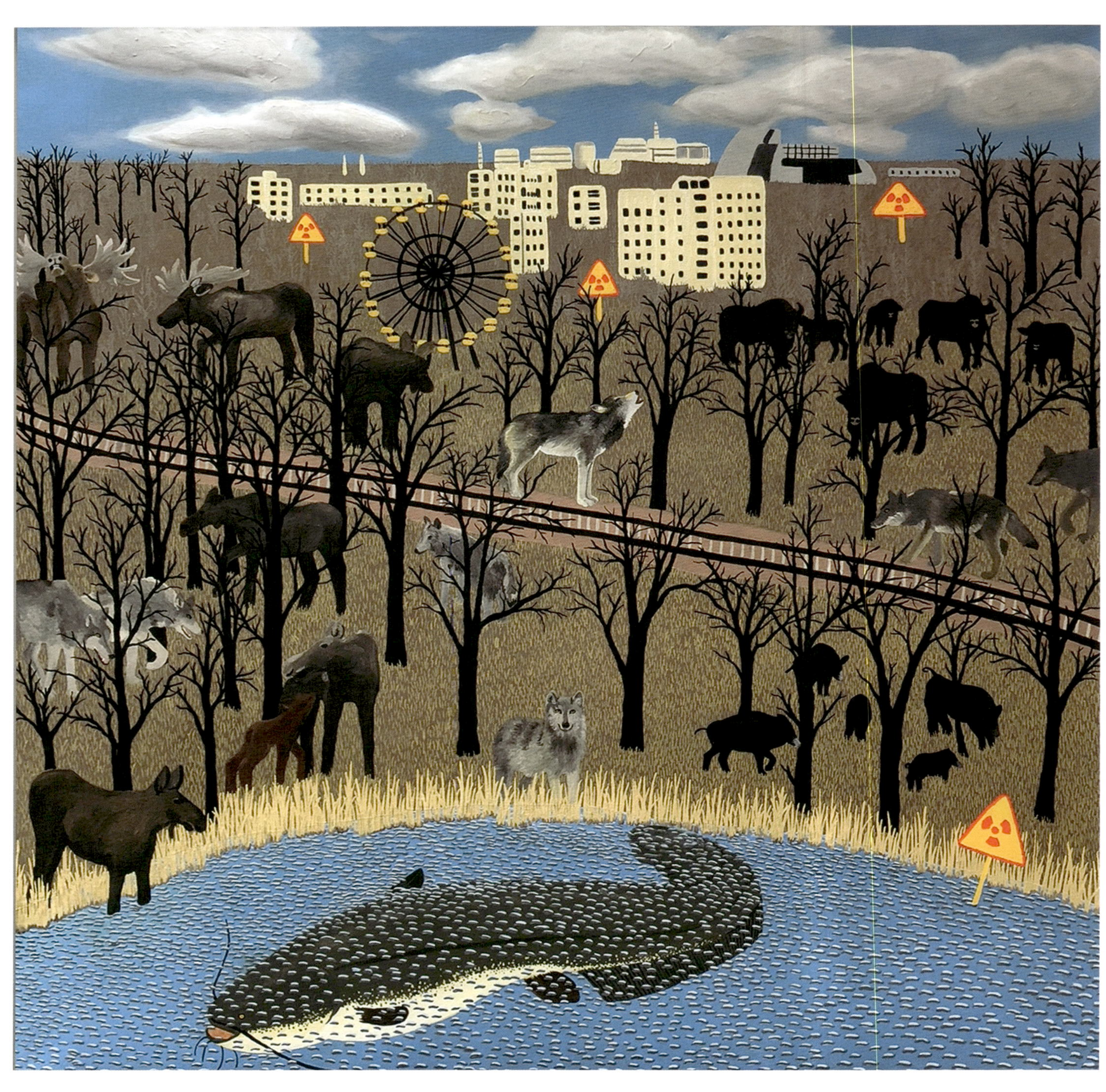

68. *Chernobyl*, 2017
Oil on canvas, 36 × 36 in. (91.4 × 91.4 cm)

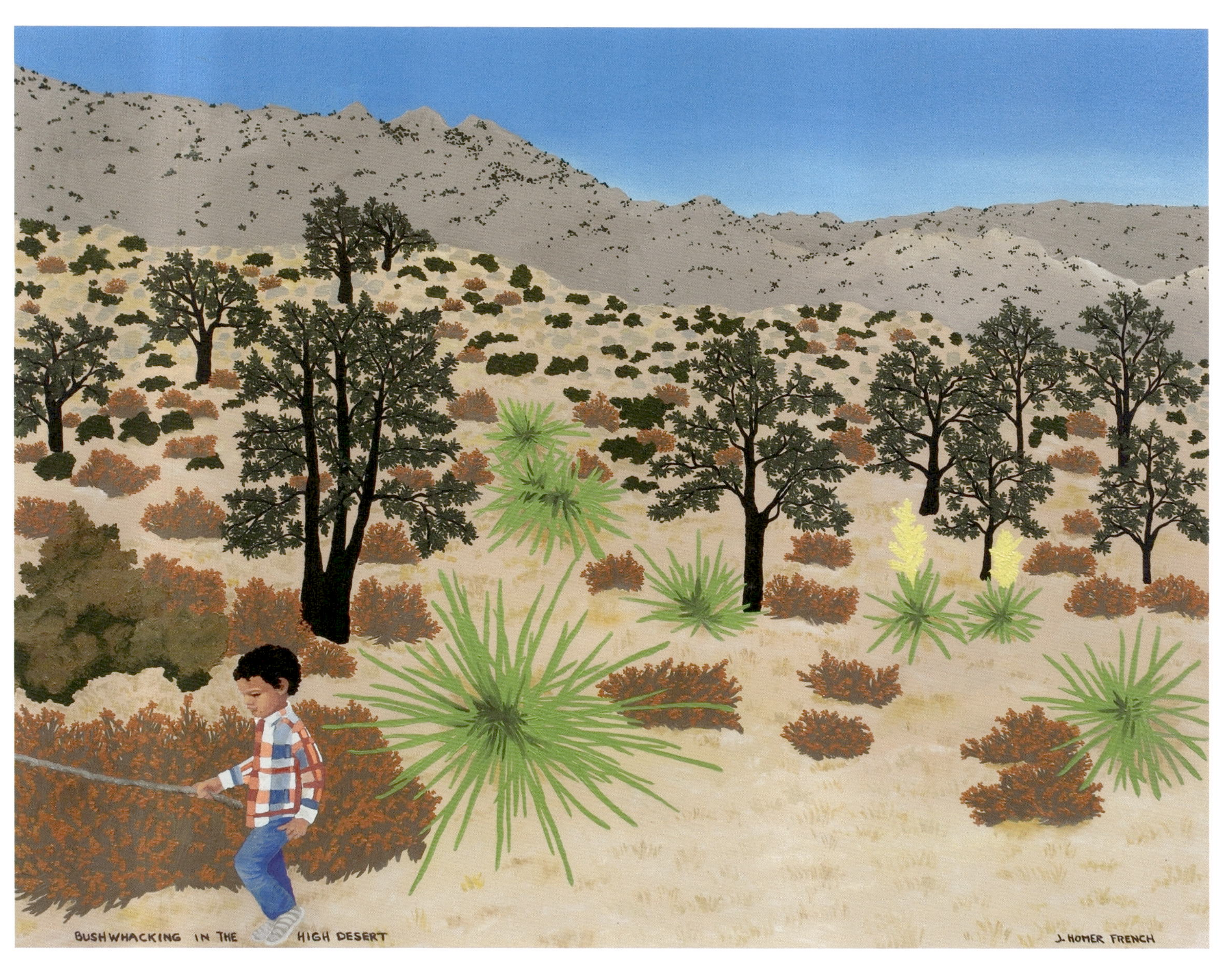

69. *Bushwhacking in the High Desert*, 2021
Oil on canvas, 24 × 30 in. (61 × 76.2 cm)

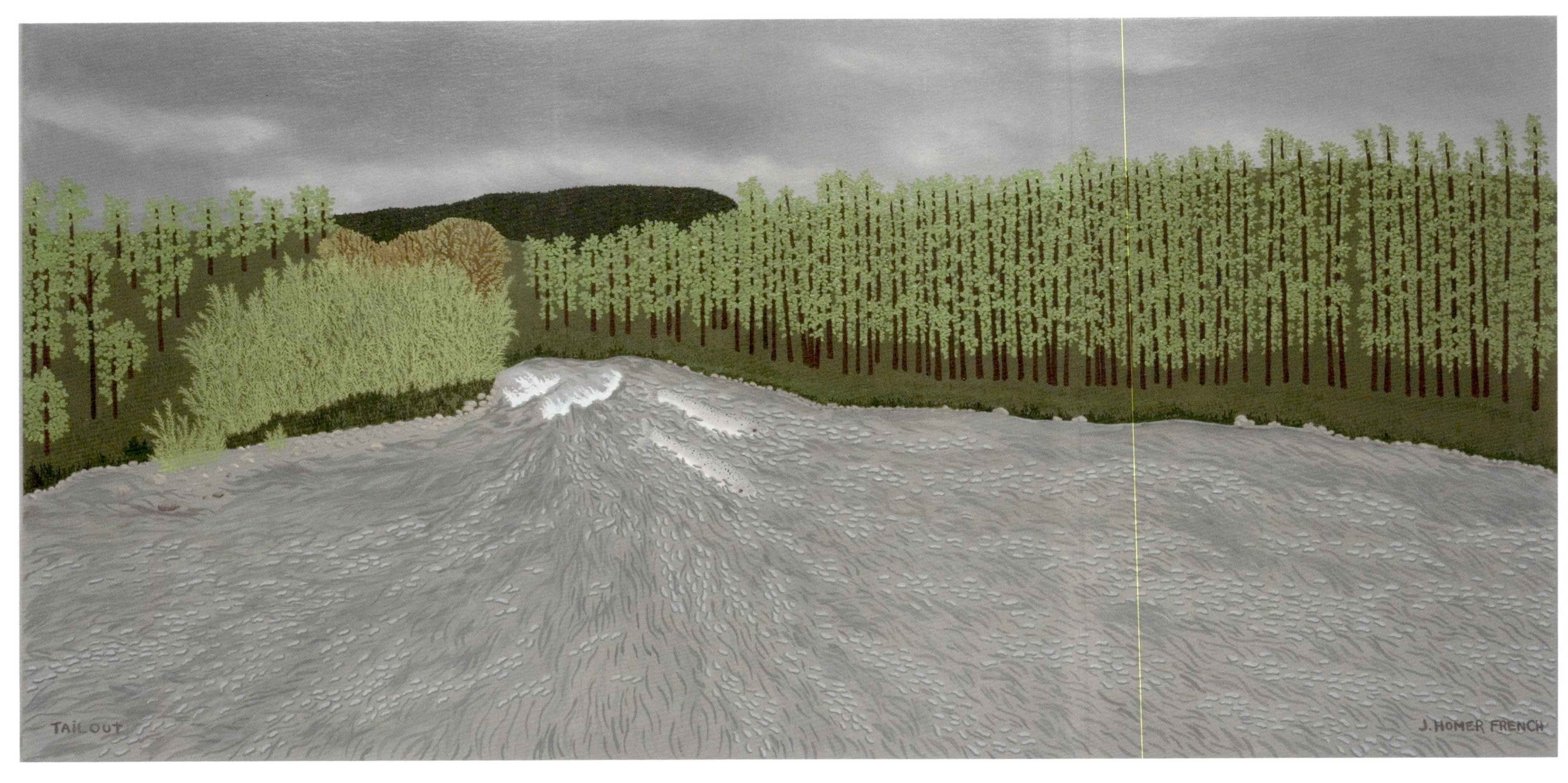

70. *Tailout*, 2018
Oil on canvas, 24 × 48 in. (61 × 121.9 cm)

98

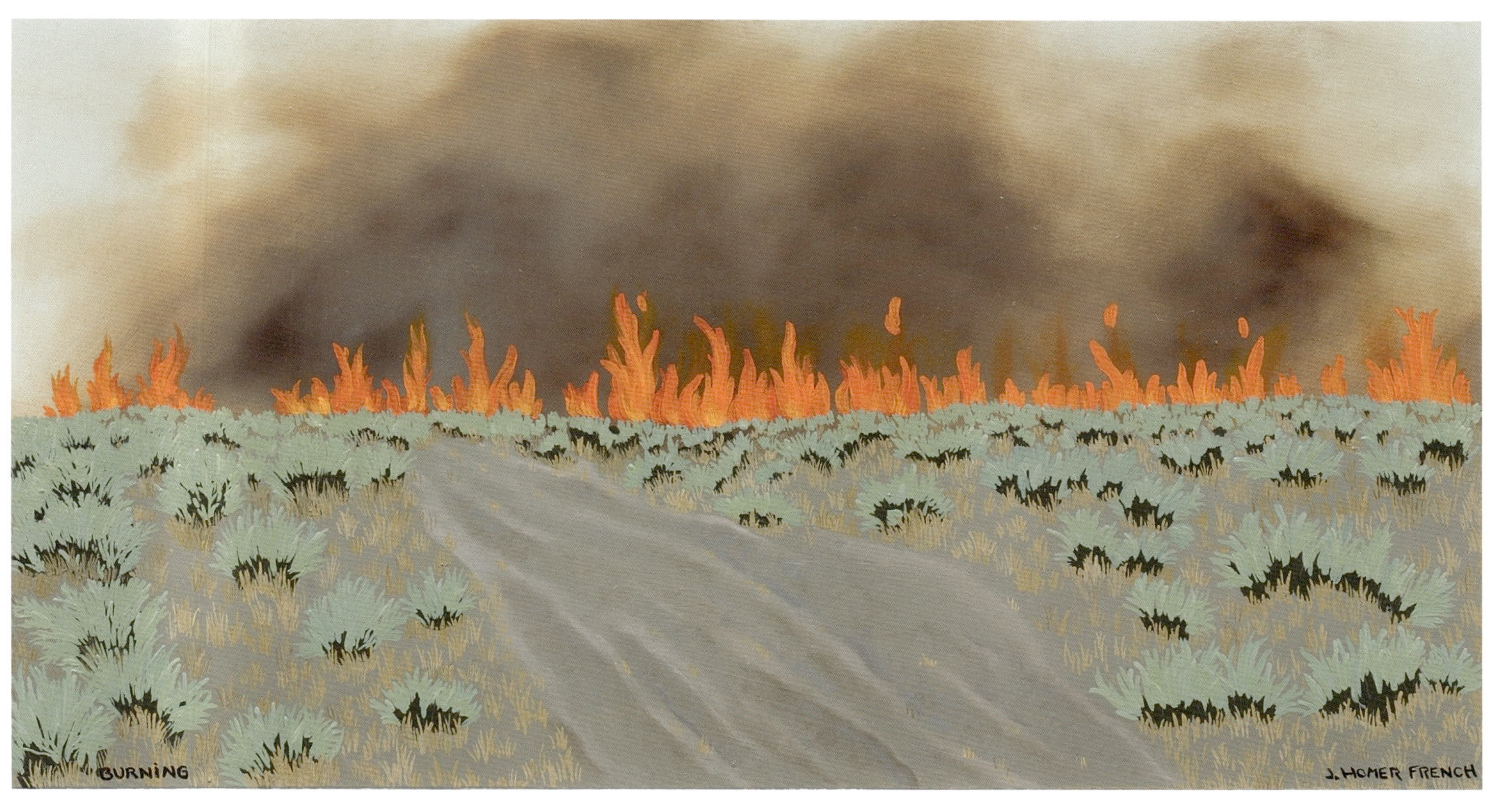

71. *Burning*, 2020
Oil on masonite, 12 × 21⅜ in. (30.5 × 54.9 cm)

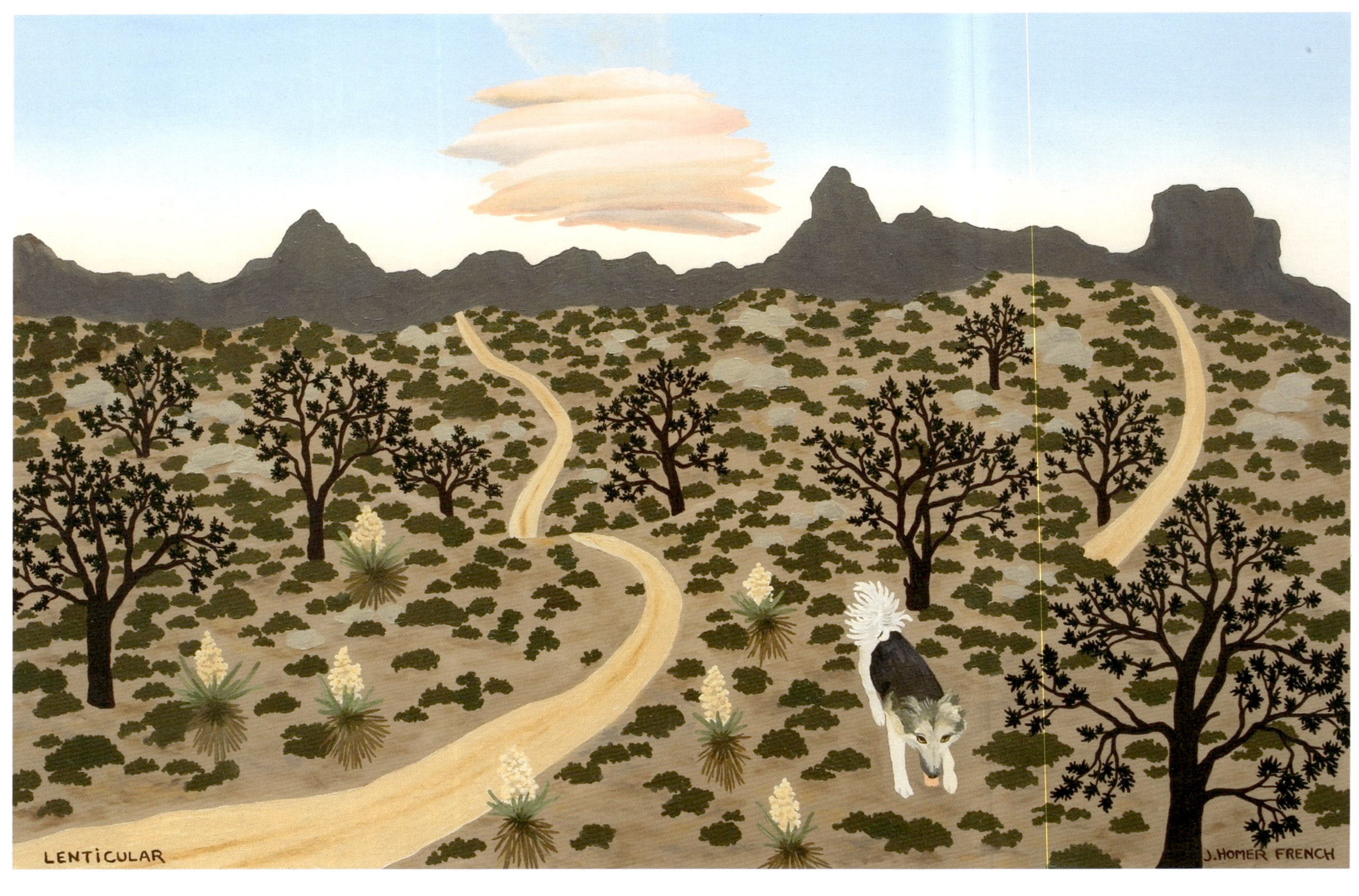

72. *Lenticular*, 2019
Oil on canvas, 20 × 30 in. (50.8 × 76.2 cm)

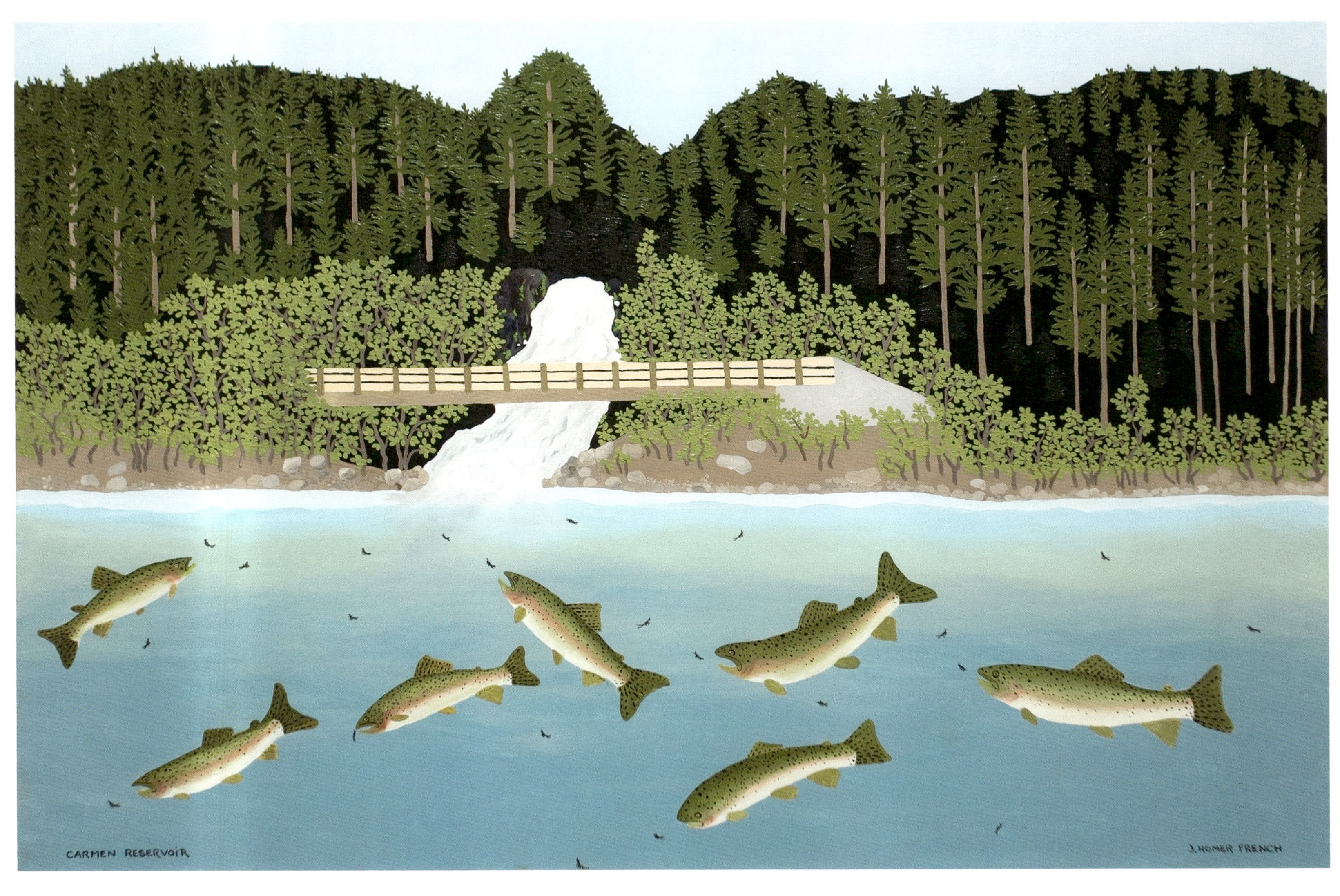

73. *Carmen Reservoir*, 2017
Oil on canvas, 24 × 36 in. (61 × 91.4 cm)

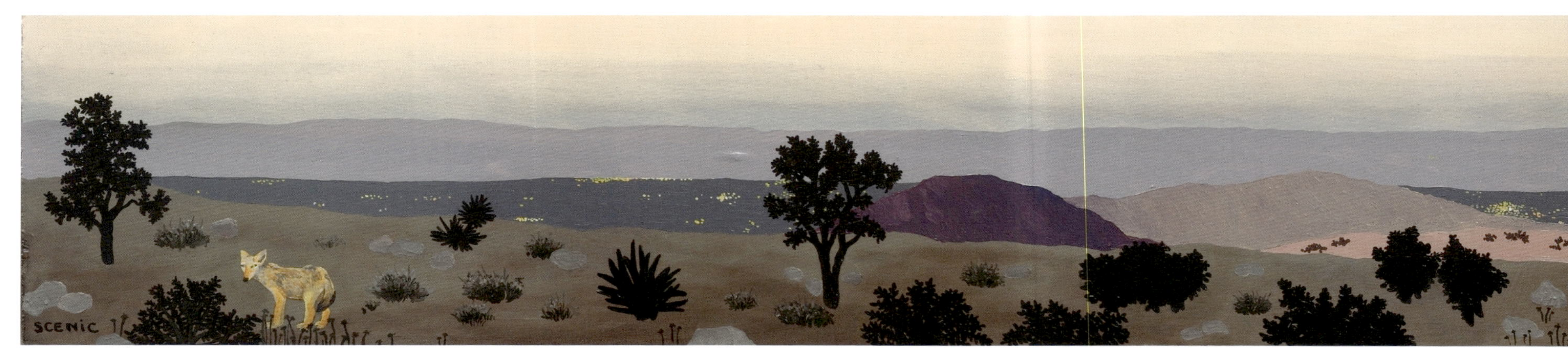

SCENIC

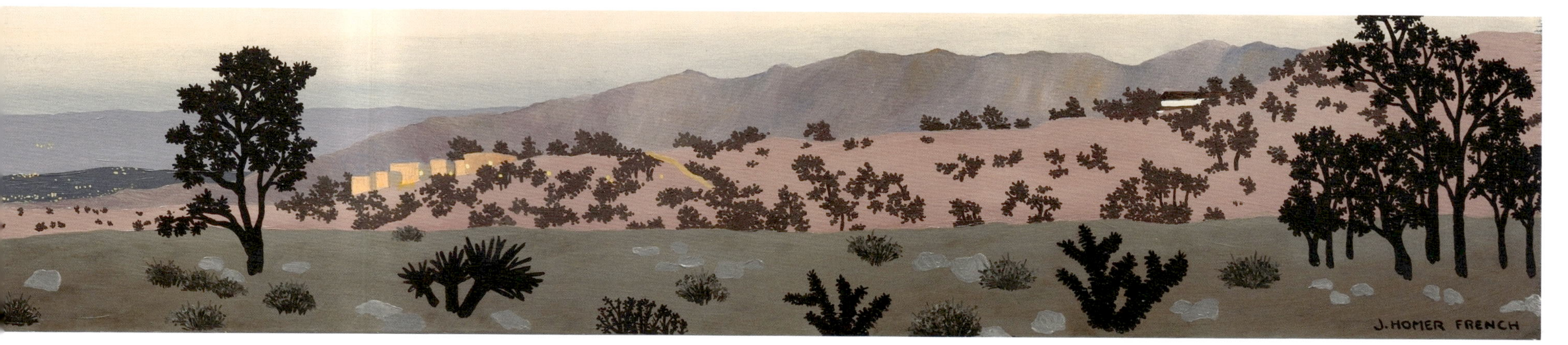

74. *Scenic*, 2019
Oil on plywood, 6½ × 61 × ¾ in. (16.5 × 154.9 × 1.9 cm)

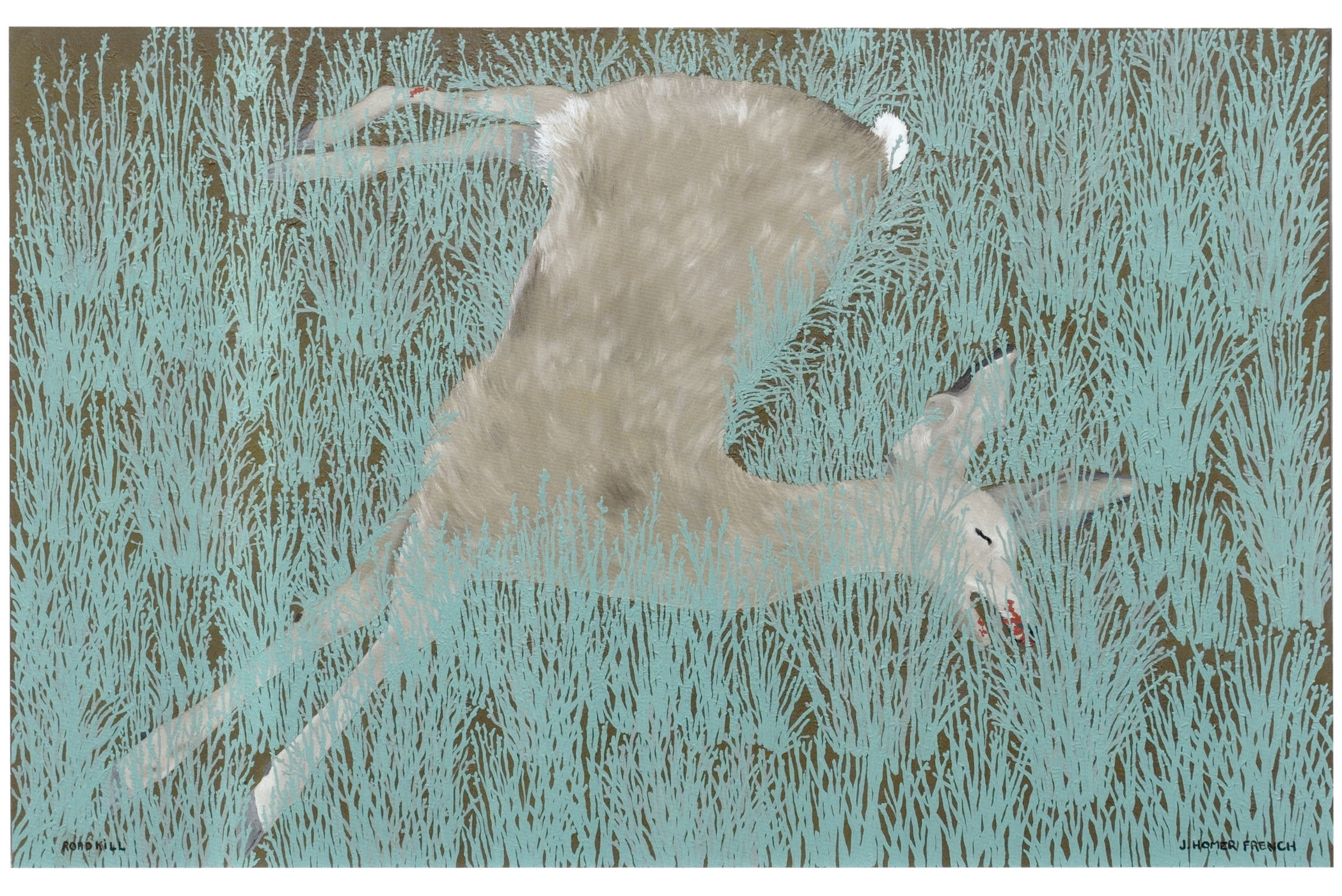

75. *Road Kill (Again)*, 1998
Oil on canvas, 24 × 36 × 2 in. (61 × 91.4 × 5.1 cm)

105

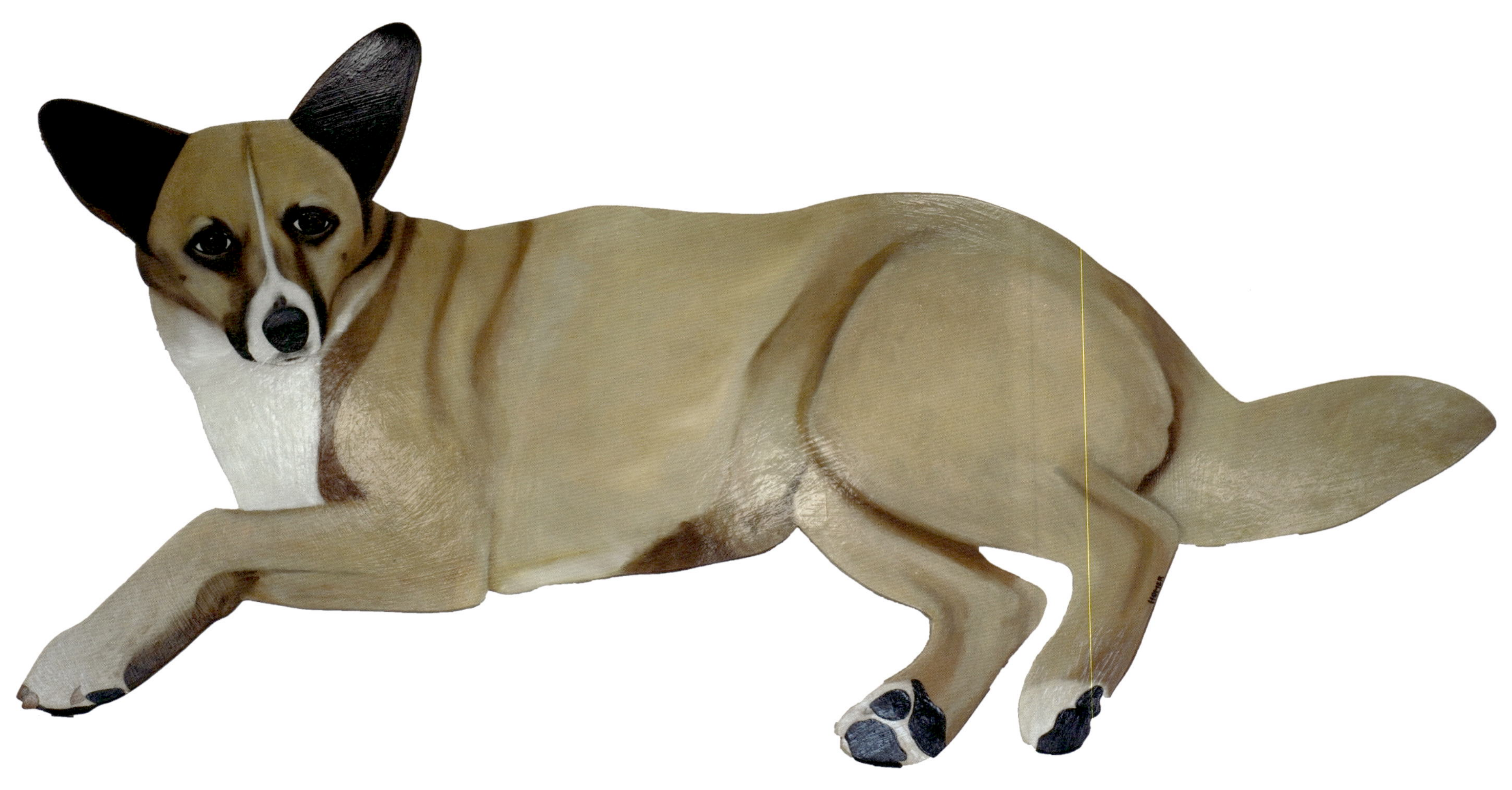

76. *Dingo Dog*, 1993
Oil on plywood, 32 × 60 in. (81.3 × 152.4 cm)

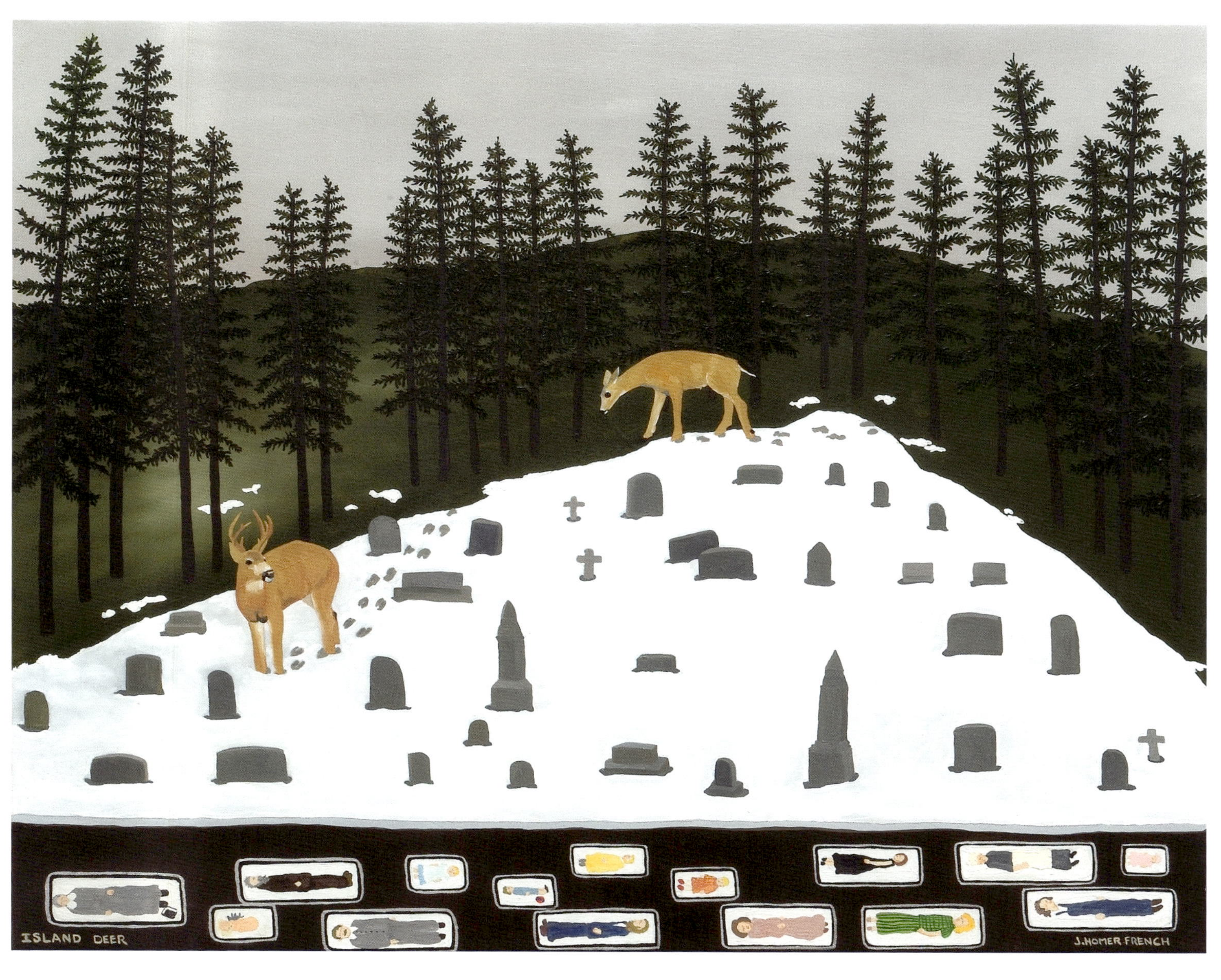

77. *Island Deer*, 2020
Oil on canvas, 24 × 30 in. (61 × 76.2 cm)

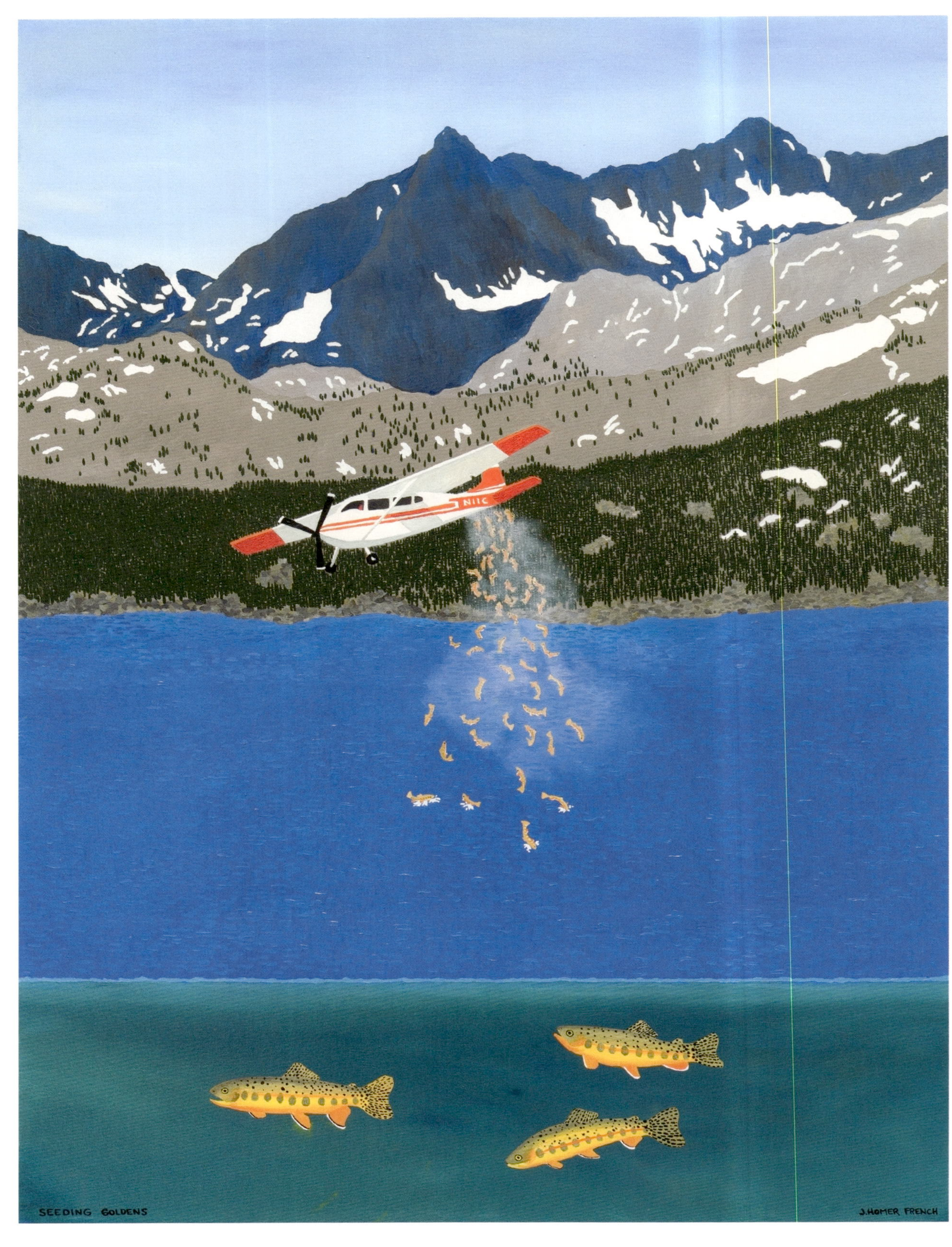

78. *Seeding Goldens*, 2020
Oil on canvas, 40 × 30 in. (101.6 × 76.2 cm)

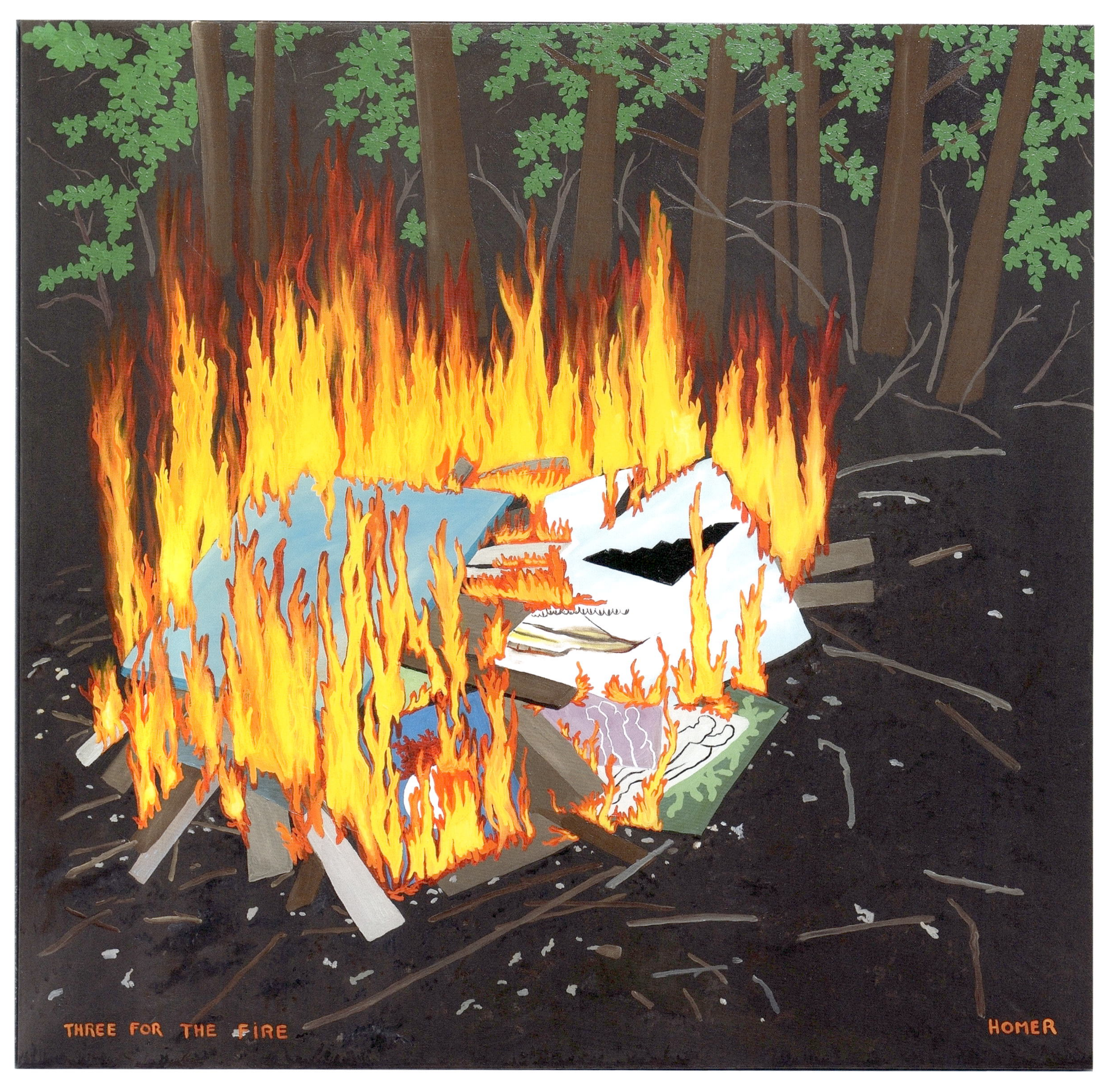

79. *Three for the Fire*, 2006
Oil on canvas, 36 × 36 in. (91.4 × 91.4 cm)

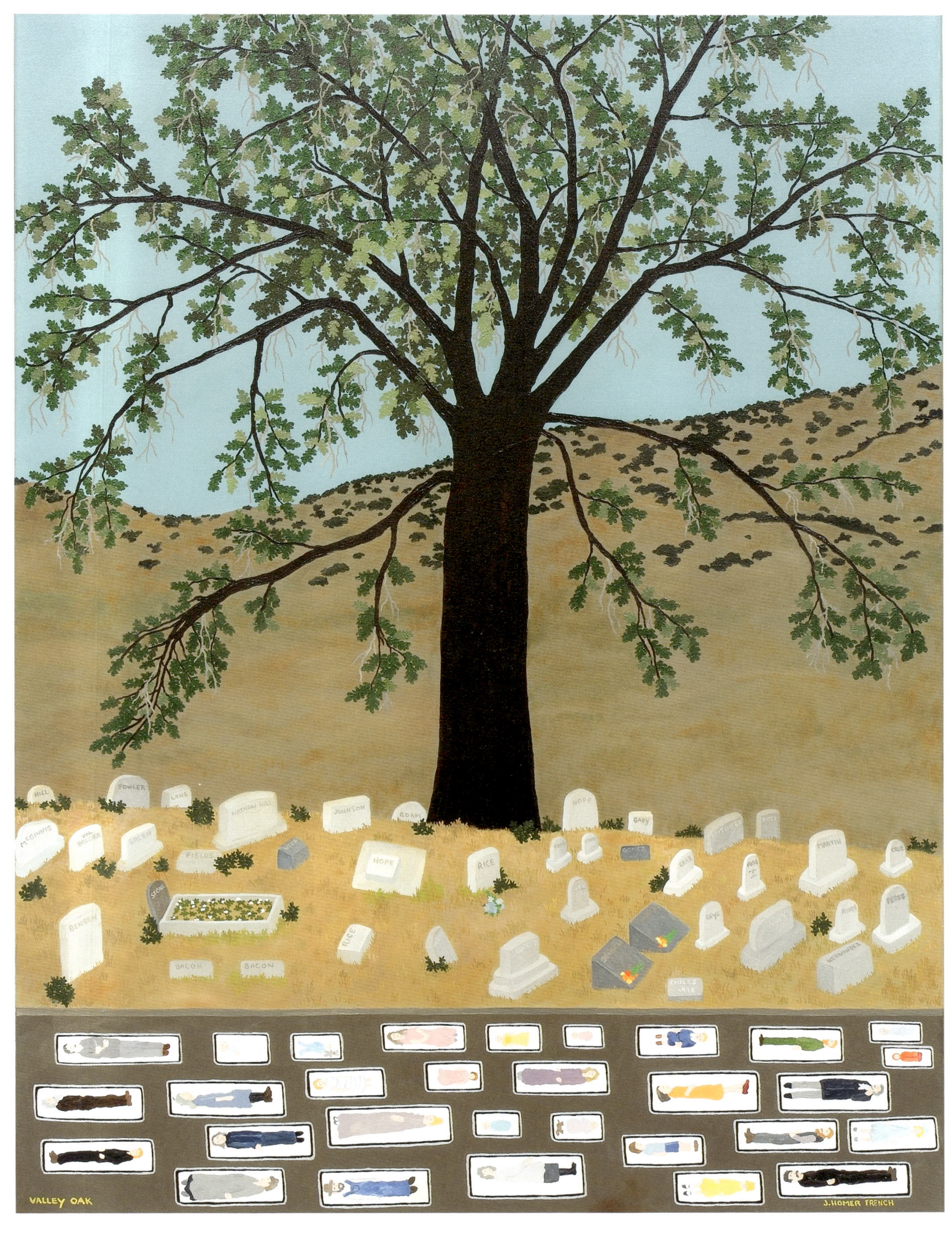

80. *Valley Oak*, 2020
Oil on canvas, 48 × 36 in. (121.9 × 91.4 cm)

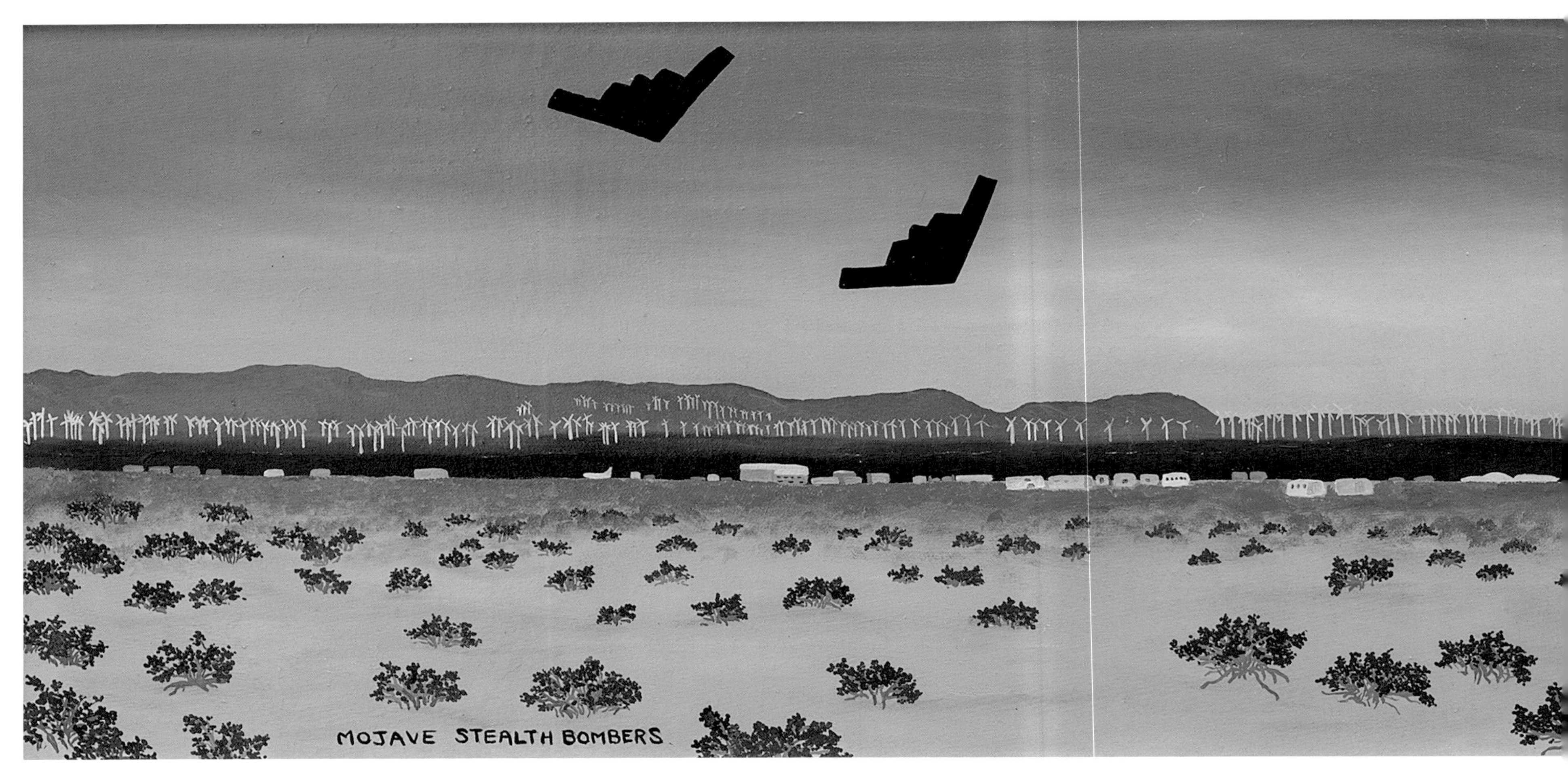
MOJAVE STEALTH BOMBERS

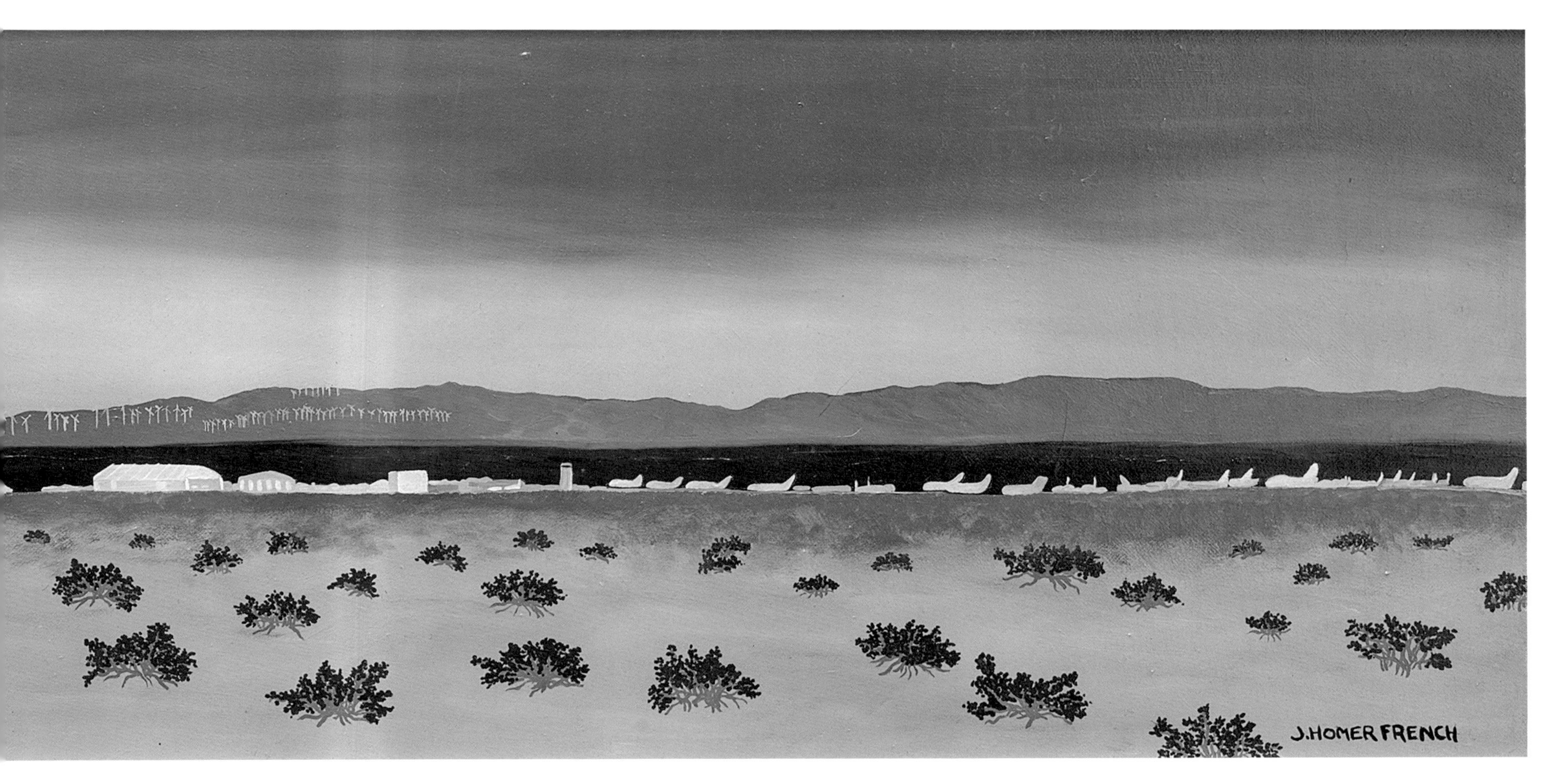

81. *Mojave Stealth Bombers*, 2013
Oil on canvas, 12 × 47 in. (30.5 × 119.4 cm)

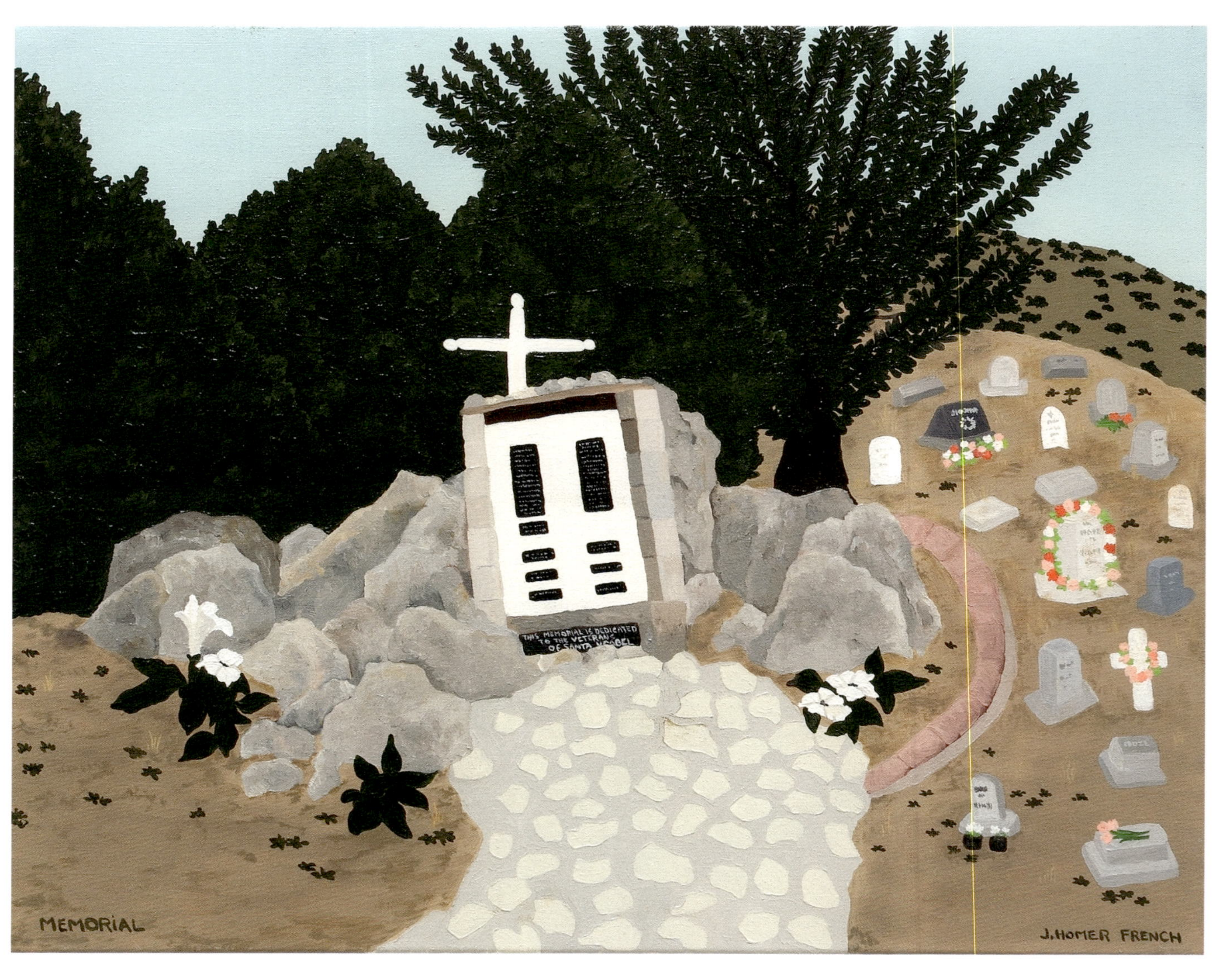

82. *Memorial*, 2019
Oil on canvas, 16 × 20 in. (40.6 × 50.8 cm)

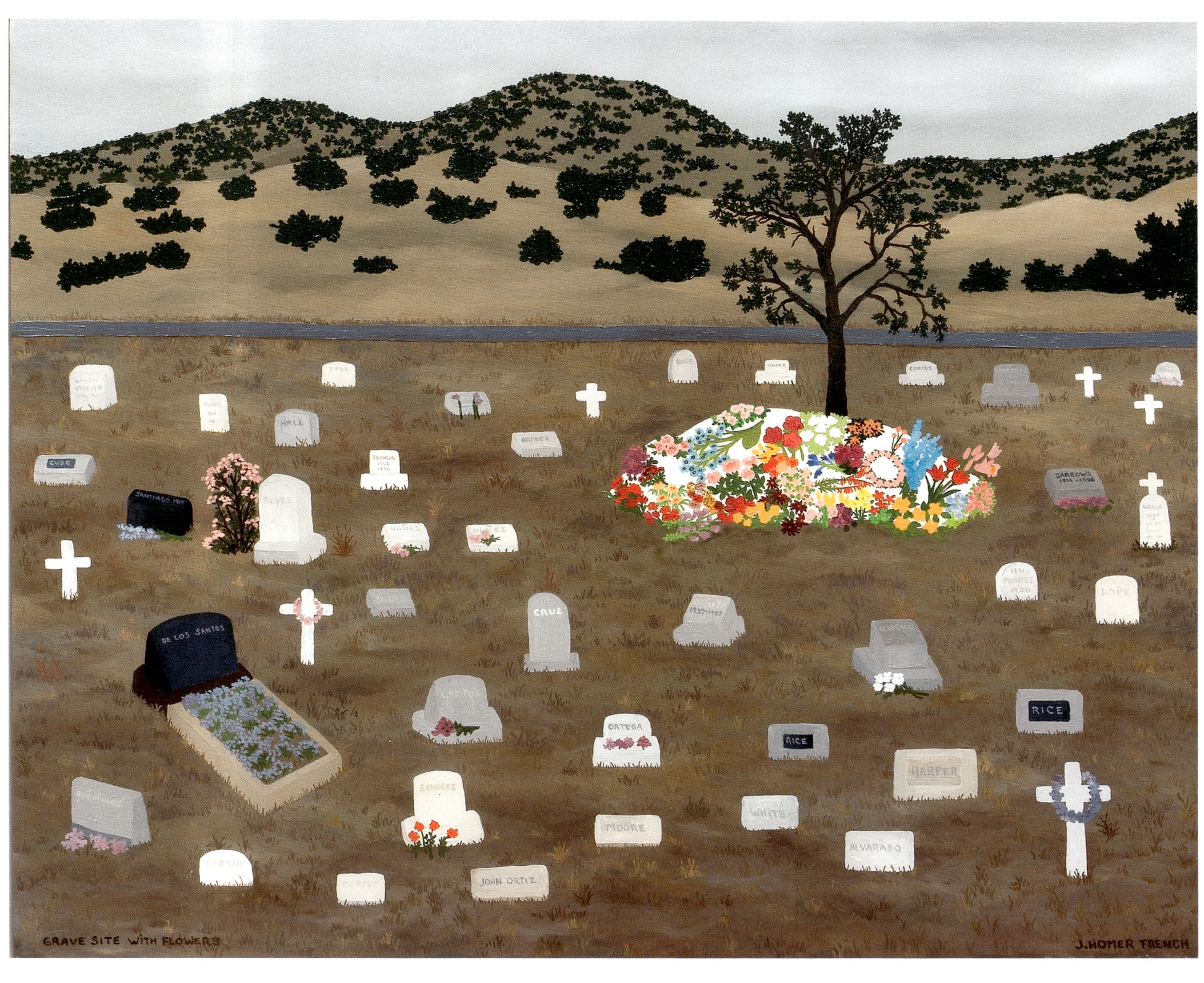

83. *Grave Site with Flowers*, 2019
Oil on canvas, 26 × 32 in. (66 × 81.3 cm)

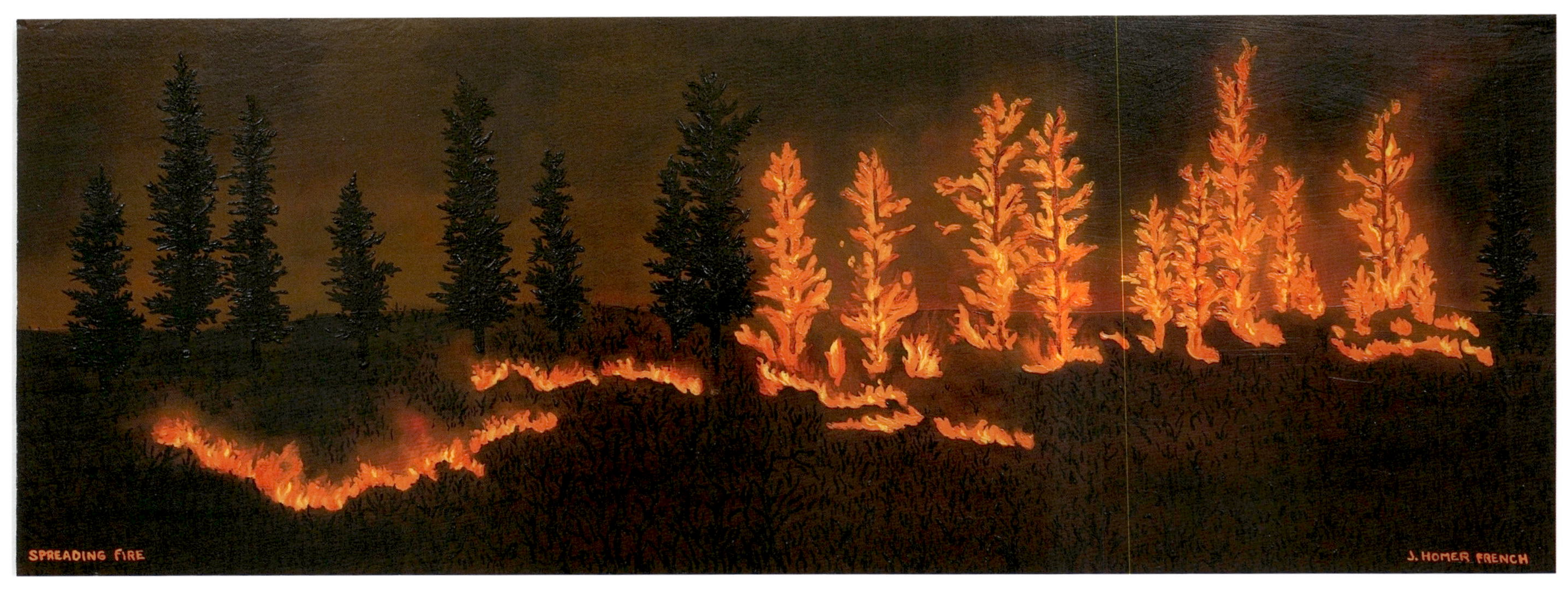

84. *Spreading Fire*, 2022
Oil on wood, 12 × 32 in. (30.5 × 81.3 cm)

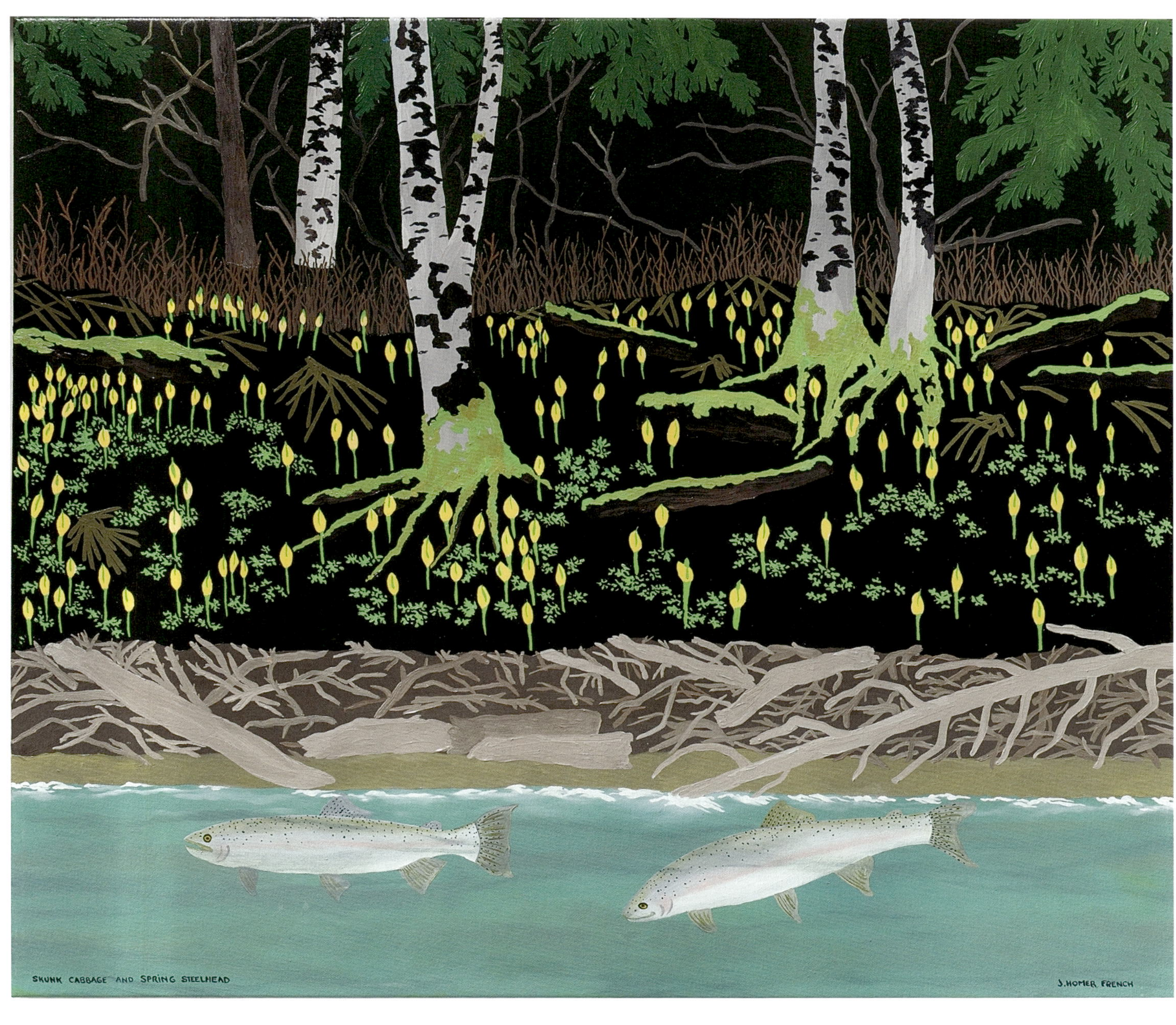

85. *Skunk Cabbage and Spring Steelhead*, 2021
Oil on canvas, 26 × 30 in. (66 × 76.2 cm)

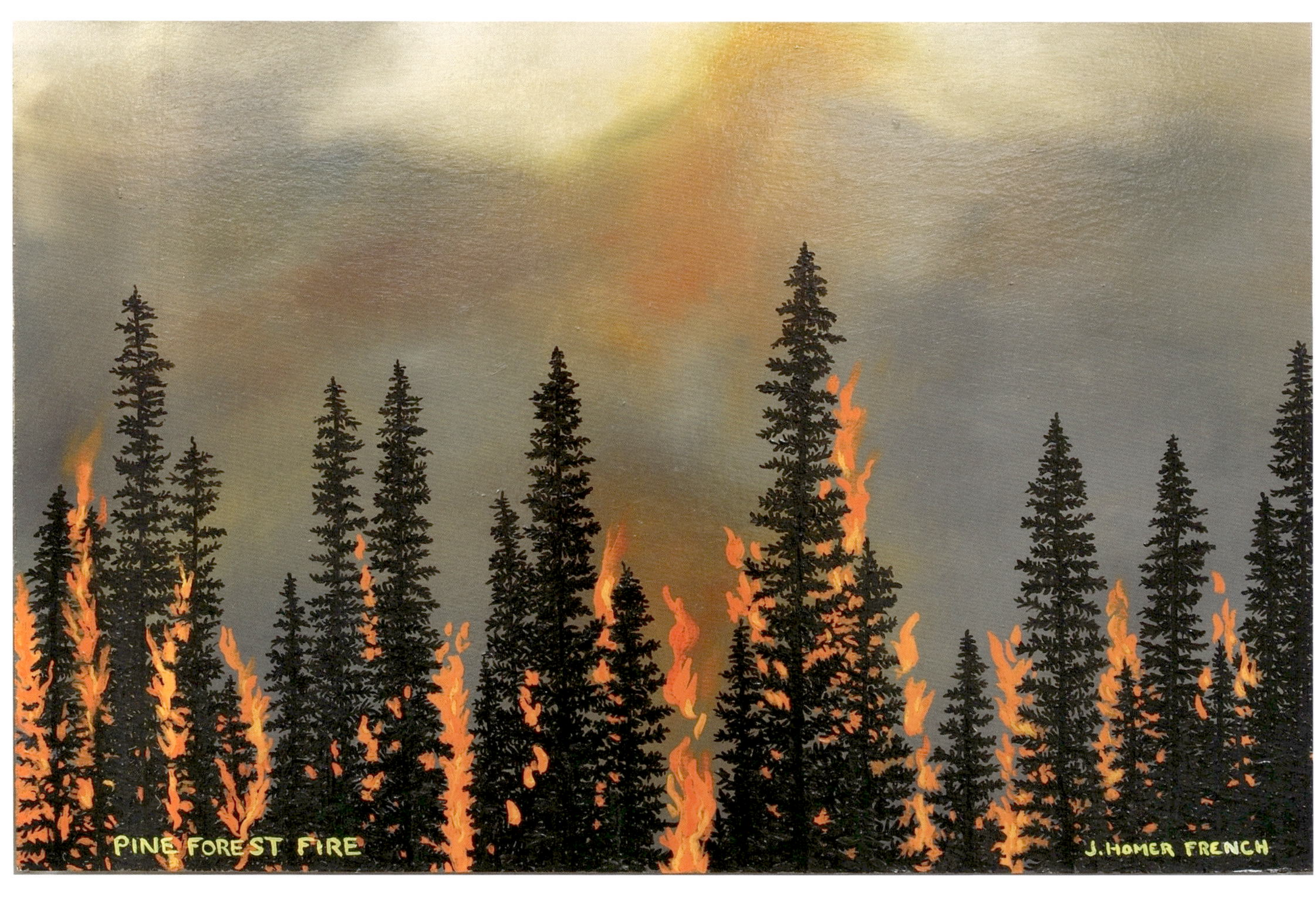

86. *Pine Forest Fire*, 2019
Oil on plywood, 12 × 17½ in. (30.5 × 44.5 cm)

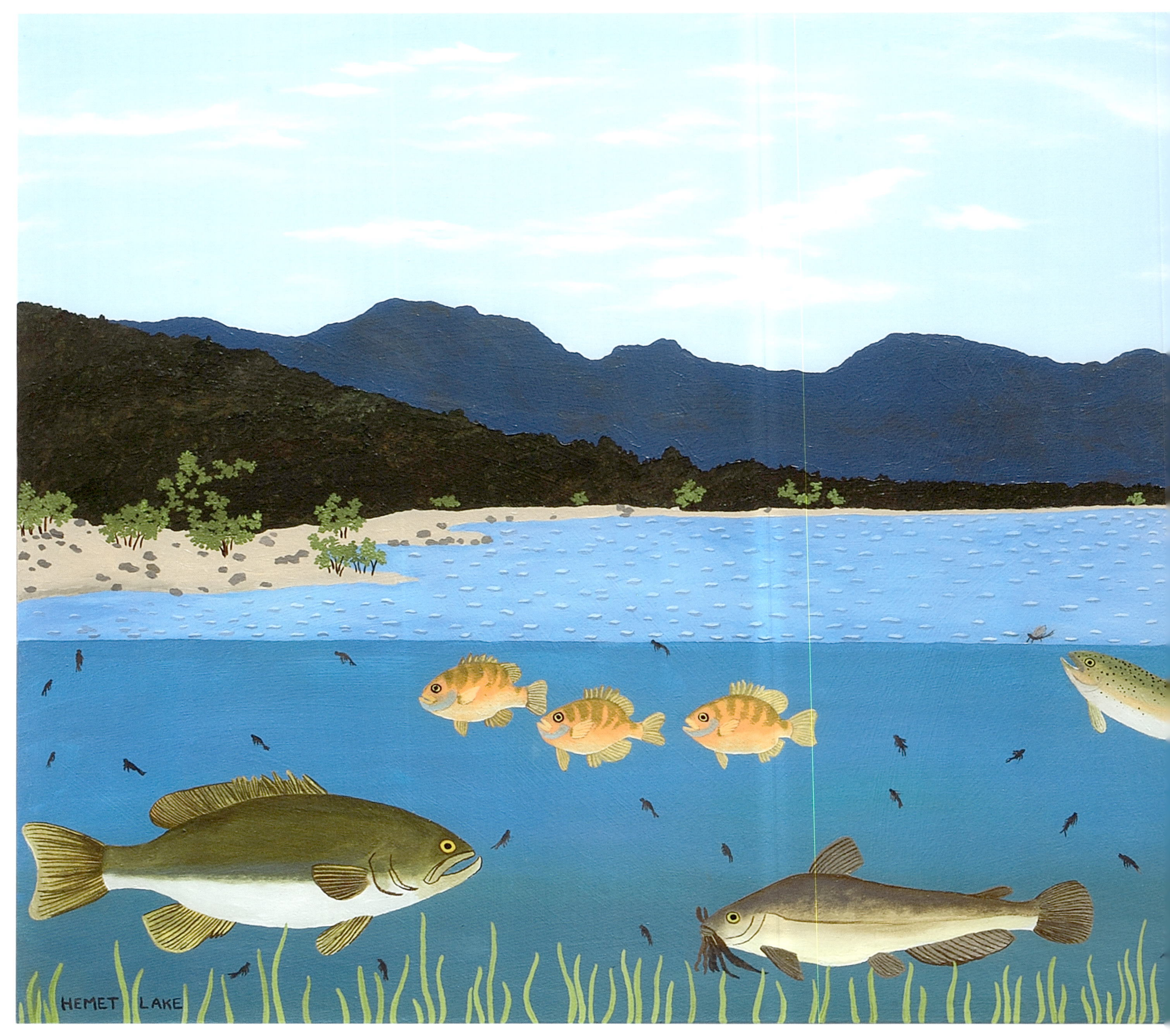
HEMET LAKE

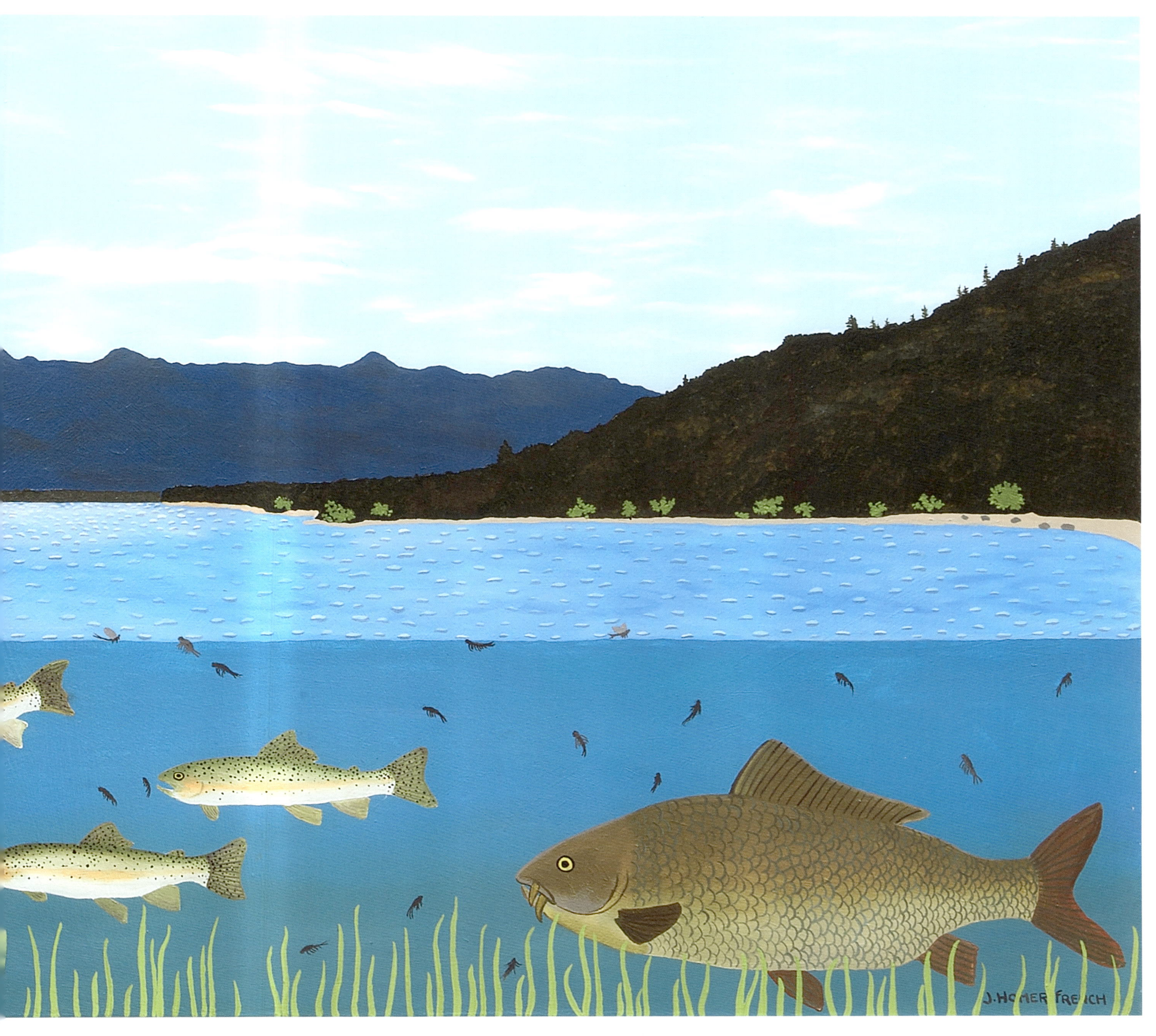

87. *Hemet Lake*, 2018
Oil on canvas, 24 × 52 in. (61 × 132.1 cm)

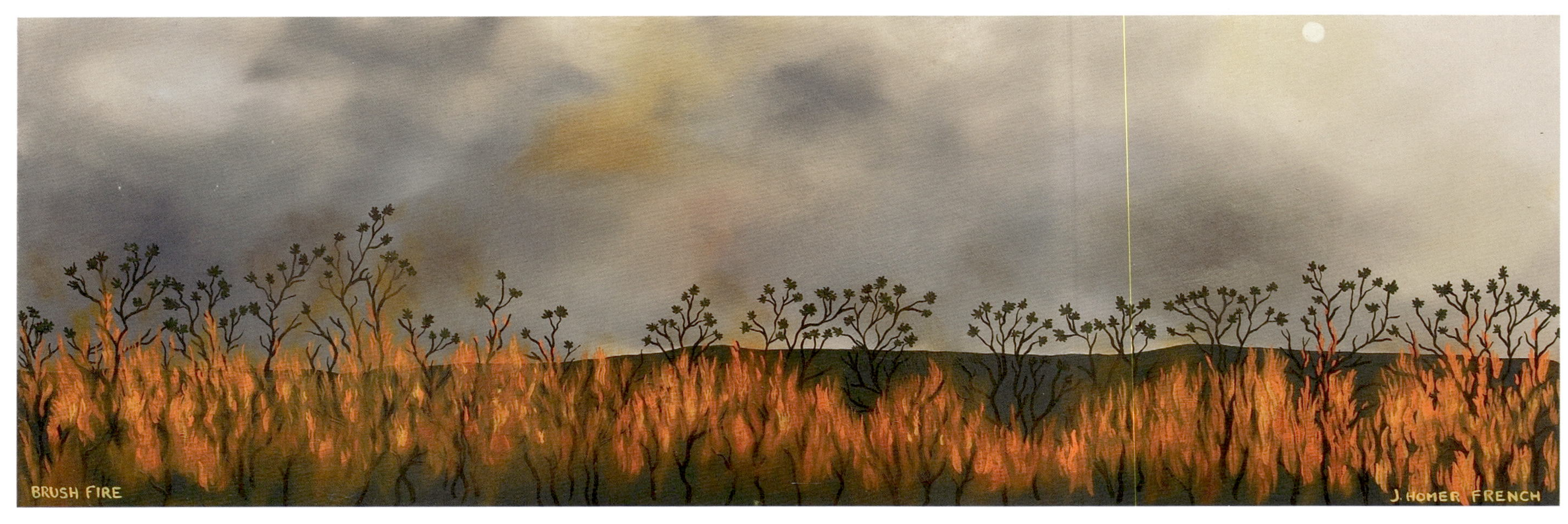

88. *Brush Fire*, 2019
Oil on plywood, 12 × 36 in. (30.5 × 91.4 cm)

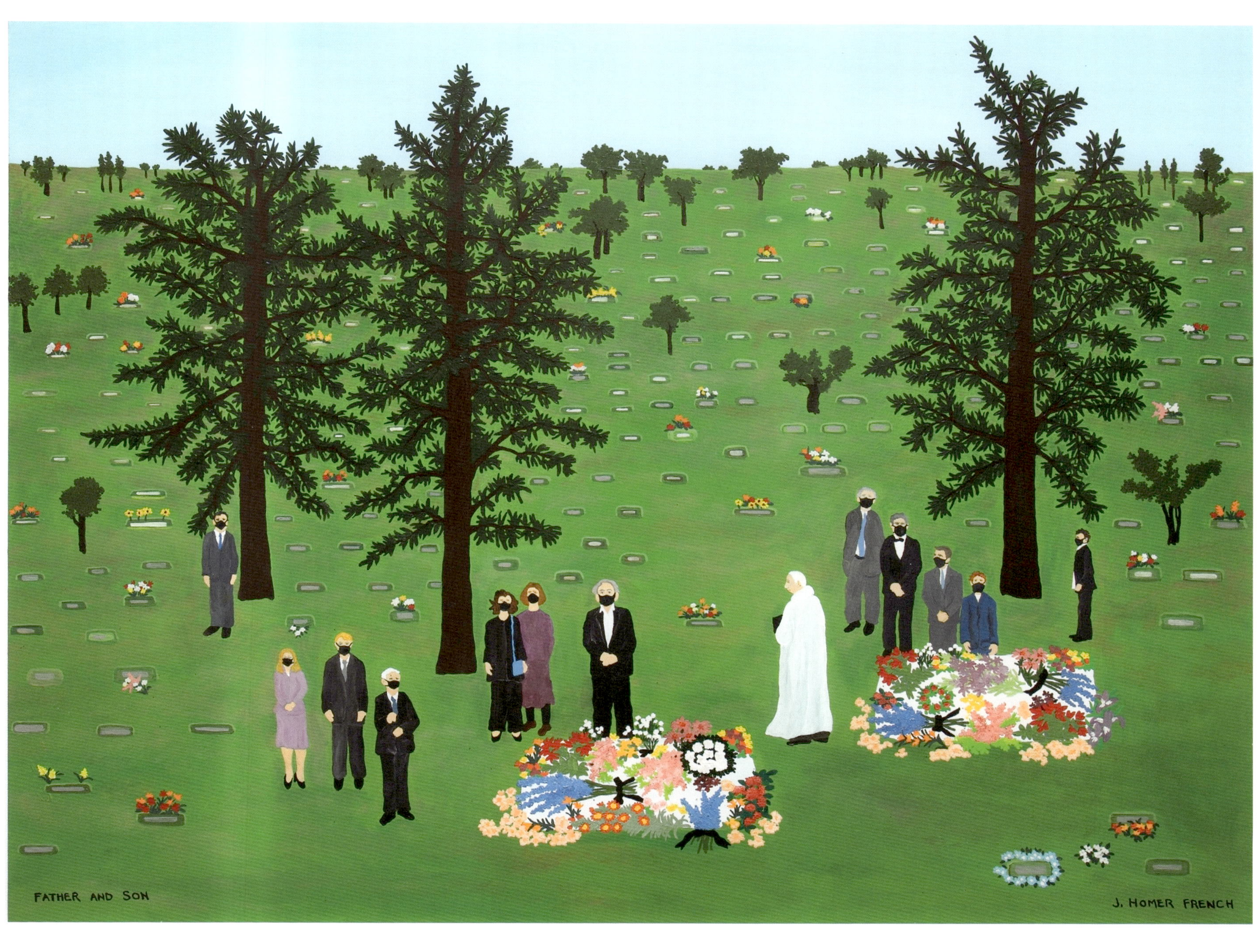

89. *Father and Son*, 2022
Oil on canvas, 30 × 40 in. (76.2 × 101.6 cm)

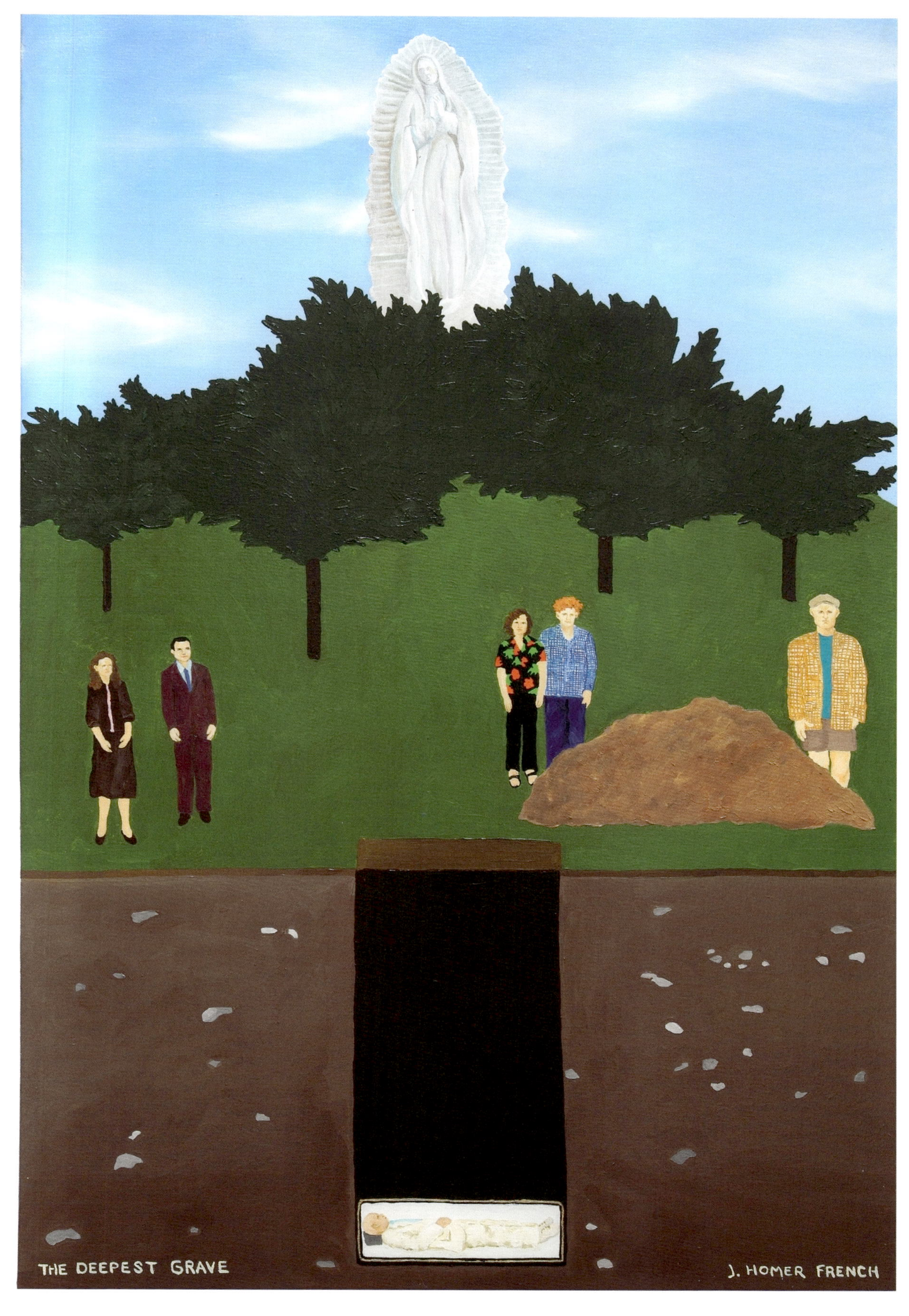

90. *The Deepest Grave*, 2022
Oil on canvas, 36 × 24 in. (91.4 × 61 cm)

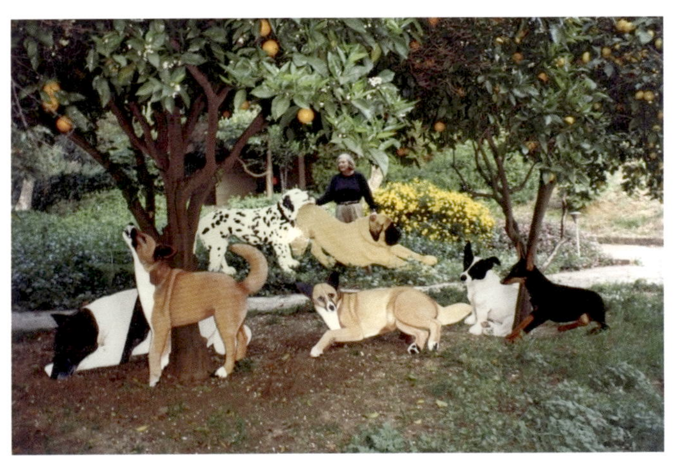

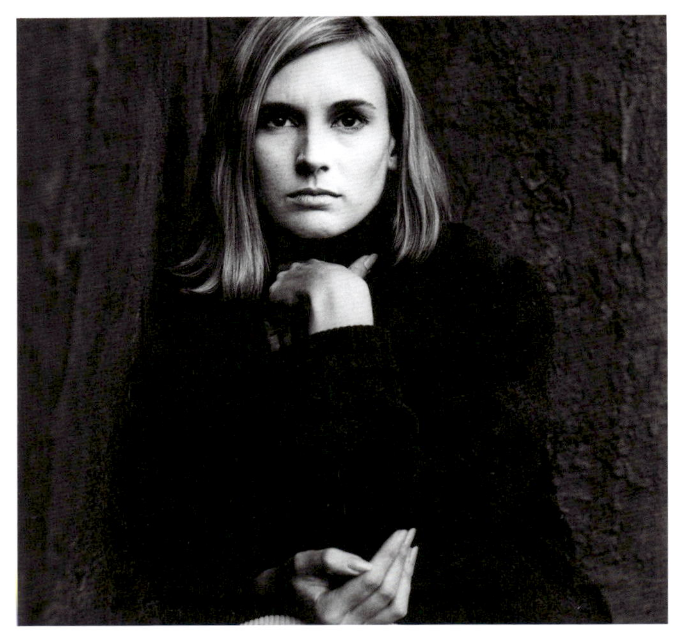

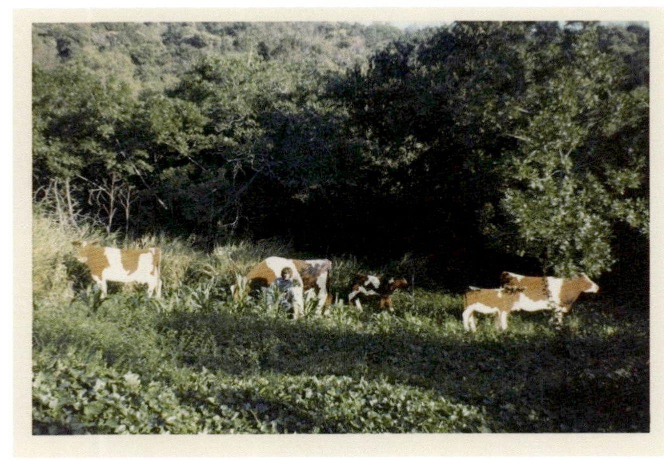

Biography

A pack of French's plywood
cut out dog paintings. Beverly
Hills, CA, c. early 1990s
Photo by Amy French

A modeling photo of French
by Kenn Mori, c. 1966

The artist missed the cows
she grew up around, so made
a small herd (oil on plywood)
near her home in Los Angeles,
c. late 1970s. Photographer
unknown

Following page
The artist on the Mackenzie
River, Oregon, c. 2008
Photo by Robin French

Jessie Homer French (b. 1940, New York, New York, lives and works in Mountain Center, California) is a self-taught, self-proclaimed "regional narrative painter" who routinely, perhaps even obsessively, paints archetypes of death, nature, and rural life. Through a simplified language of apparently naïve, flat colors and calm brushstrokes, her paintings emerge as a continuous analysis of her surroundings and reveal a personal and profound attitude to a local and transient type of composition, in which creation and destruction coexist with exemplary candor. She has held solo exhibitions at MASSIMODECARLO, Milan, London, Hong Kong, and Paris; Various Small Fires, Los Angeles, Dallas, and Seoul; Mother's Tankstation, Dublin and London; the Armory Center for the Arts, Pasadena, California; Craig Krull Gallery, Santa Monica, California; Winchester Gallery, Victoria, British Columbia; and Ankrum Gallery, Los Angeles. Her work has also been included in group exhibitions at Francois Ghebaly, Los Angeles; CLEARING, New York; the Palm Springs Art Museum; Laguna Art Museum, Laguna Beach; Samuel Freeman Gallery, Santa Monica; and the Blanton Museum of Art at the University of Texas, Austin. French's work is included in the permanent collection of the Dallas Museum of Art, Palm Spring Art Museum, and the Smithsonian American Art Museum. She was included in the 59th Venice Biennale in 2022 and the 2023 edition of Made in LA. In September 2023 she presented a project with High-Line Art in New York City.

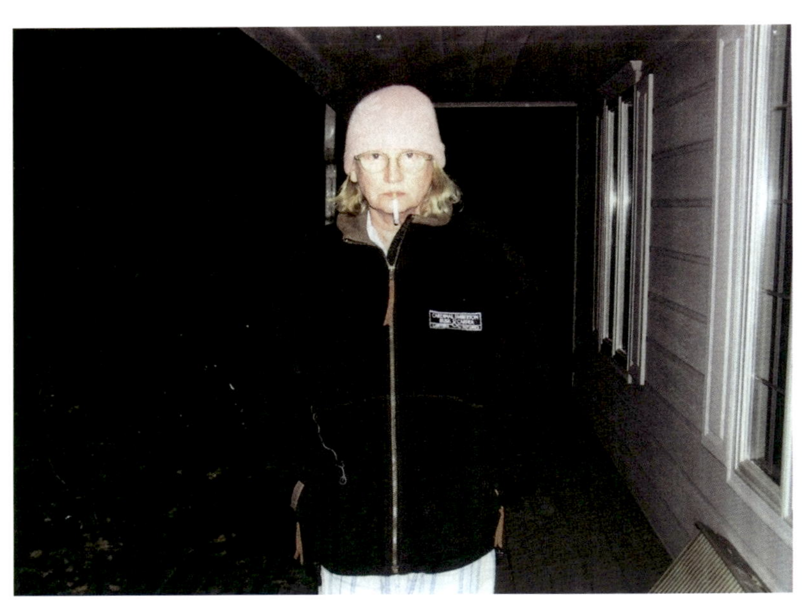